# ❋ Giants of Gaia ❋

# GIANTS OF GAIA

NICHOLAS R. MANN
&
MARCIA SUTTON, PH.D.

BROTHERHOOD OF LIFE, INC.
ALBUQUERQUE, NEW MEXICO

# CONTENTS

# ILLUSTRATIONS

# INTRODUCTION

ho are the Giants? Why do the legends of every culture say that giants once lived upon the earth? What are the Giants saying to us today? How can we hear them?

Giants were born of *Gaia,* the Earth Goddess, in the time before Time. Their shapes can be seen in mountains and gorges. Their features emerge from rocks and trees. They travel in the sky as clouds and storms. They are the elements. They are Nature. They enspirit all living things with the life force. Some legends even say they created humans.

Giants have always assisted humans. The Titan Prometheus brought humans the gift of fire. Giants of the American Southwest brought medicine power and songs. Ancestral giants of the Aborigines sang the landscape into existence. Giants moved megaliths into stone circles and built the walls of cities. Their allies, the dragons, brought currents of energy and powers of transformation to human endeavors.

*Giants of Gaia* shows that giants exist not just in ancient myth. They still walk between the inner and outer worlds. Giants arise when the divide is dropped between imagination and reality, body and mind, earth and spirit. Giants emerge naturally as we come into harmony with the world. Giants assist us whenever we listen to the intelligence of our bodies, to the wisdom of the mountains and forests, rocks and rivers. Giants awaken when we follow the paths into the magical landscapes of our total being. This book talks to the magician in us, the poet, child and mystic in us.

# GIANTS AROUND
# THE WORLD

C H A P T E R   O N E

# "HERE BE GIANTS"

*At first there is nothing. Just vast empty blackness, void and silent. As I slowly become aware of myself I know that I am falling. There is somewhere I must have come from and somewhere I am going toward. There is an above and a below.*

*The speed of my fall increases. It is toward a tiny distant point of light. I become aware that space is divided into quadrants. The instant I realize I am approaching the Earth, the four quadrants close in. I slow down and come to rest just above the surface of the Earth. It is a desert landscape. At the place where the quadrants meet there is a huge monolithic rock. It is about a mile wide and a thousand feet high. It has faces upon it. They look in the direction of each of the quadrants which divide space. Each face is strongly featured and cleanly cut. They are slightly smiling. They are giants.*

*As I watch, I become aware of a constant flickering. It is the passing of day and night. I look closely and see changes coming over the landscape. Some green comes and goes. The thought occurs to me that this must be trees. Then I see a temple being built at the foot of one of the giants. I cannot see the builders, only the temple rapidly rising, tier upon tier of stone. I notice that the faces of the giants are becoming eroded. Their clean features are being worn away. Soon they become discernible only to someone, like myself, who knows that they are there. The temple crumbles away. Then another temple comes. It is bigger and lasts longer than the first. I have the thought that the faces of the giants must be invisible to the builders. Soon it too crumbles to the ground. The last temple to occupy the site, small like the first, comes up and as quickly erodes away.*

*A long period of time sets in. Nothing happens around the worn rock. Then a shift occurs. Something alters in the movement of time. It seems to reverse direction. Changes begin again. As slowly as they went, the faces on the rock return. At length, the four faces are as strong and as clear as when they first appeared. Then I awake. I am resolved to find out more about the giants.*

---

## SEEING GIANTS

The thing about giants is that they are very large. Very large beings are attributed with all sorts of powers beyond human ability. People have a tendency to enlarge mythic heroes, deities and opponents until they become gigantic. Important cultural figures from the past gain giant status. Living or recently living people such as presidents, artists and athletes are looked on as "giants." The size of a fish that was caught gets exaggerated with each retelling of the tale. In ancient Latin and Greek cultures, *gigans* or *gigantes* meant huge real beings. But in modern culture, gigantic merely means very large.

Whether or not we believe in giants, our words for the landscape often imply that it was made by a giant or that an enormous body is located there. We see giants in rock formations, in the patterns of the clouds. We refer to the mouth of a river, the fingers of a lake, the elbow of a stream, a headland jutting into the sea, the foothills of a mountain chain, the heartland of a nation. Place names also reflect this. The summit of Mont Blanc is known as the "Giant's Tooth." There are basaltic rocks in the Irish Sea called the Giant's Causeway. Legend says they were made when a giant in Ireland attempted to reach his lover in Scotland. The native name for an unusual round landform in New

Mexico is Giant's Head. The islands of Martha's Vineyard, Nantucket and the Elizabeth Islands are said in Indian legend to have been made by the good giantess Quant and her husband Maushop. And there are many large chasms around the world known as the Giant's Leap, Ditch or Canyon.

"Giant" as used in this book is a concept meaning a way of *seeing* that is large, inclusive and long lasting. Seeing giants means seeing connections between the inner and the outer worlds. They are a way to connect with the greatest forces we can imagine. Giants are a way of expressing whatever surpasses human power and size. Giants are a signal that something is analogous to the human but vast in scale. We shall see that science is now thinking in the terms which ancient people used to describe giants.

The Graeco-Latin word *gigans* derives from the Sanskrit *gô-jan,* meaning "earth" and "giant." *Gigans* meant a mighty being, one capable of giving birth. One group of giants in Greek myth were called the *Gege-neës* which means the "Earthborn." *Ge* or *gi,* from which we get *geo,* means the earth. The French and the older form of the English word for giant is *geante* which literally means "earth before." *Ante* refers to the "first" or "before." *Ante* forms the root of the word Atlantis, one of the mythical antediluvian worlds wherein dwelt the giants.

In Greek and Hittite myth this was the time of the first mother of all, Ge, Gaea or Gaia. In Hindu myth she is Gaya. She is the Great Goddess from whose dance the earth was born. She is "great" because she gave birth to the world, the mountains, the oceans, the creatures, the giants and encompassed them all. A being of Gaia is a Gaian or a Giant. They are creators in the time of the "first earth" or the "earth before" this time.

The giants exist outside of time. They seem magical because they originated before time and magic were separated into real and unreal. In Chinese myth a primordial being called P'an Ku was the giant from whose body the earth was formed. His flesh was the earth, his sweat the rain, his tears the rivers, his breath was the wind and his voice was thunder. He named creation. On dying, the body of P'an Ku formed the five holy mountains and his eyes became the sun and moon. Likewise, around the world there are myths which tell of creation being made from the body of a giant. Gayomart was a huge light-giving figure at the time of the creation of the Persian cosmos. Ymir was the giant whose dismembered body formed the Scandinavian cosmos. The head of the Hindu giant Purusha formed the heavens, the navel became the atmosphere and the feet the earth.

Because giants are found in the myths of almost all cultures around the world, they must mean something important and deep in terms of the human mind. While the modern mind dwells on breaking down wholes into parts and analyzing details by using words and logic, the archaic mind operated in the reverse way. It synthesized parts into wholes by using symbols and pictures. The archaic mind had an entirely different notion of time and space. Anything that fit the internal images and symbols of the mind was possible. In this mindframe, we ourselves can create. We can cause to come into being anything we need. And what we create will fit our images and our cultural mythology. To have giants, all we need is to think giants.

Children retain the age-old ability to bridge what we now call fantasy and reality. In Wales, where the national flag depicts a red dragon, we recently were taking the children of friends on an outing to a spectacular megalithic mound. We told the children we were going dragon hunting. They immediately asked, "Are the dragons still alive?" Nearby in Cornwall, there are more giant stories and giant place names than anywhere else in the British Isles. There on St. Michael's Mount, we watched a child of five peer down the Giant's Well and tell her father, "But I don't *see* any giants!"

What we see depends on our cultural conditioning and our encoded images. Celtic tradition is rich in tiny humanoid fairies, huge human-like giants and non-human, serpentine dragons. Native Americans energize their world with the spirit power of the animals. They give animal names to their clans, totems and the six directions. In Asia and Australia, the spirits of the ancestors are the source of the features of the world. In Africa and Haiti, the matching of internal and external landscapes comes through voodoo, trance, animistic forces, sorcery, and fetishes. In India, every conceivable divine creative force has a goddess or god to manifest it. In the three desert religions—Judaism, Christianity, and Islam—the forces are explained by an almighty male god and a hierarchy of prophets and saints. In all cultures, ritual is the activity used to translate from the inner to the outer worlds and back again. We will look at this in detail in Part III.

The way we have of seeing and relating to the world results from our cosmology or worldview. The prevailing explanation of the origin of the universe, its dynamic changes, and inherent structure are all contained in the cosmology of a people. This is expressed in language. *Cosmos* means "world" and "order." It was coined by the Greeks to mean the world as distinct from "chaos." The suffix *-logy* means the study of something and *Logos* means "word" or "speech."

Each culture orders, describes and explains the same things in life, but often in different ways. One way is no better than another but one may work better in a particular situation. A culture's worldview is molded by its experiences and is contained in its ideas and language. Learning a language automatically predisposes a person to see the world in terms of the ideas, values and beliefs of that particular cosmology. Cosmologies provide ways of thinking and speaking about the world which allow us to locate ourselves in a congruent, meaningful way within it. They make sense of the world. The cosmology tells the people whether or not to believe in giants, to see giants, to interact with giants.

Every cosmology comes complete with a cosmography. Cosmography provides the actual spatial and temporal dimensions of the worldview. It is the "map" of nature, the world and the location of everything within it. The map is carried in the mind of a people and is projected onto the physical world. We see what we need to see and what we expect to see.

The cosmography of the universe is described in creation myth. Creation myths explain the spiritual origins of a people and describe the dimensions of their world. They typically create an Underworld where dragons and serpents live, an Overworld where sky deities live, and a Middleworld where the humans live. In Christian cosmography, this is hell, heaven and earth. In Native American thinking, this is "the below," "the above" and "the middle place." Giants, as we shall see in Part II, are able to move between these dimensions.

Creation myths are also present in the secular world. The cosmographical map of science implicitly contains the idea that everything can be reduced to something simpler which lies behind it. The ultimate "something" is the Big Bang which should be describable as one simple equation. This is a popular creation myth of the Western scientific world.

## THE DIMENSION OF GIANTS

In conditions of gravity and atmosphere such as on Earth, increasing size ordinarily means decreasing speed. Of course, brute strength can overcome gravity. But in the popular imagination, the cost of increasing strength seems to be decreasing intelligence.

Hence the dinosaurs were strong but were erroneously thought to be utterly stupid. Giants are also usually depicted as dumb and easily outwitted. Unlike dinosaurs, though, there is no firm evidence of an actual race of giants on earth. There is no fossil evidence of massive humanoid femurs. There are no gigantic primate ribs, hominid pelvises and great jaw bones complete with tiny craniums. On every occasion when bones of "giants" were exhibited they turned out to be those of an animal or a deliberate hoax.

It may be useful to clear up the matter of human giants at this point. People who become very large are not infrequently born. Apart from the tall, slender Watusi people of Africa, they are of two types. The first are glandular giants. They are usually ill-proportioned and unhealthy. The second are inherent giants. These latter can reach heights around eight feet, are normally proportioned, and live normal lives. There are many famous examples, such as Captain Martin Bates and Anna Swan Bates of Ohio. Anna was just under eight feet tall and weighed around 400 pounds. Unfortunately the children of this popular couple died at birth.[1]

As well as large animals, alive like the elephant or extinct like mammoths, there are reports of giant creatures similar to humans. These, like the Yeti, Bigfoot or Sasquatch, live in wild and remote places. It is probably best to respect the privacy of these shy beings and, until they chose to emerge, treat them as part of the phenomenon of mythical giants.

There is another possibility of giants that needs to be considered. Up until about half a million years ago we had a relative in the genus *Australopithecus*. They were vegetarians and compared to us at that time they were fairly large and slow. Speculation as to why the Australopithecines became extinct has included the idea that they were wiped out by the genus *Homo*, which is us. Perhaps there was at first an alliance between us. The lumbering apemen could have followed humans about, scavenging from them, until an over-dependence upon humans was developed. One scenario suggests that our ancestors broke the alliance and replaced the gentle Australopithecines with dogs.[2] It is possible we carry a genetic memory of the time in our early ancestry when we co-existed with this distinct but similar genus.

We will leave dinosaurs, mammoths and ancient memories of other hominids aside for the moment. Whoever or whatever the "true giants" in our myths are, they do seem to have bypassed ordinary, physical evolution. Perhaps by so doing they intended to stay smart.

If they are indeed smart then why are giants often portrayed as dumb and grotesque in popular mythology? Here is a possible answer. The tendency of humans throughout history has been to portray their opponents in as ferocious and contemptuous terms as possible. After all, there would be no glory in defeating rather small and pathetic enemies. So the enemy was always huge, monstrous, terrifying, often cannibalistic and, because of the need of being held in contempt, stupid. Giants in this context came to represent the archetypal "Other" as opposed to the collective "Us." Sometimes the "Other" was an opposing culture. Sometimes it was forces of nature made to seem hostile. Tales of victory exaggerated the opponents' size and strength—Goliath—while exaggerating the cunning and skill employed by the often diminutive heroes to defeat them—David, or Jack the Giant Killer.

Today there is evidence that bulk is by no means synonymous with stupidity. Elephants are renowned for their wisdom. The dinosaurs are now realized to have been far more intelligent and complex than originally thought. And where gravity is reduced, as it is in water, some truly amazing species live.

Dolphins and whales have often been symbolically connected with giants. These sea beings may not be able to avoid the depredations of human hunters, but accumulating evidence shows they are enormously intelligent and have been so for over 30 million years. In such a timeframe the events of the past couple of centuries may not be applicable to cetaceans where an entirely different set of criteria for intelligence may prevail. The whales and dolphins may be dreamers, skilled interpreters of the subconscious realms. They may have realized that compassion is the true principle of a spiritual life. They may be stargazers. Their amazing "sonar" makes them telepathic. Certainly they are deep ecologists in harmony with their environment. They may be composers, orchestrating harmonies into epics which take years to sing.

Judged from our standards we know very little about other life forms. By imagining ourselves into their forms, into the dimensions in which they move, we may make the leap which allows us to comprehend the giants.

The first step is to slow down. Imagine an old record slowing from 78 revolutions per minute to 45, to 33, to 1 revolution not per minute but per hour. Then we might be getting there! The sort of intelligence at work here is certainly not quick by our standards but there is no reason to say it is not profound. In fact it immediately has the advantage of embracing the workings of things which take a lot of our time. Time, by our standard, crushes the little ant. The insect barely adjusts to change before another change is upon it. But a tree thinks deeper. It can live for centuries in its life on Earth, adapting, accommodating, changing. What can bigger things than that do? What can the oceans, the planet, the Sun do? What is the order of such pervasive, powerful, gigantic intelligence?

This opens up several ideas about different dimensions. It may be argued that an insect in its dimension can no more comprehend humans than humans can comprehend bigger beings in bigger dimensions. Each is separate. The insect has a full life by its standards. There is no reason to assume that bigger beings are any more aware of us or compassionately disposed to us than we are to insects. It may be that giants can not even hear us, let alone talk to us. Time and space, quantum physics tells us, are all relative. Unless we can change our way of seeing, then ants, trees, giants and humans may continue to inhabit entirely different spectrums of energy in mutually exclusive physical universes.

It is startling to realize that the cosmology of traditional science actually prevents us from thinking in the dimensions of giants. We are taught to analyze, to break the world down into small parts. We are taught to study detail and mechanical cause and effect. We study ores or atoms or capillaries in their separate contexts instead of perceiving the whole. And the whole is huge, complex, with every part having an effect on every other part. Our ancestors looked at the world as a complex whole. They saw every part of it moving with the breath of a unifying spirit. The same wind which moved the clouds and the trees moved in them. Their cosmos had living mountains with blood vessels of lava, copper, iron and gold. It had living beings with blood vessels pumping the life force of the universe. And from this way of thinking, they saw giants.

## THE REFLEXIVE UNIVERSE

**O**ne appealing idea about the universe is that, by virtue of its infinite nature, it is able to accommodate everything. In an infinite universe everything, by definition, is possible, even if some things are improbable.

Children wonder why scientists in the space program work so hard to find out if there is life on Mars, Venus and Jupiter. Why question if extraterrestrial life exists? To young minds the answer is obvious. There is life everywhere throughout the universe. But scientists will not find it if they insist on it being exclusively human. Sending a ship containing drawings and equations out into space to contact other life is as pointless as sending books to a wolf pack or crucifixes to a microbe colony.

The word "reflexive" describes the obliging nature of the infinite universe. By this is meant that the universe has the capacity to positively respond to any theory about it. The universe is user-friendly. It can provide proof for any cosmological scheme, scientific or mystical, foisted upon it. The "proof" found, of course, does not constitute the truth about the nature of the universe. It only proves the contents of our own minds.

When we do not encounter what we expect, we need to broaden our thinking instead of cutting off all other possibilities. Even though there are no humanoids living on Mars, this does not mean that Mars is a "dead" planet. In the same way, even though it is unlikely that a huge man or woman lives in the local forest or up on the mountain, this does not mean that life forms in a dimension physically and conceptually distinct from our own cannot exist. Indeed, if the cellular, atomic and sub-atomic worlds exist, then why not the giant?

In a universe of such diverse and multi-dimensional possibility, the idea of giants provides a very useful way of thinking about anything bigger or other than ourselves. Naturally, the tendency has been to see other forms of life including the giants in our own anthropomorphic image. Until the Yeti emerge, we must discard the idea of there being actual big people living down the road. But giants are still a splendid concept which, in the words of Lévi-Strauss, have always been "good to think."[3]

Thinking in terms of giants enables us to see and understand what otherwise may be too vast to be comprehensible. Organizing nature into giants—the primordial image of which is the Earth Goddess, Gaia—gives us a way to directly relate to the world. Giants give us the vocabulary and mode of perception to make the huge Unknown into something personal, comprehensible and less fearsome.

People are going to be talking giants for as long as there are people. And giants, fairies, elementals, devas, gnomes and elves are going to be talking humans as long as there are giants, fairies, elementals, devas, gnomes and elves. We are real, but we might be myths in their dimension. They are real, but are treated as mythical in our dimension. As myths they are not susceptible to empirical proof. But they are very alive in our creation stories and symbols.

Giants are also real in the dimension which bridges mind and matter. Everyday, space ships bearing messages from other worlds might be beaming into us and we scarcely notice them. Everyday the giants might be creating a spectacular show of winds, lights, colors and patterns of growth, and we take them for granted. Instead of dismissing the beings of the Other World or scientifically "explaining" them, we might be better off to borrow from our ancestors the idea of an inspirited world—an *animus mundi*. For "here be giants." Here is a way of thinking, of relating to the world as a magnificently living, magical and enchanting place.

## GIANTOLOGY

**M**uch of the support for thinking ideas like these comes from recent revolutionary changes in science. Quantum theory and relativity have enabled scientists to recognize their own subjective and participatory role in the universe. Each of the traditional sciences is making a paradigm shift away from old orthodoxy in which the universe was compared to a machine. In the old thinking, scientists only had to get into a position where they could see all the chains of mechanical causality and arrive at the simple underlying law or equation. Then, like gods, with a little tinkering here and an adjustment there, anything would be possible!

The universe is more than a machine. Mechanical causality between separate things is now recognized by most scientists as an idealization which can never be put into practice. Things are intricately connected in far more mysterious ways. The "underlying" levels of reality are not simpler but as or even more complex than this one. Scientists like David Bohm, Rupert Sheldrake and James Lovelock are postulating the presence of intelligence not so much in things as in the interrelationships between things. Information, mind, cognition and patterns are emphasized by them rather than mechanical interactions.

Intelligence does not belong just to humans but to all life. David Bohm suggests the universe is structured by an "implicate order" in which apparently random sets of isolated, competing and chaotic entities are actually intelligently ordered sets having relationship to the whole.[4] James Lovelock built his hypothesis of the Earth being a living, intelligent organism—now spoken of as the "Gaia Theory"—upon such ideas.[5] Rupert Sheldrake suggests that the information for the creation of the external world is held in "morphogenetic fields"—sets of archetypal blueprints that underlie reality.[6] These concepts tell us of a universe generated by non-physical, intelligent, larger-than-life forces. This sounds like it could be a modern definition of giants! We will look more at this in Part II.

Jungian psychology offers additional support in terms of archetypes. These are deeply imbedded patterns. They usually take the form of pictures which we hold of creation and the basic aspects of life, such as Mother, Earth, Animal, Death. Jung studied the prehistoric, unconscious development of the human mind. When humans first internalized images, the archaic mind thought only in pictures and symbols. Today we would call this the right hemisphere of the brain. The "archaic remnants" or prehistoric images are the prototypes for all subsequent images of that basic pattern. The memory of our ancestral cousin, Australopithecus, might have formed the archetypal pattern for all subsequent images of the giant. The universal image of the dragon may derive from an archetypal memory of the time when dinosaurs dominated life on earth. Is it possible these patterns go back even further and derive from a "cellular consciousness?" They could originate from a time when the bacteria and cells which make up our being were the only form of life on earth.

To have these images is as normal for humans as it is for bees to have the instinct to "dance" the direction to a food source, geese to migrate in formation, or ants to organize into societies. These images live within us, in our minds and in our genetic coding. They exist in our conditioning, in our heritage, beliefs, ideas and values. These concepts and images come to consciousness in dreams, visions and symbols. They both satisfy the archaic mind with its knowledge of the past and give meaning to our lives in the present. The right hemisphere deals easily with fantasy and timelessness, and sees globally rather than in fragments. In the right hemisphere where archetypes exist, anything is possible, including giants.

Archetypes underlie the surface world. On one level the archetypes could be cultural history, on another level they could be cellular encoding. Every pattern of the evolution of life on earth could be present in the cells of our bodies. We stand as giants in relation to those cells. Those cells in the totality of life on earth stand as giants to us. We exist in them. Is this where we need to look to understand the giants? Are giants the larger-than-life evolutionary memories of our own bodies? Are they the unconscious contents of our own minds? Are they our ancestors—from the bacteria breeding in the first swamps of life to the dinosaurs, primates and hominids, and eventually the culture-heroes looming hugely on the screens of our dream world?

Another place where a great deal of interest in underlying forces was generated was at the Findhorn Community. Impelled by what they felt was spiritual guidance, a small group of people settled in mobile homes on some barren sand dunes beside a military air base in northeastern Scotland. They contacted the intelligence or basic pattern "behind" the forms of the plant world and were able to create conditions in which the plants thrived. Not only were they able to grow plants that should not have grown there at all, but in many cases the plants were prolific and huge. The founding members of Findhorn, Dorothy Maclean, Eileen and Peter Caddy, called the forces behind the plants "devas" and in some cases "elementals." There was a daffodil deva, a cabbage deva, soil and wind elementals and devas for animals too. "Deva" incidentally, originates in India and refers to a benevolent deity or spirit. Eventually, broader forces were discerned which worked on the level of overseeing a landscape, a forest, a valley, and these were called "angels."

The key to fertility in the barren landscape was cooperation with these beings. Devas were fields of energy, the ideal pattern after which all plants of the same type were made. By cooperating with the archetypal pattern through attunement in meditation and prayer it was possible for its energy to manifest in a "perfect" form in the outer world. Devas thus co-existed everywhere around the world as immanent and apparently immortal forces and could enter into manifestation whenever conditions were right. Devas thus come very close to the "morphogenetic fields" and the "implicate order" of the new physics. Could they be the landscape giants?

## Spirit of Place

At the same time that ideas were becoming conscious in Western thought about spirit beings underlying the plant, mineral and animal worlds, a great surge of interest began in sacred sites. For centuries, ancient sacred sites had only received the attention of archaeologists. They had become, in effect, dead museums. Now they began to be visited by people who once again had spiritual intentions. Something was shifting in the collective consciousness away from a heavenly focus and back to the idea of a sacred earth.

In thinking about sites in the landscape which had spiritual traditions around them, the idea of giants was often found to be useful. Giants were "good to think" when it came to getting reacquainted with the world as a sacred place. Many sacred sites had giants associated with them in name and legend. And today, gigantic formations such as chakra systems, earth temples and zodiac patterns in the landscape are being identified, bringing the attributes of giants into present time. People feel that landscapes are inspirited when they can experience, visualize and describe them in terms of a unifying gigantic pattern or presence.

The new reverence for sacred places has a close connection to the growth of environmental awareness and the ideas of ecology. Strong earth-honoring attitudes and holistic concepts about the living, intelligent forces of the "spirit of place" can help to heal the dualistic division in our thinking in which body and matter are not spiritual. It is no accident that at the same time as ideas about ecology, sacred sites, archetypes and devas were developing, scientists were moving into a new, participatory view of the universe inspired by quantum physics. Everything began to be seen in relation to everything else.

Ideas whose time have come are interpreted according to the eyes of the interpreters. Where scientists see "patterns" and "energy fields," Jungian psychologists see "archetypes," people on a spiritual path see "devas" and "angels," ecologists see the "ecosystem" or the "biosphere" and folklorists see "fairies" and "giants." What is happening here? Could they all be right? Is something stirring behind our conscious minds, awaiting the growth of our perception?

This book will trace the manifestation of giants wherever they have appeared in the landscape. The authors believe that the true nature of giants emerges from their interrelationship between us and the surrounding world. The book may ask as many questions about the phenomenon as it answers, but it will show that there is a good reason for the renaissance of the giants. They provide a useful construct with which to think today.

Giants have a history, a compelling presence in the maps of our minds and imaginations. They are available to every mind of any age or ancestry. They can take us beyond ourselves into unexplored terrain. They make connections between fact and fiction, between the inner and the outer worlds. They stimulate the use of the whole brain. Above all, the giants—the offspring of Gaia—are about the beautiful planet which accommodates us, gives us a home, and with which we can interact to recreate the vision of a sacred earth. ⁂

# THE WAR IN HEAVEN

*In the beginning was the black nothingness of the night. Then a swirling mist arose. It was the dance of the goddess Gaia. Her white veils swirled around her and concealed her body as she danced. The veils spun faster and faster until the form of the goddess emerged.*

*The Giants and Titans worked willingly with Gaia in the creation of life. They made the winds, the clouds, the ocean currents, the heat of summer and the cold of winter. They gave unique shapes to each mountain and valley. They saw to it that life flourished all over the earth. They made the dress of Gaia beautiful and combed out her hair so that it shone in the darkness of the night. They showed the creatures of the earth how to live together. And when they had done this, the Giants brought forth the people. They shaped them from earth and made many gifts for them. The people received so many gifts, in fact, that they stood up and said they could do anything they liked.*

*The Giants told the people that Gaia, their mother, had taught them differently. She had reminded them they were a part of all things. She had told them that everyone and everything had to be together in order to continue the self-creation of life. The people did not listen. They made war on each other. And, like gods and goddesses, they threw out the Giants from their lives…*

All cultures have giants in their ancient past. From Ireland to Japan, Africa to Siberia, Chile to Alaska, stories and legends abound of beings who resembled gigantic humans and possessed magical powers. We have giants in story, such as David and Goliath, Jack and the Beanstalk, or St. Christopher who carried Christ across the river in flood. We have giants in myth, such as Gogmagog and Ysbaddaden, the leaders of their ancient British race, or the Giants and Titans who challenged Zeus for Olympus. We have the signs that giants left behind such as the rocky islands in the English Channel made by their passing from Europe to Britain. We are told of their helping humanity such as in the construction of walls of cities and the building of megalithic sites like Stonehenge. We are told of their gifts to humanity, such as the Titan Prometheus bringing fire, or the giant figure of Sakaraka'amche who spread himself over the land to give medicinal plants to the Yavapai of Arizona.

On the other hand we have stories of giants as hostile and violent beings. On earth, human heroes are often pitted against giants. The cruel giant Ricca or Retho made himself a cloak from the beards of those he had slain. He was defeated by King Arthur and banished below Mt. Arvaius, which is now Snowdon in north Wales. In the Anglo-Saxon saga *Beowulf* the hero slays the giant Grendel and his terrible mother. They are monstrous man-eating ogres. The reason for the Flood in the Old Testament is said to be partly because of the need to rid the earth of evil giants. In the heavens, the gods fought viciously to control the giants and curb their powers. Often banished from heavenly realms to those below the earth, giants could cause mischief by drying up rivers, destroying crops, flocks and mountains. The giant Enceladus, buried by Zeus beneath the island of Sicily, causes Mt. Etna to erupt when he turns in his grave.

Since the Greek gods were immortal, it is puzzling why they so fiercely contested the giants, who were neither mortal nor immortal. What was at issue here? Why was there a war between the giants and the gods? The giants seem like a before-Time bridge or preamble to human presence on earth. Their ambivalent mortality is closer to the human condition, where Western tradition says we have mortal bodies and immortal souls. Perhaps another issue was at stake in the battle, an issue which was to alter the cosmology of much of the world. The unified chthonian ("earth arising") cosmos of the giants was replaced by a divided cosmos in which concepts of divine immortality and a transcendent soul distinct from the body became predominant.

In Classical mythology it is said that the Titans were the children of Gaia. By herself (parthenogenesis) Gaia created the Sky which was called Ouranos, the Mountains called Ourea, and the Sea called Pontus. She then took the Sky as her lover. Out of their union the Titans were born. These included Oceanus, Cronos, Hyperion, Themis and Phoebe.[1]

The *Gigantes,* the giants, were born out of a ruthless pattern of descent, characteristic of Greek male deities, in which the son overthrows the father. In this case, the giants were born from Gaia when she was impregnated by the blood of her mutilated mate Ouranos. Ouranos had been forcing Gaia, out of jealousy, to hold her children within her body. Gaia, in pain, urged her son, the Titan Cronos or "Time," to castrate Ouranos. Cronos did the deed and from the drops of blood falling upon the earth Gaia was said to have given birth to the Giants. They included Enceladus, Porphyrion, Pallas and Alcyoneus. They had the heads of men and bodies ending in serpents.[2] However, some of Gaia's children from her original union with Ouranos were also called giants. They were the hundred-handed giants, Briareus, Gyges and Cottus. Then there were the giant one-eyed Cyclopes.

As a result of this multiple usage, and because giant has come to replace Titan as the word for large human-like beings, we feel it permissible to call the collective offspring of Gaia, the Giants.

In the *Odyssey,* the ancient epic of Homer, the hero Odysseus visits the island where the race of one-eyed giant shepherds, the Cyclopes, live. They are an independent, self-sufficient race, who have no need to cultivate the soil. Polyphemos, the most formidable of the giant Cyclopes, imprisons Odysseus and his companions after they have entered his cave and helped themselves to the food there. He begins to devour them two at a time. The wily Odysseus plots their escape. First, they introduce the Cyclops to wine. Then they drive a sharpened stake into his one eye while he sleeps. When the other giants come to his aid and ask who did this to him, Polyphemos replies "Nobody," the name Odysseus had told him was his. The other Cyclopes leave. Every night the flock of sheep belonging to the remaining Cyclops came into the cave and left for pasture the next morning. Odysseus observed that the now-blind Polyphemos merely ran his finger along the back of the sheep as they departed. One morning Odysseus had his men hang onto the thick fleece on the underside of the departing sheep to avoid detection. In this manner they made their escape.[3]

In this classic story about giants, Homer's intent is to show the cunning of Odysseus against a rather stupid but powerful and dangerous foe. However the story contains some points which show our hero poorly and the giants in a rather better light.

The first point is that the Cyclopes are devoted to their sheep. They are the archetypal good shepherds living close to nature. Polyphemos knows each sheep by name and handles them gently. There is no suggestion of their being eaten. This is in contrast to the hostility he directs at the humans, whom he did not invite into his cave. They provoke his anger with their arrogance, and they literally have no name. Cannibalism seems almost an addition to the story to justify the aggressive actions of Odysseus.

In the north of Europe there is a race of beings similar to the Cyclopes. They are the Gruagachs, "hairy giants," or club-carrying Wild Herdsmen. In Scotland, where they are called Fachans, they are shown with one eye, one leg and one arm. They are the protectors of cattle with a close affinity to the trees. They are devoted to the land, but are held in awe or dread.

The second point is that the other giants come the moment one of their number is in distress. They are concerned for the well-being of Polyphemos. They only depart after he insists several times that "Nobody" did this to him. While Odysseus was cleverly avoiding blame by the "Nobody" ploy, the giants were revealing their more honorable trait of solidarity. Although the poem wants to paint the Cyclopes as unsocial savages, they are a caring bunch whose only crime seems to be that they do not live in cities or plough the soil. The sense from the poem is that they live an idyllic life and wish only to be left in peace.

The third, and rather different, point is that the Cyclopes live in caves. They are at home with earth and stone. The name Cyclopean is given to massive and well-joined masonry such as the walls in the early Greek cities of Mycenae and Tiryns. In the *Aeneid* the Cyclopes build the wall around Elysium. In Scandinavian myth the giants build the wall around Asgard. In Britain the giants are responsible for colossal earthworks which divide the land. The implication is that only a race of giants could have the strength and skill to achieve such monumental feats in earth and stone. The giants are raw nature, wild and men-devouring. Yet at the same time they are city building and culture creating. They cross the divide at the beginning of time between wild and civilized, between subhuman and more-than-human.

We see this crossing over in Greek mythology. The Pantheon—all the deities of the Greek people—was larger in early tradition than it was later after the war in heaven. At first it included the primordial mother goddesses: Euronyme, the cosmic mother of all, Gaia, the earth goddess and Rhea, the mother of Zeus. Also included were the Giants and Titans. Titans were a family of cosmic beings, the earliest deities of creation. They were the children of Ouranus the night sky and Gaia the earth and fertility goddess. They set the first people on earth during the paradise known as the Golden Age and helped them with many gifts. Their offspring included the major Olympian gods who, eventually led by Zeus, overthrew the Titans in order to win the war in heaven.

One of the wisest of the Titans was Prometheus, "Forethought." He was the offspring of the Titan Iapetus and one of the Titanesses of the oceans, probably Themis. Some traditions say he made the human race from clay. He worked constantly to benefit the mortals of earth, often aiding them against the demands of the gods. One of his creations was a boy so beautiful that Prometheus dared not allow Zeus to see him. Zeus grew increasingly incensed with actions like this. He decided humans had been given quite enough and forbade Prometheus to give them the gift of fire. Prometheus concealed fire in a fennel root and carried it to earth. For his role as benefactor to humans, Prometheus was condemned by Zeus to be forever chained to a rock. His perpetually renewing liver was to be torn at by an eagle.[4]

Some traditions say that Zeus discovered the potion that Gaia was seeking to make her children immortal and kept it for himself. Zeus was the son of Gaia's daughter Rhea. He had overthrown his father, Cronos, and ruled in his place. Gaia eventually encouraged the Giants to attack Zeus for his arrogant and high-handed ways. War broke out between the giants and the gods and goddesses of Olympus. The Olympians enlisted Heracles in the struggle. They had been told by an oracle that they could never defeat the Giants without mortal aid. Heracles shot the giants Alcyoneus, Ephialtes and Porphyrion with arrows. Poseidon threw a piece of the island of Cos on Polybotes.

*A Gruagach. A Cyclops from Northern Europe*

Enceladus was buried below Sicily. Athena slew Pallas, taking his skin as her shield. The thunderbolts of Zeus, the arrows of Heracles and the weapons of the other Olympians dispatched the remaining giants.[5]

When the war in heaven was over, Mount Olympus was established as the home of the gods and goddesses who were arranged in the cosmological order that we know so well. Zeus was at the top of a hierarchy, with his brother Poseidon ruling the sea. The goddesses were demoted from being creators and were consigned to minor roles as wives and protectors. The Titans and Giants were relegated to the "time before Time." They were condemned like Prometheus to eternal punishment, or like Atlas to be forever carrying the weight of the world upon their shoulders. They were made to suffer the assaults of whirlwind and ice in deserted, dark and barren lands. They became the *Ge-antes*, the beings of the "earth before."

This pattern of early presence in the Cosmos, beneficial cooperation with humans, then conflict with gods or heroes, and banishment to elemental realms appears in many of the world traditions concerning giants. How can we resolve the ambivalence which surrounds giants? How can we resolve the conflict between their ancient role as benefactors and their subsequent role as terrible beings?

## IN THE BEGINNING

The answer to this question lies in the historical process of the growing divide in the Western mind between the concept of nature and the concept of culture. Let us define what we mean by "culture." Every race, tribe or society has a culture: ideas and beliefs held in the mind and taught to offspring. It is also their style of life, their traditions and customs manifested in the material world.

People who have not developed many material manifestations may have a rich culture. So it is a mistake to define some people as "primitive" and lacking in culture and some as more cultured or "civilized" on the basis of their material existence. Indeed, little material development may mean an intensely developed spiritual life just as high materialism may mean little spirituality. "Culture" therefore does not mean "civilization" which carries a value judgement in our society.

Anthropologists speak of a split between the world of nature and the world of people, called the "nature versus culture" dichotomy. However in this book we are not going to perpetuate that dichotomy because it tends to demean nature and elevate culture. We will use the term "nature-culture" for those people close to the natural world with little material development. And we will use "urban-culture" for those people living more removed from the natural world, in built, urban environments. This will avoid any value judgement about "primitive" versus "civilized."

Originally, the human experience was closely tied to the land. There was no separation between nature and how humans lived. Self-identity came from the reciprocal relationships of life. The external world was perceived in terms of human experience and human experience was perceived in terms of the external world. The world was not objectified. Henri Frankfort characterized this as an "I-Thou" relationship. Ernst Cassirer wrote of it as "sympathetic identification." The anthropologist Levy-Bruhl called it "participation mystique." It could be expressed as: there is nothing outside of us that is not also within us, and there is nothing within us that is not also outside of us.

The experience of "self" or "mind" extended beyond the individual body to the tribe, even into animals and the whole of nature. In his book *Steps to an Ecology of Mind*, the anthropologist Gregory Bateson saw the mind *in* nature as the only unit of evolution worthy of examination.[6] Perception was a function of the whole person with no division between mind and body. The "self" or the body-mind confronted the world as a living presence, as a constant revelation, in which everything was infused with spirit. In this world, storms had a reason for coming, trees a reason for falling, the sun a reason for rising, rivers a reason for flooding, animals a reason for giving themselves to the hunter. All things—the sun, animals, trees, rivers and mountains—had a spirit.

In such a world the key to good fortune, fertility and abundance lay in actively and purposefully participating in the central drama of creation. This is described in each culture's creation myth. To the extent that this drama is enacted, dreamt, danced, sung, ritualized and realized in sacred forms, so the people are in harmony with the Cosmos. The act of the sun rising and "singing the sun rise" are synonymous. One reciprocated the other. The act of creating a ritual dance mask of a nature spirit is not to represent the spirit, it is the actual face of the deity.

The original deity was the undifferentiated Great Goddess. She contained all things, both male and female. Her body, Nature, was the primordial giant. In her body, the people found relationship, connectedness, meaning and identity. From her came the giant forces of creation, constantly unfolding and emerging in an eternal now. The central image of the primordial goddess is the womb. Her cycle is birth, change and death. Her power was often represented as a serpent, dragon or lightning flash. In the next chapter we shall see that giant forms manifested and were created in the living landscape to invoke and encourage the participation in the great drama of the cycle of life.

With settlement and the development of villages and then towns and cities, attitudes toward the world underwent a transformative process. The people became increasingly separated from nature. Awareness of the individual self became more important. "I" came to mean the historical self existing in linear time with fixed memories, thoughts and cultural goals. The local spirits of place became separated from the unified body of human experience—"Us"—and became increasingly differentiated— the "Other."

As language developed and became more of a tool for abstract thought, new concepts about life evolved. Language and ideas became widely divergent from the natural world. Writing meant that language no longer needed an active thinker. Concepts achieved an illusory objectivity. Complex cultural practices were created through language and writing. These included laws, sacraments, philosophies and religions.

The natural world was still there, however, and humans still needed to cooperate with it. The ancient spirits of place became projections of the urban-culture's worldview. They became less natural and more like individual humans with distinct characteristics. They became the giants, ogres, fairies, cyclopes, undines, dryads, gnomes and the now distinct male and female deities of place in the local traditions. Eventually these latter became the gods and goddesses.

When people lived *in* nature, they took the elements as they came. Their cultural practices expressed this. The spirits of the living earth were subtle, diverse, huge, reaching into every dimension of life. They were mind and matter, without distinction. But once people moved to villages and towns removed from nature, in which self or mind meant "Us," they needed to make the world a safe place to live in. At that point the ancient spirits of the rivers, the weather, the animals, the forests, the "Other," were perceived as potentially hostile and had to be tamed.

Now that people had taken themselves out of the natural world, it began to be seen as being full of malevolent forces. Urban-culture was easily threatened. It required a high degree of planning, organization and control. The dangers of urban living, systematically created by humans in their cultures, were projected back onto the natural world as though the elemental forces had suddenly turned demonic. Respect and awe for the spirit of the Other—formerly met in the immanent experience of the natural world—became replaced by fear.

In her book *On Longing*, Susan Stewart reminds us that the human body is our gauge for perceiving scale. The body of the Other, the giant, is the antithesis. Human scale represents symmetry and balance. Gigantic scale is made to be grotesque and disproportionate. Our human-scaled world is interior, contained, domestic and cultural. The gigantic is exterior, uncontainable, potentially hostile and overly natural. "Our most fundamental relation to the gigantic is articulated in our relation to *landscape* [italics added], our immediate and lived relation to nature as it surrounds us.... The gigantic becomes an explanation for the environment."[7] From this we can see that the body becomes the central metaphor for describing and relating to the environment. With the growing divide between nature and culture it is easy to see how the gigantic forces of the world became the object of fear.

Why did people demonize the world though? Why did all that was not "Us" become evil? As farmers know today, and as all people who have lived on the land know, the living elemental forces are capricious, indifferent and arbitrary but not evil. How and when did the change in thought occur?

## THE FALL

When people lived on the land, directly participated in the seasonal cycles and relied on the gifts of nature, they respected the powers of wind, sun, earth, water and fire. They worked with them through ritual re-enactment of the myths of creation. When people began to live in urban areas, they built walls and houses and dams to keep out natural forces. They cleared forests and hills, domesticated animals, forced growth and created cosmologies at odds with the cycles of nature.

If nature seemed to oppose human will it was deemed evil, as if willfully obstructing human plans. If a road was built across a watercourse and the road was consistently flooded, the water rather than the road was at fault. If a village was built across a migration path and wolves or tarantulas continued in their territorial habits, the animals rather than the village had to go. If a town was built on a fault line, earthquakes were described as "disasters" rather than as inevitable occurrences of that area.

Mythology and religion in the Western Hemisphere developed very differently from those in the Eastern part of the world. After the war in heaven, the Greek gods became ascendent, replacing the Great Goddess and her attendant giants. The gods became irrevocably separate from humans in status, immortality and power. Judaism and Christianity continued this split. As Western urban-cultures developed, they tended toward a dualistic cosmology. This is in contrast to Eastern thought which generally accepted polarity and paradox in concepts such as yin/yang. In Western dualism, mental categories such as heaven and hell, within and without, mortal and immortal, believer and infidel, mind and body, spirit and matter, tame and wild, became absolute. One side was good and the other evil.

If a cosmology emphasizes dualism and puts twin forces in opposition, thinking will tend to be developed in the left hemisphere of the brain. This hemisphere operates with logic and binary function. As a result, the language of such thinkers will contain black and white categories, reinforcing the dualistic cosmology. In contrast, if a cosmology emphasizes unity and polarity, thinking will tend to be developed in the right hemisphere of the brain. This hemisphere operates with images and holistic function. As a result, the language of such thinkers will accommodate the whole, reinforcing the unified cosmology.

In ancient times the forces of nature were perceived directly by the body-wisdom of the senses. Under Western dualism, the forces of nature were removed to the level of concepts through the growth of mental ideas. For example, in place of the experience of time as an emergent periodicity determined by the amount of walking between two places, time became an absolute measure. It now took *this* amount of time to walk between the two places. Landscape became a commodity rather than an experience. This linear concept introduced the idea of there being "not enough time." Religions which eliminated the concept of the birth-death-rebirth cycle contributed to belief in linear time by postulating a single-life existence.

Another idea adopted by Western cosmology was hierarchical order. Those forces which seemed helpful to urban life took on a high, divine or human nature. Those forces which appeared outside or inimical to culture took on a low, animal-like nature. The divide between earth and heaven was made complete and the image of the universe became vertical: a ladder, pyramid or triangle. This division is clear in cultures which extolled urban living, intellectual progress, a good god "up" in heaven and evil "down" on earth. In the cosmology of these peoples—the Jews, Greeks, Romans and subsequently the Christians—the natural world became something which was to be cultivated, ordered and dominated. The wild places beyond human control became demonized.

Forests became places to be feared, to be avoided, the haunt of ghosts and witches. Wild animals became the metaphor for everything that was evil, including the "animal" nature of the body. The Earth Goddess Gaia, Pan, the Giants and beings from the Otherworld were relegated to dark chasms, mountains and wildernesses. There they entered the category of evil, identified with the "Devil." In Greek mythology this was accomplished by the citified deities of Olympus fighting and defeating those forces which were chthonic and wild—the Giants and Titans.

A similar process is revealed in the cosmologies of the desert religions. There the forces of heaven are pitted against the forces of the Devil, most of whom are recognizable as the ancient chthonian deities of the Middle East. The Great Goddess herself had to disappear. Her complex changing nature was identified with "chaos" as opposed to the ordered world of the "cosmos" that the new urban cultures desired. The old temples echoing the organic forms of earth were replaced by the square, abstract lines of temples constructed in contrast to the earth.

The giants of the Old Testament are the actual historical opponents of Israel writ large. Israel's enemies were made exterior, huge and evil. When the Hebrews arrived in Palestine the enemy Canaanites are described in the Bible as giants. The greatest of the Canaanites, Goliath, was killed by the "miniature" David. By this parable the Old Testament implies that the smallest of the Israelites is more than a match for the largest of their enemies. Nimrod, whose other name Gibbor means giant, was the builder of the Tower of Babel. Moses killed the one giant, Og, who survived the flood.

Other Old Testament giants represent huge, ancient, established cultures against which the small nomadic tribe of Israelites struggled.

Among the Greeks the first task of heroes who are the founders of cities is to clear the land of malevolent beings which included the giants. An example is Theseus the founder of Athens. He not only clears the immediate vicinity of giants and other monsters but goes to Crete and kills the Minotaur there. The giants rapidly became the subdued forces of the natural world, or the conquered forces from other cultures. It is ironic that the beings who became the deities of the newly emerging urban-cultures had chthonian—earth arising—origins and even giant origins. Both Zeus and Yahweh began life as the giant Thunder Spirits of mountains and became enthroned huge men with beards. Athena began as an owl and rock spirit from Anatolia and became the matronly deity of the Athenian city state.

By this point in history, the division between natural forces and urban dwellers had become thoroughly enshrined in language and in cosmology. This found expression in books of law such as the Bible. The whole structure of the cosmos now affirmed that divine law proclaimed the natural as evil and the urban as good. This worldview suited the patriarchal, monotheistic practices of a struggling desert people. As a result, giants became everything the Judaeo-Christian culture did not want to be, that is: solitary, evil, violent, hostile, naked, cannibalistic and identified with the natural world—the "Other." Giants were used to clearly establish the boundaries. They defined who was "in" and who was "out."

It is unfortunate that the Christian Church had to take the Old Testament literally. Here the giants were the wicked forces of the "Other." Christianity went to great lengths to prove that the giants were historical beings. It said they came from the line of Cain. In the process it perpetuated fear of actual evil beings existing upon the earth. The cosmological dualism that a fundamentalist reading of the Bible created in people's minds consisted of real demons and a real devil on earth. This arose as a result of accepting a real angelic hierarchy and a real god in heaven.

By the time mainstream European culture became thoroughly Christianized, giants had become negative and evil. Christian theologians, like Augustine, took the dim Old Testament view of giants. But there were places where the ancient memory of good giants could still be found. Saint Christopher, "Christ carrier," was an extremely popular good giant in medieval Europe. Effigies of him were paraded in many cities until his cult was banned by the Church. Gog and Magog, ancient British giants, became adopted through popular demand by the City of London for their defense of the land. Statues of them were set up in the city Guildhall. In the folk traditions of Europe the giants were inclined to be friendly if approached in the right way. Rùbezahl was a kind giant of Bohemia. The giant of Grabbist Hill in Britain would help fishermen. The Gruagachs or Fachans, Wild Herdsmen, would protect cattle if offerings were left to them. Some of the giants in literature were also friendly, but this was usually because they had been tamed and made Christian. Jonathan Swift's good giant, Gulliver, was very helpful and moral. The good giants of Rabelais were all Christian and his bad giants were definitely not.

On the whole, the idea of good giants in the literary, Christian line of European thought is anti-traditional. Heracles or Hercules, who could be construed as a good giant/culture hero, is denied giant status. He remains in the category of Theseus, a human giant-killer. During the war in heaven he killed many of the giants. But Hercules did appeal to local folk culture as a good giant. His representation in the great hill figure at Cerne Abbas in England was likely made by local people in the spirit of the original, pre-Biblical, view of giants.

*A female Gruagach*

## THE LANGUAGE OF GIANTS

Ever since the process which contorted nature to fit urban categories began, we have thought of giants in human terms. But in fact giants are the elemental forces of the world. Giants *are* nature.

Until the war in heaven was fought, which drove away the unifying cosmology of the Great Goddess and created good and evil, people lived in harmony with giants in the elemental sense. Wherever the ancient wisdom of human bodies with their complex senses and intuition was valued, people moved in harmony with the giants. When the river flooded, the giant was spreading its body, arching its back. When the volcano exploded, the giant was troubled by dark dreams. When the forests burned, the breath of the giant was cleansing the earth. When hurricanes flattened coastlines and lightning flashed, the giants were walking in the sky. When new green growth spread a mantle over the ground, the giant was putting on new clothes. When the setting sun made patterns in the clouds, the giants were at play. When the giants of nature began their fertility rites so could the humans.

These direct experiences of life are the language of the giants. They could be participated in, even increased, through "sympathetic magic." Sympathetic magic is based on the principle that like resonates with like. If a result is desired, it is created on a miniature scale. Through proportional equivalence, something small can effect its greater likeness: pouring water on the ground can bring rain, strewing pennies around the house can bring wealth. Through creating something on a larger scale, sympathy is achieved with the gigantic forces of the cosmos.

It is difficult for us today to think in these terms as a result of the establishment of the scientific cosmology with its mind-matter division and mechanical and linear notions of cause and effect. It would be just as hard for a tribal person not to think in these terms. Their language predisposes them toward synchronicity, communion of mind and matter, sympathetic resonance and non-linear time and space.

Is it possible to find in the idea of giants a key for unlocking the ancient secrets of the sacred way of life? Can they offer a way of relating to the world around us which reunites earth and spirit as they were in our ancient inheritance? Can the idea of giants provide us with a way of being with the world which ensures the future for generations to come?

The clues to this ancient way of being may reside in the somatic memories of our own bodies. Our bodies have a history upon the earth of such length that the cosmologies of the past few thousand years are but a veneer. Clues to the giants may lie in the huge forms which lay across the landscape: the mountain ranges, rivers, plains, woods and forests. Clues to the language of giants may lie in traditions where people interacted with natural forms to produce myths and shrines, and cultures which enhanced the patterns and powers in the landscape. We now turn to this subject, for in the landscape itself is written a language which promises the restoration of a sacred world. ✵

### CHAPTER THREE

# GIANTS IN BRITAIN

I walk toward a cluster of shadows made visible on the horizon by the dim memory of the setting sun. It is eerily quiet. The shadows become larger until they tower up before me. I can make out massive standing stones capped with roughly hewn lintels. I pass through one of the portals made by the suspended stones. The starry sky is momentarily blacked out above my head. The huge trilithon seems to be falling as its dark shadow forms an ancient symbol framed by stars.

I stand in the center of the circle. I lift up my arms to the sky. The age-old cry of mortals is soundlessly voiced against the timelessness of the place. At that moment, far below me, something stirs. A breath of wind ripples through the night air. The thought "Giants!" comes to me. At the same instant the image of a finger rising upwards toward the surface of the earth passes before my mind's eye. It rises rapidly until it slows and stops at the surface. Just the tip of the little finger of a huge being is crowned by the ring of stones. The hanging stones begin to spin, to dance before my eye. I do not know whether the sky is turning, the stones, the giant or myself. It is enough to join in the dance.

———————————

illiam Blake wrote that the giant Albion once lived freely in his native land of Britain. But then his spirit was held immobile, imprisoned by the chains of a false religious morality and the materialism of an Industrial Age about to begin. Blake prophesied a time when Albion would shake off the chains which bound him, break free of tyranny, and rise to restore a sacred "New Jerusalem" on earth.

Although Blake drew upon history for his visionary work, he could not have known fully of the vast network of ancient sites covering the British landscape because that network was only just being unearthed by the antiquarians. He had probably visited and marvelled at the "Giants' Dance," the local name for Stonehenge. But the full story of the gigantic earthworks and thousands of standing stones connected over hundreds of miles had not yet been written. If Blake had known the reality of giants in the British landscape, what would his unique imagination have been inspired to write of the true nature of the giant Albion?

The fact is that ever since the beginning of the Neolithic Age people had joined together to create huge complexes of earth and stone in the landscape. This occurred not just in Britain but across Europe and some say across the globe. These landscape structures must have had a profound purpose. And among the hill figures, barrows, mounds, henges, avenues, dolmens, menhirs and stone circles, there always lurks the figure of a giant.

Researchers into these complex sites have been awed by their scale and driven to explain them in both scientific and mystical terms. One suggestion is that they form a magical technology for dealing with the energies of the earth. All the sites in an area, or even across the country, connect in a vast pattern whose purpose was to invoke benevolent cosmic forces.

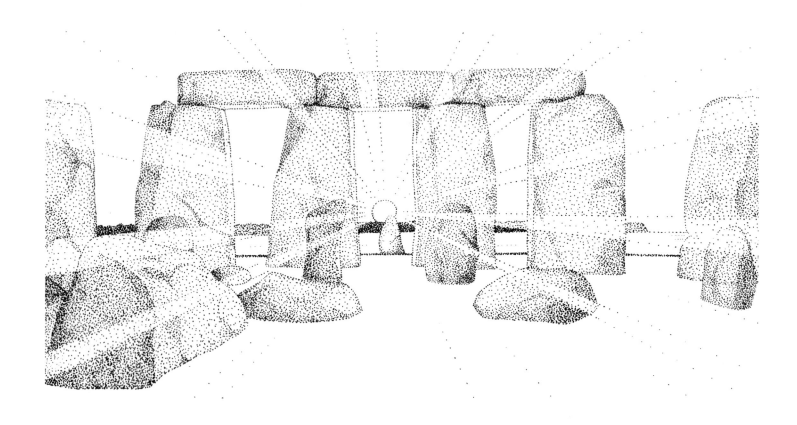

Telluric currents, subtle forces and electromagnetic energy which could respond to the implantation of stones at specific sites have all been suggested. The stones would act like acupuncture needles along the meridians of a body, resulting in the improvement of health and fertility. In this case the body was that of the landscape giant.

John Michell in his seminal book *The View Over Atlantis*, made the case for many of these ideas. He wrote:

> *A great scientific instrument lies sprawled over the entire surface of the globe. At some period, thousands of years ago, almost every corner of the world was visited by people with a particular task to accomplish. With the help of some remarkable power, by which they could cut and raise enormous blocks of stone, these men created vast astronomical instruments, circles of erect pillars, pyramids, underground tunnels, cyclopean stone platforms, whose course from horizon to horizon was marked by stones, mounds and earthworks.*[1]

Empirical evidence supporting such ideas has not been easily forthcoming. Like the elements of wind and water, the paths of the giant spirits of the earth were subtle and could not be grasped by the hands and ideas of physical science. Let us examine some of the sites about which such claims have been made and assess the evidence. As this book is mostly concerned with the Western world this is where we shall begin.

*A dolmen in western Ireland*

## DOLMENS

The first evidence of megalithic ("large stone") construction occurs in the form of dolmens which begin to appear in France, Portugal and Spain from about 5,000 BCE. BCE means "before the common era" and replaces BC. Likewise, CE means "common era" and replaces AD. This avoids an implicit theism while keeping the familiar structure of dating intact.

Dol-men in the Celtic language of Brittany means "table stone." A dolmen is comprised of large orthostats or upright stones arranged to form a chamber with a capstone on top. Most dolmens were originally covered by a mound of earth or stones, but have since been unearthed and left bare. By the fourth millennium (4000-3000 BCE), dolmens had become highly developed throughout western Europe. Dolmens with long stone passageways, multiple chambers and huge capstones became the norm.[2] Seen as burial mounds by later cultures, their huge size and colossal stones often led people to believe the dolmens were the work of a bygone race of giants.

## NEW GRANGE

A truly sophisticated example of the developed dolmen is New Grange in County Meath, Ireland. New Grange is a huge chambered mound located about 30 miles north of Dublin. It is on a ridge beside the Boyne River. Built around 3,300 BCE, it vies for being the oldest stone structure in the world. It is almost a thousand years older than the stone pyramids at Giza in Egypt.

The mound covering the extraordinary interior is some 300 feet wide and 36 feet high. It was carefully built of layers of gravel and soil and then covered with quartz stones to reflect light. These were carried from the Wicklow Mountains over 50 miles away in the

to a chamber about 12 feet wide. Three smaller side chambers open off the main one, which has a corbelled roof rising about 16 feet high. The roof has not leaked in over five thousand years! Sixteen of the upright stones in the passage are deeply carved, as well as many in the chambers. The symbols mostly consist of circles, spirals, cup marks, crescents, wavy lines, triangles, chevrons and diamond shapes or lozenges.

At the Winter Solstice a beam of light from the rising sun moves down the passageway all the way to the end chamber where it illuminates a beautiful design of carved

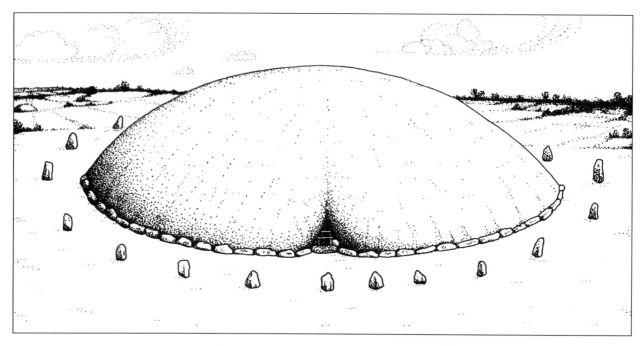

south. All around the base of the covering mound are massive recumbent stones, 97 in all, many of which have symbols carved upon them. Surrounding the mound is a circle of standing stones.

The interior of New Grange consists of a 62-foot-long passageway strikingly lined with orthostats, leading

*New Grange. View from the southeast. (After Martin Brennan)*

spirals. This purposely constructed and breathtaking alignment reveals that the prehistoric people, often considered "barbaric" or "primitive," understood the solar calendar perfectly. They were first-class planners and architects. They wrote messages in stone and created some of the world's most enduring art. In all those accomplishments, they conceptualized and built a giant: an enormous yoni complete with vagina and womb, penetrated on the darkest day of the year by the life-giving shaft of returning sunlight.

Grave robbers, antiquarians and archaeologists have sifted this astounding site for centuries. Recently it was "restored" by the Irish Office of Public Works and now receives busloads of visitors. Despite the restoration, New Grange remains a powerful place with traces of the magic and immense importance that once accompanied the rituals there. Whether glimpsing the huge mound from a distance at sunset across the Boyne River, or crouching inside along the passage and brushing past the massive, silent presence of carved stones, it is possible to feel awe at being in the presence of the ancient mind of our ancestors. That mind understood giants.

New Grange was built near two other chambered mounds which are equally dazzling in conception and design.

Knowth to the northwest of New Grange is an even larger mound and possesses two passages oriented east and west. Dowth to the northeast has several chambers which have significant bearings to the other mounds and to the solar calendar. The area lies in a bend of the River Boyne and has 30 smaller mounds which also lie in precise geometrical relation to each other.[3] If one considers the amount of labor which went into hauling and erecting the megaliths, carving symbols upon them and constructing dozens of huge mounds, the organization and social cooperation required becomes immediately apparent. Add to this the symbolic, geometrical and astronomical sophistication of the sites, and we encounter brilliant thinking and the ability to depict concepts which are huge in scope. It would be equivalent to putting a person on the moon today.

What did the Neolithic Irish people think they were doing when they conceived the stone and earth complex of the Boyne Valley? Why was New Grange at least partially covered in quartz? Who was going to see it and from where? What is the significance of the rays of the sun entering the dark passage of the mound at Winter Solstice? What do the carvings on the stones tell us?

Answers to questions like these are always viewed through the particular lens each researcher brings to bear. We are introducing bias in viewing the Boyne Valley through the lens of the giants. We find the imaginations of the builders to be concerned with the cycles of time, the division of space, the procurement of fertility and with the elements of the Irish landscape, of which the mounds then became a part.

The River Boyne flows through rich agricultural land. Because of its abundance it very likely was a site chosen by the first settlers of Ireland and thus became a center of origin. In fact the Hill of Tara, where ancient Irish sovereigns were crowned, is only ten miles away. The county name, Meath, means "middle place." It lies halfway between the northern and southern shores of the island, on the Irish Sea. In Irish mythology rivers are seen as powerful spirits who later became identified as deities, such as the god Nechtan, whose name means "serpent."[4] Where European rivers have retained their ancient name it usually refers to a serpent. The land itself is often spoken of in terms of a deity, usually feminine. The Boyne Valley is no exception to this in being named after a goddess, Boanne.

*The reconstructed entrance to New Grange. The light of the Winter Solstice rising sun enters the mound through the light box over the entrance*

One legend tells of the impregnation of Boanne by deities called Elcmar by some, Oengus or Nechtan by others. They are solar, serpent or river gods. A simple interpretation would inform us that the Boyne over-flowed its banks in the spring and fertilized the sur-rounding land. A more mythic and magical interpretation of the legend would explain the beauti-ful symbols on the entrance stone of New Grange. The

wavy lines coming up out of the ground at the base of the stone could depict the river. Does the narrow line in the center of the stone represent the vulva of the goddess or the impregnating beam of light? It can hardly be a coincidence that the line on the stone pre-cisely marks where the beam of light enters the pas-sageway of stones at the Winter Solstice and reaches the central chamber. We are looking at elaborate sex-ual symbolism.

Why was this planned for the Winter Solstice? Why not orient the sacred structure for some other time? Well, if the concern of the builders was primarily agricultural, then the turning of the sun on the horizon at this time was of great importance. It meant that the nights would become shorter, the days would become

*Kerb stone from New Grange. This stone is on a line directly through the mound from the entrance*

warmer, and the cycle of the year ideal for growing plants would begin. In effect, it meant that what the river accomplished every spring with its rich nutrient-depositing floods, was now accomplished on a greater cosmic scale through what is called "sym-pathetic magic." So they constructed a place where the solar spirit could mate with the earth spirit. Perhaps the New Grange builders even thought that without the sun spirit impregnating the mound of the earth spirit at the Winter Solstice, the cycle of the sea-sons would not be renewed and the cold and darkness would go on.

If this interpretation is correct we can see that the ancient people of the Boyne Valley thought in gigantic terms. They were intensely interested in their place in the world, in time and space, and in the recurrent forces of the seasons which ensured the abundance of their lives. Not content to be passive witnesses to the compelling and somewhat indifferent passing of these giant forces, they created replicas of them. The upturned buttocks of New Grange covered in shining white quartz were designed to be seen by the passing giant of the sun and were an invitation, an encourage-ment, to perform the act which guaranteed the fertility of the coming year.

Studies of the symbols carved upon the stones in the Boyne Valley yield equivocal interpretations. There is some agreement however that triangles, chevrons, lozenges and cup marks are sexual in character. Paleolithic studies have suggested that the pubic triangle was the commonest simple sign for a woman. Other symbols convincingly depict calendars and show methods of counting off solar and lunar time. This would seem to account for zig zags, "sun dials," cres-cents and other linear and notched symbols.[5] The remaining symbols are mostly spi-rals. Perhaps these depict the movement of energy itself. The spirals could be the cycles of life, swirling clouds, water and air, serpent or dragon energy and kundalini sexual energy. Perhaps the spirals depict the long-awaited fusion of elemental earth and sky forces that took place at the winter solstice.

The symbols carved upon Irish megaliths give support for interpreting the Boyne Valley structures as the means by which Stone Age humans participated in the cycle of life. They perceived and thought about this life cycle in terms of giants. There is a Summer Solstice alignment through the large mound of Dowth and alignments to Spring and Autumn Equinoxes through the passageways of the huge Knowth mound. These are markers to encourage the procession of the giants through the cycle of the year.

## INTERPRETING CHAMBERED MOUNDS

Chambered mounds or dolmens occur in many parts of the world. Though their simplest form consists of several orthostats forming a portal covered by an immense capstone, later this form was repeatedly connected so that some dolmens have more than 10 capstones. The greatest incidence of dolmens is in Neolithic Europe. They spread throughout Britain, Ireland, Scotland, France, Holland, the Iberian peninsula and Malta in the Mediterranean. "Tholoi" or round subterranean chambers also occur in Crete. Developed forms of these appear later on the Greek mainland, notably at Mycenae late in the second millennium BCE. Dolmens were built, probably in the last two thousand years, in Ethiopia, Japan and even in the north-eastern United States! These latter could have been influenced by European examples.

They represent either the last vestiges of the spreading megalithic impulse, or independent development.[6]

On a very fundamental level the dolmens are openings into the earth. They are the womb of the Great Goddess, the original prototype for the giants. They are the caves in which the ancient ancestors once celebrated the stages and events of life and death. Burials in them show the wish to return the deceased to the earth, the place from which they came. But of the tens of thousands of Neolithic people who existed, apparently only a small percentage were buried or their ashes deposited in dolmens. All the mysteries of life's stages were likely to have been ritually enacted within the chambers of dolmens: birthing, adolescent initiation, mating, menstrual retreat, healings, shamanic journeys, dying, and the honoring of buried ancestors.

Many dolmens are accompanied by standing stones called menhirs. Men-hir translates from Breton as "long stone." We interpret this juxtaposition of dolmen and menhir to be symbols of a giant enactment of intercourse. The phallic nature of these stones in Britain and France is unmistakable. They are tall and narrow, often rounded at the top and sometimes shaped to show the head or glans of the penis. Those that remain in existence range in height from a few feet to over 30 feet. Folk custom to the present day is to pay a visit to menhirs to encourage fertility.

Sexual expression was refreshingly explicit for Neolithic people. Their structures emphatically tell of the enormous importance of creation as carried out in fertility of plants, animals and humans. The gigantic size of mounds and menhirs is an accurate guide to the importance they gave to impregnation and birth. The structures also hint at the enormous power they attributed to earth and sky, and how they invited that power to move through their lives. We explore these sexual themes more fully in Chapter 12.

Examples are plentiful of a female mound accompanied by a male menhir. One standing stone near the New Grange mound is just topped by the winter solstice sun as it shines into the passageway. In Brittany, the several varieties of dolmens that occur are often accompanied by menhirs. In some cases, as at Les Pierres Plats, the menhir stands just beside the entrance. In several places, such as Gavr'inis, an old menhir fell or was broken and used as the capstone for the chamber. And at the extremely old site where the two dolmens of Table des Marchands and Er-Grah were built, they were accompanied by a colossal menhir, Le Grand Menhir Brisé, now fallen, which at 60 feet was the tallest in the megalithic world.

There are many examples of dolmens and their menhirs which are aligned to significant astronomical azimuths on the horizon. Stoney Littleton long barrow near Bath in England is illuminated by the rising sun on the Winter Solstice. Le Grand Menhir Brisé may have been a foresight to the eight extreme rising and

*The huge sculpted menhir at Dol, Brittany*

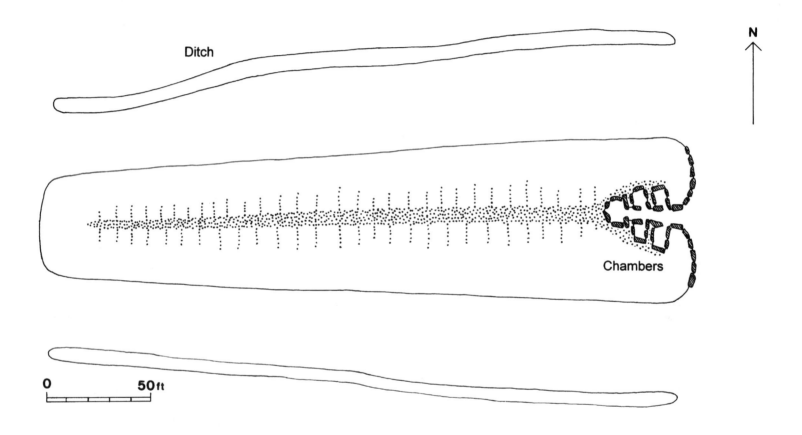

Ditch

N

Chambers

0    50ft

West Kennet Long Barrow

setting points of the moon. The huge mound-covered dolmen at Gavr'inis or "Island of Goats" in the Gulf of Morbihan is aligned to the sun at Winter Solstice and also to the major southern moonrise. It is also situated to interact with a tidal river mouth which is now visible as an underwater river. Gavr'inis is so powerful it quivers. Its placement was deliberate and its power was multifold. Nearly every megalith inside Gavr'inis is deeply carved with undulating lines of energy. These include serpents, "goddess figurines" and spirals similar to those at New Grange but likely to be slightly earlier, circa 3,500 BCE.[7]

The numbers of dolmens run into thousands. It is to one remarkable example in central southern England that we now will turn for further interpretation of giant thinking and the megalithic mind.

## WEST KENNET LONG BARROW

West Kennet Long Barrow lies not far from Silbury Hill. Silbury is the most gargantuan human-made structure in prehistoric Europe. Both sites are just a few fields away from the enormous Avebury stone circle and avenues. The area as a whole can truly be described as the most varied and mysterious sacred landscape of the Neolithic Age.

The long barrow is an elongated mound stretching 340 feet along the ridgetop just south of Silbury Hill. It has been tested by the trials of time, but somehow has retained its full, if somewhat broken, length. It still lies dramatically outlined on the skyline to a height of almost 10 feet. It was piled up with earth taken from ditches neatly dug on either side about 40 feet away. The date of construction is estimated to be about 3,250 BCE, and is likely to be earlier.

In his excavations, Stuart Piggot found that the long barrow had been constructed along a central core of boulders, heaped about 6 feet high, which ran like a spine along the entire length of the mound. Reinforcing the spinelike imagery were short spurs of boulders which ran regularly off either side of the central core. Each rib was composed of 6 stones. At one end of the long barrow was an entrance leading into a passage and five stone-lined chambers. These chambers contained 46 articulated burials; this is far too few over a thousand-year period to justify an exclusive funerary purpose.[8]

At the eastern end of the barrow a shallow forecourt lined by megaliths was built at the entrance. The barrow lies east-west and on the equinoxes the rising sun originally penetrated the entire length of the passageway to illuminate the end chamber. The sun can no longer do this as five massive stones were put up to block the entrance forecourt around 2,600 BCE. At the same time the interior was filled with deposits.

Excavations have shown that this sealing process was done very carefully after the interior had been in continuous use for almost a thousand years.

At the end of the 25 foot long, 8 foot high passageway a large, roughly circular, corbelled chamber was constructed. On either side of the passageway four smaller and lower chambers were made, two on each side. Orthostats lining the passage and chambers create the impression of ancient presences. When ground plans of the interior orthostats were drawn in this century, it was clear that the five megalithic chambers formed the shape of a rather plump, squatting female figure of a type with precedents in the Paleolithic Age. The entrance to the interior was through the passageway that, by its explicit location, formed the vagina of the mound goddess.

Aerial views of the barrow revealed an even larger goddess on the outside. The earthworks of the barrow as a whole formed the outline of a rectangular visual image of the goddess almost a tenth of a mile long. The forecourt, passageway and inner chambers formed her vagina. The goddess was not just symbolically represented as might be the case in spiral carvings, but the mound and its entrance were created on a scale which constituted her actual body. The overall shape is a very close match to rectangular Neolithic goddess stones found in Britain and Ireland. It also matches images of the goddess carved on stones in the dolmens of Brittany.[9] Interestingly, the barrow takes its name from the nearby spring and stream, the Kennet. Authorities agree "Kennet" derives from, or is the origin of, the Anglo-Saxon word for the female genitals, the cunt.

Why was the entrance forecourt, no doubt the scene of ritual, blocked off after so many years of use? The answer might be that the time of the closing of the barrow coincided with the completion of the construction of Silbury Hill, c. 2,600 BCE. Every year around harvest time, further levels were added to this massive earthwork, until, after centuries of labor, the desired height and shape had been achieved. The base of Silbury covers over 5 acres and the hill is 130 feet high. The traditions about it have always been that a great treasure is concealed within. In some versions the treasure is gold and belonged to a great king called Sil. The gold and the name hint at solar and female attributes. For Sul is the ancient British name for the sun and, contrary to modern gender practice, was the name of the solar goddess.

From here it is easy to speculate that Sul-bury Hill, clearly visible from the West Cunnet Long Barrow about a mile away, is the pregnant belly of the Great Goddess. The hill is an expression in the landscape of the all-embracing power of the primordial giant, the Great Goddess. Since the Great Mother of All, by definition, contains both female and male powers, perhaps the completed hill assured fertility permanently. If that was the case, impregnation by having the equinox sun shine into the goddess's open vulva in the nearby barrow was no longer needed. Michael Dames develops ideas along these lines in his books, which we shall discuss in the chapters on sexuality and on ritual.

For now we shall note that many other barrows in Britain have giant associations. Several are called Giants' Graves. There is a Giants' Hill. In nearby Oxfordshire a barrow very similar to West Kennet called Waylands Smithy has the legend of a helpful giant blacksmith associated with it. The parallels involving fertility and giants are fairly evident between the West Kennet-Silbury complex, the dolmens and menhirs of Brittany, and the Boyne Valley in Ireland. But the ancient British builders created one unique pattern upon the landscape in their wish to invoke and participate in the giant forces of life.

## THE BUILDERS OF STONEHENGE

William Blake's vision of the giant Albion shaking off his chains and rising to restore the sacred order of the land of Britain is a potent theme in British mythology. Giants have always been said to reside in Britain. Caxton's *Chronicle of England* tells us it was settled by a Lady Albine, her 32 giant daughters and sons, Albion and Gogmagog. In Geoffrey of Monmouth's fictitious account of the Trojan Brutus, who changed the name of the land from Albion to Britain, he and his comrades have to drive off the giants who live there (Cornwall being a particularly favorite haunt for them). After a battle in which Albion was slain, Brutus' lieutenant, Corineus, hurled Gogmagog into the sea.[10] An island in Plymouth Sound is said to be where he landed and is known as Lan-Goemagog or Gogmagog's Leap. A figure of at least one giant was carved into a hillside overlooking this island.

Geoffrey of Monmouth also provides us with the colorful story about the construction of Stonehenge. Aurelius Ambrosius and Uther Pendragon, the father of King Arthur, are leaders who combat the invasion of Britain by the Saxons. When Aurelius wishes to commemorate the defeat of the Saxons with a lasting monument, Merlin is proposed to him as the architect. Merlin suggests that he transport the enormous stones of "the Giants' Ring which is on Mount Killaraus in Ireland," but adds "there is no one alive strong enough to move them." Merlin goes on to say that the stones have great medicinal power and that originally "the Giants transported them from the remotest confines of Africa and set them up in Ireland at a time when they inhabited that country." When the Britons fail to move the stones of the Giants' Ring, Merlin provides the magical means of shipping them over to Britain and putting them up on Salisbury Plain.[11]

This story was, of course, dismissed as historical fiction. Aurelius is factual enough, but his time was the fifth century CE and Stonehenge in its present form was completed 2,300 years earlier. The stones however include among their number the "Blue Stones" which have been convincingly shown to have originated in the Prescelly Mountains of southern Wales. These phallic-like stones were transported from Wales long before the squarish sarsen stones which support the lintels appeared on the site. Could Geoffrey's story contain a memory of this extraordinary feat? The connection with giants still lives on today with the traditional local name for Stonehenge being the Giants' Dance.

There are many other stories of giants associated with places in Britain. Sometimes the giant is benevolent and sometimes malevolent. The earlier the story the more beneficent the giant. In the early Welsh *Mabinogion,* for example, Bran the

Blessed, a Celtic king of Britain, is so huge he had to wade across the sea when he attacked Ireland. Eventually his head was set up on White Hill—the site of the Tower of London—and its presence alone secured Britain against invasion. The giant who lived in the ancient barrow of Wayland's Smithy was definitely benevolent. Giant stories are often around places which involved stupendous feats of labor, such as the megalithic sites, or the great earthen dikes. They are found around huge human or animal forms cut into hillsides. They also appear in places that were connected with others across the landscape to form a figure on a massive scale.

## ST. MICHAEL IN THE LANDSCAPE

An example of this is provided by the story of St. Michael's Mount in Cornwall. St. Michael's Mount is a small but steep and rocky island just off the Cornish coast near Land's End. At low tide it can be reached on foot across a causeway. According to legend it was built by the giant Cormoran and his wife Cormelian. They built the island from white granite. One day, while the lazy Comoran slept, it occurred to Cormelian it would be easier to collect the much closer greenstone. As she returned with the stone in her apron, Comoran awoke, saw what she was doing and aimed a kick at her. The apron strings broke and the greenstone rock fell to form the causeway which connects the Mount to the mainland.

Comoran went on to torment the local population. He stole their livestock and chased their wives. One day a bright local lad called Jack decided to confront the giant about this in his stronghold. Jack went over to the island and dug a deep pit. This is the well which can still be seen on the ascent route. He then stood before it and taunted Cormoran with insults. As the giant came rushing down the path of the mount, Jack whipped out a polished disk and the giant, blinded by the reflection of the sun in the disk, fell into the pit.

This legend of "Jack the Giant Killer" uses the sun to defeat the giant. The folk legend contains a memory of the ancient spirits to which such mounts were usually dedicated and of an astonishing solar alignment formed by sites across the British landscape.

Across the English Channel Mont-Saint-Michel is an island almost identical to St. Michael's Mount. Though larger, it has the same steep aspect and originally it too could only be reached on foot at low tide. It and its sister island Tombelaine were said to have been made by the giants Grant-Gosier and Galamelle. Geoffrey of Monmouth tells us of a visit Arthur paid to the island to deal with the maiden-violating, man-eating giant who lived there. It is interesting to note that both

*St. Michael's Mount*

islands became sanctuaries of St. Michael. His task as leader of the heavenly forces was to defeat and banish the ancient pagan earth forces. While St. Michael's chthonic or earth arising foes are usually depicted as serpents, in these two cases they are explicitly identified as giants. Jack and Arthur are the human heroes.

Although the parallels between the two mounts are fascinating, it is to the British mount and the land-

which runs through southern England. Many elevated St. Michael churches, including those on St. Michael's Mount, Brentor, Burrowbridge Mump and Glastonbury Tor, lie on a line several hundred miles in length.[12] It is not a mathematically precise alignment, but the connect-the-dots arrangement creates a linear figure of striking length and meaning. Many of the prominent hills with St. Michael churches have associations with giants, dragons or other pagan symbols. The line also connects other ancient sacred sites besides hills. The Hurlers stone circles in Cornwall, the great Avebury circle, and the major pagan ritual center of Avalon at Glastonbury in Somerset are on the

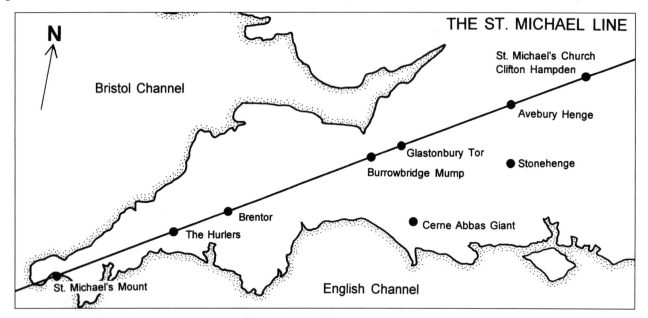

**THE ST. MICHAEL LINE**

N

Bristol Channel

St. Michael's Church
Clifton Hampden

Avebury Henge

Glastonbury Tor
Burrowbridge Mump

Stonehenge

Brentor

The Hurlers

Cerne Abbas Giant

St. Michael's Mount

English Channel

scape pattern of which it is a part that we shall now turn. We will see why the Christian church needed to specifically charge the Archangel Michael with banishing the giant chthonian forces in order to suppress the powerful pagan pattern that had been built across the landscape of Britain.

In *The View Over Atlantis* John Michell describes an extraordinary alignment of hilltop shrines dedicated to St. Michael and other dragon-slaying saints

line. The fact that some of the most important sacred places in Britain were placed on the alignment would seem to confirm that the awareness of this geographic connection was conscious on the part of ancient Britons.

A feature of the "St. Michael Line" or the "Dragon Line" is that it is oriented to sunrise and sunset on the cross-quarter days. These are the points midway between solstice and equinox and form the four main Celtic festivals of the year. The festivals which the rising sun indicates are Beltane or May Day on May 1 and Llughnasad or Lammas at the beginning of August. The setting sun pointed to by the line indicates the festival of Samhain or Hallowe'en at the end of October and the festival of Imbolc or Candlemas in early February. These days are considered "Celtic" but we know they were also important to Britons thousands of years earlier because many of the megalithic sites include alignments to the rising or setting sun on those days. Stonehenge possesses all these alignments, plus the well-known summer solstice—winter solstice line, and Stonehenge is certainly not Celtic!

This orientation meant that if observers stood on one of two hills in the alignment which were visible to each other, such as Glastonbury Tor and Burrowbridge Mump, they saw the sun rise or set over the other hill depending on the time of year. As the cross-quarter days are fire festivals it is likely that fires were lit on these hills at those times. It is possible to imagine a line of beacon fires running between Avebury and St. Michael's Mount as the sun rose over the line on May 1 and as the sun set over the line on October 31. One carried the energy of the summer as the year waxed, the other honored the winter as the year waned.

It is hard to know what the ancient Britons practiced on these sites or know what they thought they were doing. Whatever they may have done, the line and its shrines express a cosmology in the landscape on a gigantic scale. Any rites performed at appropriate times on the linear figure of the landscape giant would have been sure, through sympathetic magic, to have encouraged the turning of the great cosmic forces which gave and supported life.

The story of Jack and the giant on St. Michael's Mount reveals details of an ancient solar ritual. It is by design that the causeway to the Mount, the well down which the giant fell, the path down which he came and thus the flash of light which Jack projected onto him, are all on the alignment which then continues for over 250 miles across the landscape. Perhaps precise knowledge of solar timing is also shown to be critical in the story. The sun would have its most dazzling power when reflected directly, that is from the southwest, behind the giant's head. This would be later in the day, or on a calendar scale, in the darker part of the year. We know the Druids kindled fires on the high beacon sites. Perhaps this story also reveals that they reflected light along the alignment from highly burnished surfaces. Fire and light, gifts from the sacred sun, thus moved in the veins of a giant stretched over the land.

## SOVEREIGNTY AND KING ARTHUR

Remnants of the cosmography of the sacred earth are found in the mythology of the British Isles. There is no better illustration than in the body of material which has come to be known as the "Matter of Britain." This is a highly complex subject, fraught with pitfalls, which refers to the myths, legends, history and symbols that provide the people of Britain with a "charter" for their nature, sovereignty and, ultimately, for their destiny. The giant Albion is a personification of this theme, as is the giant monarch Bran, as is Britannia, an ancient goddess of the land.

It is a common practice to refer to a country as a person. A land can have a head, a heart, a foot, even a soul. The metaphor of the body is often employed when justifying social institutions. Without its leaders at its head, the Roman ruling class said, the body of the army or of the empire would have little intelligence, sense or direction. As long as the head of the giant British king, Bran the Blessed was intact, no matter that the rest of his body was gone, the land would remain protected.

The Matter of Britain as it has come down to us is a confusing mass of lore and elaboration. Yet several clear themes emerge when examined through the lens of the giants. Early Celtic literature names the themes as dragons, giants, cauldrons and other magical objects. The stories take place in sacred space, magical time and Other Worlds.

In the early Arthurian literature, best represented by the Welsh text the *Mabinogion*, the chief giant Ysbaddaden has a beautiful daughter called Olwen whom Culhwch cannot marry until he has performed thirty-nine impossible feats. The feats include the rescue of the Divine Child Mabon, son of Modron ("mother"), and the hunting of the great boar Twrch Trwyth for the comb and shears between his ears. This cosmographical drama takes Culhwch, Arthur and the Celtic precedents of the Arthurian knights through every element, over every land, through encounters with Other Worldly and animal beings. The story culminates in the death of the giant Ysbaddaden and the marriage of Culhwch and Olwen.[13]

The grail theme is well known. It has its origins in the magical cauldrons of the Celts, and in the primal imagery of the womb and thus of the Great Goddess. It is central to the "Matter of Britain" and has been well-documented. For now we shall look at the theme of two competing gigantic dragons that occurs at highly significant times in the literature. On one occasion, plagues ravage the land and can only be removed by entrapping two fighting dragons. They must be buried "within the strongest place...in the island." This is determined by measuring its length and breadth and finding "the exact center."[14] Later, a red dragon and a white dragon locked in combat are discovered by Merlin below the place where a king is attempting to build a castle. The king, Vortigern, is unfit to be sovereign. The chthonian forces of the land represented by the dragons reject his attempt to establish a seat of spurious sovereignty.[15]

Throughout Celtic literature, and indeed throughout the creation myths of the world, there are remains of a myth about a great cosmological serpent. In Classical mythology the *gigantes* or giants were themselves serpents. Named Avanc or Adanc of the Deep by the Celts, the serpent twists either in the world above or the world below this one. The stories of the red and the white dragon appear to be concerned with the reconciling of this cosmic polarity. In the same way as the rightful sovereign is needed to maintain the health of the land, so the balance of this polarity ensures the health of the monarch. The correct balance of mighty cosmic forces represented by the dragons means rightful sovereignty, which means the spread of sacred and auspicious forces across the land.

Uther Pendragon ("head of the dragon") appears to have reconciled these forces with the reestablishment of the kingdom of the Britons after the Roman withdrawal and the defeat of the Saxons. He adopted a royal standard which showed the red and white dragons. It is through his son Arthur that the claim to the sovereignty of Britain has been legitimated ever since. Local lore often refers to King Arthur as a giant. Although the red lion and the white unicorn have re-placed the dragons on the royal standard, the dragons still occur frequently in heraldry. Is it surprising that the arms of Lord St. Levan, the hereditary owner of St. Michael's Mount, contain them?

We are now in a position to say there is enough evidence to demonstrate that the ancient inhabitants of the British Isles purposely built sacred sites in huge patterns. It is legitimate to surmise that they saw the world in terms of gigantic forces and their intention was to work with them. The ancient Irish and Britons conceived their works on a gigantic scale, such as the New Grange and Avebury complexes and the St. Michael Line running across the breadth of southern Britain. In these works the cosmological themes of unity and polarity of giant forces are enacted again and again. In their minds, these great works conducted "energy" vital to the continuation of life. Remnants of the cosmology in which that energy is very much alive have come down to us in myth. They are evident in the themes around the "Matter of Britain."

The vision of a magical reality covering the ancient world, forming a Golden Age from which we have declined, is a reality of the mind and of an alternative cosmology. It cannot be proved by physics. Archaeologists and other academic researchers agree that the ancient architects did not use our sciences, nor did their technology conduct any form of physically measurable energy. However, we have enough evidence to see that Blake's vision of the sacred landscape once existed. Here mind and matter were in synergy. It can exist again if we look toward the holistic world of mind-body-spirit.

Throughout British mythology, especially around the "charters" which form its heart and shape the cosmography of its landscape, we find gigantic forces, usually represented by goddesses, sovereigns, giants and dragons. These are powers which have, or did once have, an enormous impact on the way the Britons perceived their world and related to it. These are the forces of the earth spirit still alive in the vibrant depths of the subconsciousness today. These are the forces whose restoration is still promised in the dreams of the re-creation of the Golden Age. A remnant of this is represented in British mythology today by Camelot and by King Arthur, "who is not dead, but sleeps." ✸

### CHAPTER FOUR

# GIANTS IN AMERICA

*I am dwelling in a small cave at the foot of a stepped pyramid. I am ashamed of my song. It is poorly sung and I forget much of it. One morning I awaken to a distant singing. It is beautiful and strong. I step outside and around the corner of the pyramid comes the singer. It is a serpent. It comes toward me with its swaying head held high. Its head is radiant with many colors. It shimmers like the feathers of the quetzal bird. The song is melodious, perfect. I can see the shapes of the song shimmering in the air around the head of the serpent. It is the most beautiful song I have ever heard.*

*Inspired, I ascend the solar pyramid. It is steep and I have to zigzag from side to side. My steps trace out the pattern on the serpent's back. At the summit I pause and catch my breath. I am aware of powers in the form of animals on every side. There are four in the directions of the earth, and one above and one below. They begin to sing as they move toward me. The animals merge and pass through me, joining heaven and earth. I breathe deeply to take in their song. As I descend the pyramid I vow never to forget this beautiful song which is now my own. I sing this song with all of my being: my body, mind, heart and spirit.*

he argument we presented in Chapter 2 is that giants were originally seen as natural forces with whom people cooperated in the direct experience of life. Later with the advent of dualistic and transcendental cosmologies, giants were seen as hostile and evil forces with whom people battled. If this argument is correct, then in places where dualism did not develop we should expect to find the original view of giants. In this worldview, giants are the benevolent if arbitrary forces of nature. They also are the larger-than-life ancestors, deities and heroes of an earth-honoring culture. To find giants in nature, we shall look at native cosmology in the Americas.

The indigenous Americans remained close to nature. They lived their experience of the great cosmic forces through the sacred mountains and the animal powers. The Thunderbirds of the sky and the beings of the Underworld were autonomous powers which could be worked with through prayer and spiritual practice. Through this cooperation and spiritual effort, harmony was established in the Middleworld of earth.

For centuries, Native Americans expressed their unity with the cosmic powers by creating mounds and animal forms—sometimes on a giant scale—in the landscape. Mounds and animals are the medium of the giants in America. Examples are the Ohio Serpent Mound, the Rock Eagle Mound in Georgia and the many pyramids of the great "Classical" American civilizations. In Mexico the pyramids with their carved animals rose up out of the jungle. In South America enormous animal and geometric figures stretched over the tablelands of Nazca in Peru and the Atacama Desert in Chile. The Plumed Serpent is a tradition that spread outward from Mexico. In southwestern United States, petroglyphs of the Plumed Serpent and many other creatures reveal the importance of animals. These animal and earth forms show the balance and fusion of the mighty celestial and terrestrial powers.

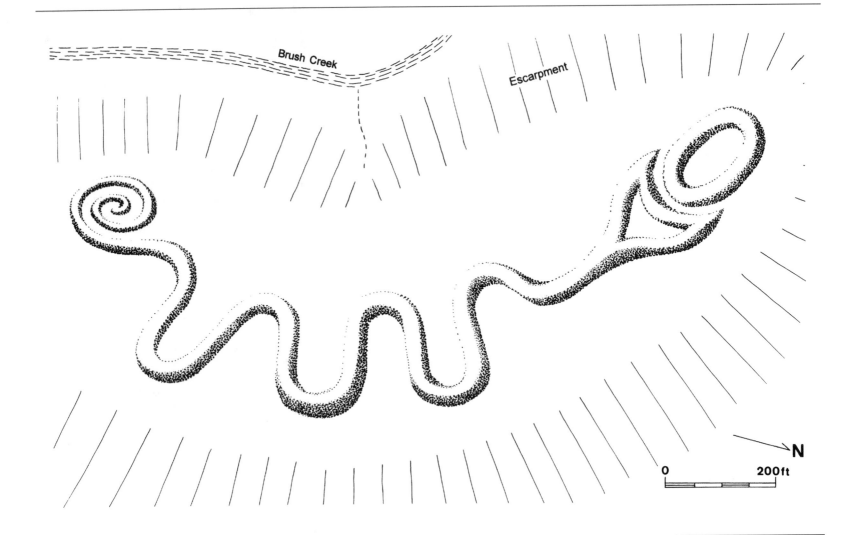

Brush Creek

Escarpment

N

0          200ft

*The Ohio Serpent Mound*

## THE MOUND BUILDERS

N ative American beliefs have been practiced without interruption for thousands of years. Descendants of the original inhabitants of North America live today on or near their ancestral lands. When we look at their early structures we see spiritual beliefs created in the physical world, knowing that in many cases people still exist who practice similar beliefs. As a result we do not need to guess or surmise the meaning of ceremonial sites and ritual practices. This is in sharp contrast to the Neolithic and Celtic sites of Britain, where the pagan practitioners were suppressed and many of their structures destroyed.

Native Americans expressed their cosmology through representations of giant forces in the landscape, as well as through non-permanent means such as sacred "sings" and dance. We will be looking at two periods of mound or "pyramid" building, at "geoglyphs" and at what is called "effigy mound" building. The mounds are just that, enormous earthworks sometimes with a flat top used for ceremonies. "Effigy," however, is a misleading word for those mounds which depict giant figures. While an effigy means an image made in the likeness of somebody or something, we usually think of it as being a likeness of a person made to be ridiculed or destroyed as evil. Native Americans however shaped likenesses of animals to honor them and call in their power. A more apt term might be "animound."

One structure stands apart from all the rest, both because it is probably very early and because no other giant figure quite like it has ever been found. The Serpent Mound near Locust Grove in Ohio is North America's most famous giant effigy. It is the figure of a serpent with a coiled tail at one end, four perfectly shaped undulations along its enormous length, and a cosmic egg between its jaws at the other end. This sinuous mound is nearly one-quarter of a mile in length, 20 feet wide, and 4 to 5 feet high. It lies on a spur of land beside a river. No burials or artifacts were found in the mound so dating is difficult, but it is believed to be earlier than the other effigy or animounds of North America. It is thought to have been built by either the Adena or Hopewell cultures who overlapped

in this region during the last centuries BCE and the first few centuries CE.

The older Adena culture at first carried out burial in simple mounds from as early as 1000 BCE. Their later, more developed mounds often contained multiple burials and artifacts which could only be acquired through extensive trade.

The Hopewell culture appeared in Illinois and Ohio at the beginning of the common era. The Hopewell built extremely elaborate mound complexes. Near Chillicothe, the Mound City Group comprises a rectan-

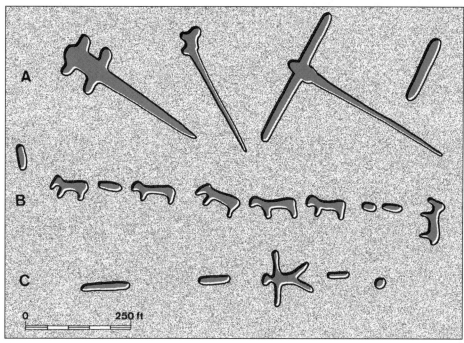

*Mounds in Wisconsin.The upper group (A) are in Lizard Mound State Park. The lower (B & C) are along an ancient trail between the Mississippi River and Lake Michigan*

gular embankment enclosing 23 mounds. By 500 CE the Hopewell culture had created its most fabulous ceremonial site at what is today Newark, Ohio. Here the embankments are up to 14 feet high, and enclose circles, squares, octagons and avenues—one over two miles long. The Octagon Mound encloses an area of 50 acres and its sides have been shown to be aligned to the extreme rising and setting points of the moon. A civil engineer, James Marshall, demonstrated that the builders used a unit of measure 187 feet long to mark out the earthworks. The same unit was employed at the great Mexican pyramid at Teotihuacan. Although

the Hopewell clearly had the means to create the Serpent Mound it does not look like any other site they built, so it either belongs to the Adena era, 500 BCE–200 CE., or is much later.

From about 500 CE, the Effigy Mounds begin to appear in Wisconsin, Iowa and Illinois. These are the gigantic landscape figures of which the enigmatic Ohio Serpent may have been the forerunner. Some are simply long mounds, but others take the form of panthers, lizards, bears, deer, birds, turtles and giants. The mounds typically lie on ridges. They did not always contain a burial and had few or no artifacts. At Lizard Mound State Park in Wisconsin, 31 effigy mounds, 3 to 4 feet in height, and up to 400 feet long lie over the landscape. These birds, lizards and panthers may have an earlier date but are most likely to have been made between 500 and 1000 CE. Another site between Lake Michigan and the Mississippi River has bears, conical and linear mounds and a

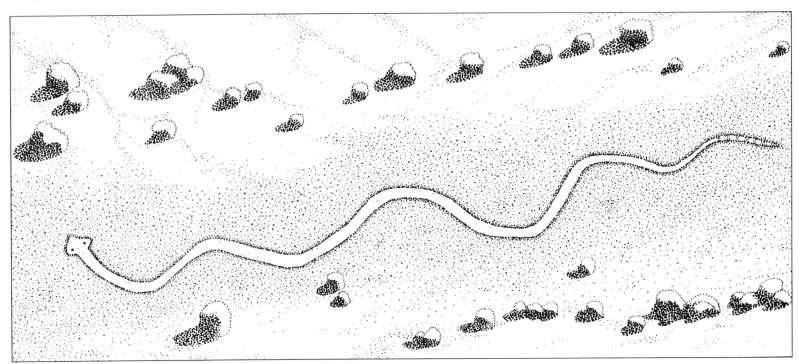

*Snake geoglyph or "intaglio" near Parker, Arizona*

giant human figure, 125 feet in length, stretched in an alignment along half a mile of high ground.[1]

In other parts of North America the Native peoples favored geoglyphs or "earth carvings." They were made by scraping away darker surface debris to expose the lighter material underneath. Near Blythe in Arizona groups of animal, anthropomorphic and spiral figures have been found in the desert. One of the human figures is 167 feet in length. At a site near Parker many geoglyphs, similar in their abstract nature to those carved on the plains of Nazca, cover a huge area. Like Nazca in Peru the designs also include animal forms. A serpent, complete with eyes and rattles, undulates for almost 150 feet across the desert floor. Still honored by Native peoples, some of these giant figures are associated with nearby dwelling sites about 2,000 years old.

After about 800 CE, the period of effigy making ceased and was followed by another florescence of giant mound building. This period is usually called the Mississippian. It peaked between 1000 and 1200 CE, with the creation of the largest ceremonial centers and earthen mounds in North America. The Mississippian people evidently were inspired by Mexican structures yet developed their techniques independently. Huge mounds, pyramidal and often terraced with a platform for a temple on the summit, were built throughout the central and eastern half of the continent.

Some examples will give a picture of these giants in the American landscape. Poverty Point Mound in Louisiana reached 60 feet in height and covered an area 700 by 800 feet. The base of Emerald Mound in Mississippi covers an area of 8 acres. Monks Mound at the Cahokia Mounds State Historic Site in Illinois is the greatest of them all. The mound covers 16 acres to rise through four terraces to a height of over 100 feet. It has been estimated that 50,000 people occupied the city and surrounding territory. The central site also included many other mounds and a circle 410 feet wide consisting of 48 posts for equinox and solstice observations. The mounds contain burials. Archaeological evidence shows these were accompanied by elaborate ritual practices and artifacts from distant places including the Toltec and Aztec civilizations in Mexico.[2]

This evidence illustrates that the pre-Columbian Native Americans were thinking in terms of giants in the landscape. The Hopewell and Mississippian periods of concentrated urban-culture focused on the construction of huge earthworks with sophisticated geometrical and astronomical properties. These are typical of the practices of the megalithic site builders in Europe. There is evidence that the mounds were built to establish harmony between the terrestrial and sacred Other Worlds in the cultural cosmography. Death and burial were primary considerations.

The Adena period 500 BCE–200 CE, when the Ohio Serpent Mound may have been created, the intermediary period 500–800 CE, and the period of geogylph making in the desert Southwest, are characterized by a less urban focus and by the construction of giant human and animal forms. This was the time of a nature-culture. Typically, the cairns, glyphs and mounds follow the lines of ridges, spurs and river courses. Unlike the giant figures on the hillsides of Britain, they could not have been seen from anywhere but the sky. Burial was not very significant and thus the focus was on the symbols themselves. What do they have to say?

## THE PLUMED SERPENT

The myths of the native peoples of North America are as diverse as their many languages and landscapes. One myth cannot be taken as representative of the whole. Yet certain themes do stand out, especially the continual presence of animals. In the creation myths it is the animals who provide for the people and lead them from one world to the next. In the coyote-raven stories the animals account for anomalies while providing humor. Some creation stories say the earth was originally inhabited by giants. Two recurrent worldview themes are that the land is upheld by a giant turtle, and that the cosmos is sustained through a dynamic polarity of earth and sky.

This cosmic polarity finds its expression in two classes of beings, both of whom are represented and thought about in giant animal terms. The first are the sky beings, the Thunderbirds. They are giant birds whose wings create thunder and whose flashing eyes are lightning. They have great powers which are ordinarily benevolent but may inadvertently cause destruction, such as a hailstorm. Birds, especially the hawks and eagles, are sacred to native peoples. Through their flight the birds carry messages to the dwelling place of spirits. For this reason feathers are used in ceremony and must always be handled reverently. The Sun Dance, one of the most important ceremonies of the Plains tribes, is dedicated to the Thunderbirds.

The second class of beings are those who live below the earth or below the waters of rivers and lakes. These are the serpents and the "mirror" beings of some of the creatures who live on the earth such as the bear and the panther. These Underworld beings have power that is arbitrary, dangerous and indifferent. They must always be honored if their power is to benefit and not harm humanity. The lines which follow are part of the Cheyenne myth of the Mississippi Serpent:

*The young man stared at the river. Rising from it was a great snake. His body was covered with bluish skin, he had twin horns on his head...."Well, my friend," said the snake-man, "...From now on I will lie here in the middle of the riverbed, and will fill it from side to side. My body will stretch out as long as the Mississippi.... Whenever you cross, you must bring a buffalo paunch, or some other of the inside meats, and drop them in the middle of the river for me to eat. Or you can drop tobacco in me for me to smoke. Whenever anybody does that, I will give him my blessing."[3]*

The Pueblo people of the Southwest also divide their deities into two groups which can be identified by the Thunderbird and Underworld categories. The Sun and other celestial and meteorological deities are "Those Above," while "Those Below" are the deities who live within Mother Earth. These include the Corn Father and Mother and the "mineral" deities such as White Shell Woman and Copper Woman.

Visitors to the many petroglyph sites of the Southwest will observe the great numbers of animals carved upon the rocks. Deer, antelope, lizards, toads, snakes, birds and Thunderbirds are common, but the most striking recurrent image is that of a horned or plumed serpent. Another motif is that of the star, some-

*Horned serpent and star petroglyph. White Rock Canyon, New Mexico*

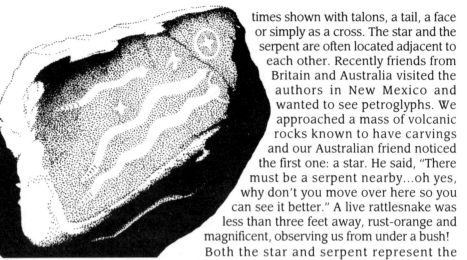

times shown with talons, a tail, a face or simply as a cross. The star and the serpent are often located adjacent to each other. Recently friends from Britain and Australia visited the authors in New Mexico and wanted to see petroglyphs. We approached a mass of volcanic rocks known to have carvings and our Australian friend noticed the first one: a star. He said, "There must be a serpent nearby...oh yes, why don't you move over here so you can see it better." A live rattlesnake was less than three feet away, rust-orange and magnificent, observing us from under a bush!

Both the star and serpent represent the Plumed Serpent deity known as Kukulcan to the Maya or as Quetzalcoatl to the Nahuatl people—descendants of the Aztec Indians. These two great civilizations of Meso-America had much contact through trade with their northern neighbors. An understanding of the Southwestern petroglyphs, geoglyphs, the Ohio Serpent Mound and the ceremonial mounds and pyramids can be gained from the Plumed Serpent deity.

Quetzalcoatl, "Feathered Serpent," is a beneficent creator deity whose power manifests through recurrent cycles. Throughout the Americas the presence of Quetzalcoatl is seen in the movement of Venus, the Morning and Evening Star. By watching the progress of the waxing or waning deity through the celestial sphere, and by observing periods when the star is not visible above the horizon, favorable or unfavorable influences or times could be deduced. At times when Quetzalcoatl is not present because Venus is not visible, the opposing forces of Tezcatlipoca, "Smoking (Black Obsidian) Mirror," prevail. Tezcatlipoca is an all-seeing warrior-shaman. Among the Maya, the Plumed Serpent was known as Kukulcan, "Feathered Vision Serpent." Kukulcan united the natural and the supernatural worlds, earth and sky, through the ability to pass between them. This was done by invoking the center of the cosmos from a sacred site, ideally a pyramid. The pyramid established the four cardinal directions, the center, the above and the below. The pyramid was the primordial sacred mountain. Through invoking the Plumed Serpent deity, unity was then established between the worlds. This interpretation can be usefully applied to the mounds and pyramids of North America to gain an understanding of the way the people saw and used them.

The urge to build the sacred mountain is not yet lost in America. There is an exact parallel between the mounds and pyramids of the ancient cultures and the architecture of modern city skylines.

The challenges presented by the huge vistas, great plains, towering mountains and mighty rivers of the American continent are resolved in the human mind when architecture—the handling of form and space—is on a gigantic scale. At the Cahokia mounds and the Mayan pyramids, the artificial mountain created the world axis around which the cosmic order was established and maintained. Today, in buildings such as the Luxor Pyramid Casino in Las Vegas and the Space Needle in Seattle, knowingly or not, this American tradition of the sacred mountain is continued.

## THE ANIMAL POWERS

*W*hen we looked at Celtic myth in the "Matter of Britain" the reconciliation of the cosmic polarity represented by two dragons, one red and one white, was accomplished by establishing right relationships upon the earth. The forces of the "above" and of the "below" were balanced by the rightful participation of the people in the cosmic drama. This was conceived of in terms of giant forces and sovereignty. But the native European tradition has been veiled by 2000 years of Roman and Christian overlay, so it is not possible to know how this was accomplished by the Celts. There are clues, and there is the even older evidence from the megalithic age, but there are no written records from either time. However, in the Americas the native tradition was flourishing—and in some places literate—at the time of the conquest, and still exists as a separate culture.

The indigenous peoples of America make no absolute divisions between culture and nature. They do not make nature an "evil" force to be conquered. Rather, they carry the universal polarity of "above" and "below" through with them as they and their deities make their journeys around the cosmos. The giant animal powers, like the Celtic dragons, represent these forces. The Plumed Serpent by its ability to pass between the Underworld, Middleworld and the Celestial world, can connect all realms and is supreme among them. On the cosmic scale the serpent is conceived of and represented as a giant. Let us take a closer look at a giant which combines all these powers.

The Ohio Serpent Mound lies beside a river—representing the Underworld forces—upon a spur of high ground looking up to the heavens. As it is today, it appears

that an egg is emerging from its mouth. This is the preferred interpretation, rather than a snake in the act of devouring an egg. Either way, the egg represents the birds and may represent the sun. Recent research has revealed astronomical alignments at the site; solar alignments are confirmed and lunar possibilities are being studied. Thus the Serpent Mound shows its as-

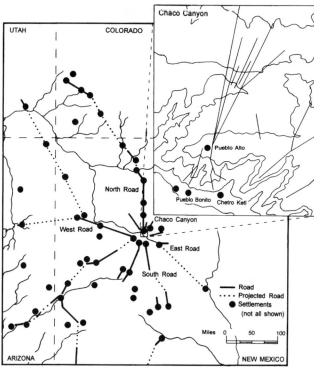

Map of the Anasazi "road" system. Inset map shows detail of roads focused on Chaco Canyon. Note straightness of roads and duplication, making them redundant for purely functional purposes. Not all roads or settlements are shown (After Kathryn Gabriel, 1991)

sociation with the heavens and with the Thunderbirds, despite its not having plumes or horns, and there is even some evidence that it did originally have these! It is therefore symbolic of the harmonious union of the powerful polar forces in the cosmos. If the Serpent Mound was built by the Adena people in or before the first century, it is the earliest representation of the deity which later was known as the Horned or Plumed Serpent. Whatever the time of construction, it is the most perfect manifestation of this power ever to be represented by a landscape giant in the North American continent.

In South America many huge figures were etched into the surface of the landscape. Their connection with the sky is made evident by the fact that some cannot be observed in their entirety from the ground. In the Atacama Desert of northern Chile, for example, one giant figure runs over the crest of the mountain. Over 1,000 feet in length this geometric figure of a man with outstretched arms and perpendicular hair was made by carrying dark rocks up onto the light colored hillsides. He is known locally as "the giant." In the surrounding arid landscape there are hundreds of other figures, including pumas, llamas, dogs, humans and unusual geometrical designs. These could have been made by the Chimu culture, or their southern neighbors, about 1,000 CE. They are possibly much older.

The Chimu were likely to have made the figures on the Nazca Plain in southern Peru. There, figures were precisely imprinted over an immense area, on a scale that was sure to please the giants and in a location where they could only be entirely seen from the air. Many people are aware that "runways" triangulate the area, but the native people also created geometrical figures and outlines of animals and plants. Unlike the figures of the Atacama though, the ones at Nazca were made by scraping away the dark desert crust to expose the lighter sand and gravel below. The Nazca markings also include lines up to 5 miles in length,

running perfectly straight over every slope. These lines have orientations to solstices and to the rising and setting points of significant stars.

There is no suggestion that the giant figures etched on the landscape by the ancient Chimu culture are anything but benign. The later Inca empire apparently felt the same. After conquering the Chimu, the Incas did not attempt to remove the lines but added their own in other areas. The Incas made sacred shrines called *huacas* at places such as mountains, rivers, forests, trees and unusual rocks, where the forces of the natural world were strong. In order to add this power to the empire, the Incas connected the huacas through a system of straight alignments called *ceques*. These lines connected the huacas in a gigantic system of sacred engineering, regardless of the ruggedness of the terrain. It has been estimated that as many as 42 ceques connecting over 500 huacas were focused on the Inca capital of Cuzco.

Similar systems of alignments have emerged from studies of the *sacbes* in Mayan Mexico, the 'avenues' of the Hopewell in Ohio and the Anasazi "roads" around Chaco Canyon in New Mexico. These well-constructed ways often ran in straight lines over great distances. The North Road out of Chaco Canyon, for example, runs for about 40 miles and is oriented almost precisely north-south. Neither the Mayan, the Hopewell nor the Anasazi lines were actually roads, according to accumulating evidence. Either they did not go to any terminus, they duplicated each other unnecessarily or were far wider than needed for efficient construction and the simple carrying of goods. Many have a characteristic not required for roads at all, which is orientation to sun, moon or stars. All their features make sense, however, if they are interpreted as paths for ritualistic movement to ceremonial centers and as an expression of the sacred cosmography on earth.[4]

To summarize this section, when natural forces are conceived in terms of giants in the Americas they are usually identified with animals. Unlike the fearsome giant in European traditions, the giant in Native American tradition is a positive force. It is a culture-bearer and creator. Where powerful beings lie under the earth, such as the Giant Horned Snake of the Eastern Woodlands, they might be considered capricious and dangerous but they are also a source of great wisdom and medicine power. They are not defeated by their polar opposites the Thunderbirds; instead, both are deemed necessary forces. They complement each other for the fullness of life.

The huge Thunderbirds painted on the dwellings of the Northwestern peoples, the giant figures of Atacama and Nazca, the gigantic serpent geoglyphs of the desert lands, the Ohio Serpent and the many mounds and pyramids of the "Classical" civilizations are direct expressions of the natural forces of the world. Dwelling on a continent with mighty rivers, mountains and canyons, the people directly echoed and personified these powers with their works. The giants were the expression of the powers that walked between them all.

The images of a giant serpent and a giant bird occur many times in American mythology. It was the sighting of an eagle with a snake in its talons which led to the foundation of the Aztec capital, Tenochtitlan, a motif present on the Mexican flag today. In the southwestern desert of the U.S. we find our next, little-known, example of giants in the natural landscape as we look at images of a huge bird and serpent.

## GIANTS OF RED ROCK COUNTRY

**S**ome of the most beautiful scenery of the southwestern United States lies in the Red Rock Country near Sedona, Arizona. In the Yavapai and subsequently the Apache tradition, this area is the emergence place of the people after fire and flood destroyed the previous worlds. The First Woman, Komidapukwia, came to the Red Rock Country in a hollow log during the flood which destroyed the first world. She knew it was safe to come out of the log because the bird who accompanied her, when released, returned with leaves—evidence of dry land. It is intriguing to note that Noah, who performed the same actions, is sometimes referred to as a giant.

Yavapai means "People of the Sun." The story of the First Woman is that she was impregnated by a sun beam shining into a cave where water dripped from a spring. She gave birth to a daughter who did what her mother did, and who eventually gave birth to a son, Sakaraka'amche. His mother was killed and so it was he and his grandmother who lived in the Red Rock Country and were responsible for many of the landscape features to be found there.

One day Sakaraka'amche wanted to know who his father was. Although his grandmother was reluctant to let him go, he climbed up to heaven. There he met Sun and Cloud, who acknowledged him as their son and gave him medicine powers.

> *They gave me four lines of lightning to descend to earth. Two on the left belonged to Cloud, two on the right belonged to Sun. I descended on the lightning flashes. I arrived at Komwidapukwia's place.*

When he arrived back on the earth he was a giant. His body stretched from one end of the Red Rock Country to the other. He said:

> *I knelt on the ground and pressed. With my hands and knees I pressed on the ground and sang. When I lifted my hands medicine plants sprouted out of the earth.*

At length, the human descendants of Komwidapukwia ("Old Woman Medicine Stone"), came to live on the earth. Sakaraka'amche taught them many things, not least of which was the gift of medicine power which could be obtained from the Red Rock Country. He told the people:

> *You open me down the middle from my head to my crotch, and turn me belly down upon the ground. Then sing around my body and you will get my songs. If you sing my songs you will keep alive.*[5]

---

*Cathedral Rock. The spires form a giant hand or two figures standing back to back*

In this story the figure of a giant is clearly a culture bringer, helping and teaching the people. His origin from the First Woman honors the Great Goddess, known simply in America as "Grandmother." Although the Yavapai and the Apache have been forced out of their sacred lands they still honor the places in their creation mythology. The natural landscape around Sedona, shaped by their founding deities, reveals many features of significance to a study of giantology.

The profile of the colossal Courthouse Rock resembles an Amer-Indian looking up into the sky. No canyon is without spires or buttes of red sandstone which assume the shape of giant figures. Two giants known as the Sentinels stand beside Soldier Pass, while across the canyon "Coffee Pot Rock" is a giant hawk. Another mundanely named formation "Steamboat Rock" is a Thunderbird, and in the center of Cathedral Rock are two giants, a man and a woman, standing back to back. But it is when an aerial view of the Red Rock Country is examined that the huge nature of the giants in the landscape can be seen.

In maps and aerial photographs a giant bird can be discerned flying through the mountains, canyons and

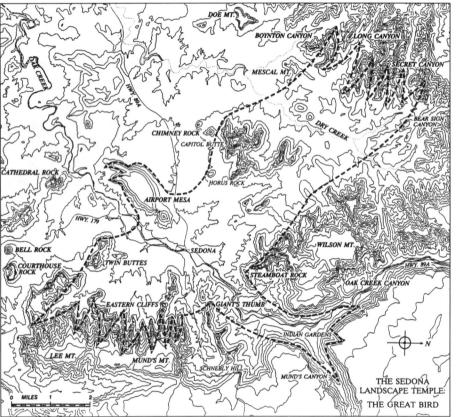

mesas of the Red Rock Country. It swoops to the southwest and measures 11 miles across its wings. Every feather of its wing tips is made by the canyons cutting deeply into the mountains. The head, including details of the beak, is delineated by a mesa.

In the center of one outstretched wing of the giant bird is a serpent formed by the features of the landscape. As noted earlier, serpents are frequent companions of birds in American mythology. Six miles in length, if extended, the serpent is formed by the sinuous twists of a set of isolated peaks. The native name for the peaks is Thunder Mountain. At its center is a natural arch known as "Devil's Bridge," an appellation commonly given to places of the serpent. A rock known as "Lizard Head" forms a possible head for the giant serpent. Pictographs (rock paintings) of snakes are common in the area, many of which are shown with horns or plumes. The snake as a symbol of cosmic energy is present in the lightning evoked by the name of Thunder Mountain.

The giant figure of the bird and the serpent are not real semblances like the animal effigies in Ohio, Wisconsin, western Arizona, Chile or Peru. They can only be perceived from the air or by studying maps. They are simulacra, unintended representations. But it is interesting to note the importance of the bird in the emergence legend of the First Woman, and the importance of serpents as a whole in American mythology. Bird and snake represent above and below. In the myth of Queztalcoatl they find their unification.

---

*The giant bird made by the features of the Sedona landscape*

It is also interesting to note the importance of giants in legend and in the landscape where the legends are said to have taken place. In the myth of First Woman she is the cosmic giant whose womb gives birth to the world and whose giant grandson becomes benefactor to the people. In the sacred places of the North American continent these themes find expression not only in human-made forms but in the natural forms of the landscape. What is the relationship between the land and the myths of origin? Here we approach the subject of "geomythics" to be explored in the following chapter. ※

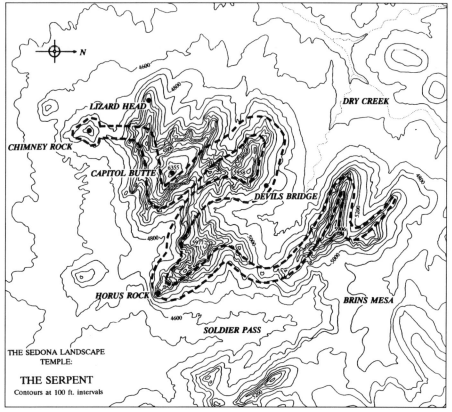

THE SEDONA LANDSCAPE TEMPLE:

**THE SERPENT**
Contours at 100 ft. intervals

*The serpent of Thunder Mountain*

### CHAPTER FIVE

# GIANTS IN AUSTRALIA

*I struggle out of the dream. I can see the patch of stars framed by the trees but I cannot tell if I am seeing it in the dream or if I am awake. A huge figure glides into the grove. There are red and white feathers on the dark form of its huge body. The grove catches the light enough, but the giant is marked by what it is not rather than by what it is. It dances in the space at the foot of my bed roll. It begins to speak. I finally wake up sweating just as its words become my words and are simultaneously spoken: "If the myths are not told and the songs are not sung then the land will die."*

---

## SONGLINES AND DREAMTIME

The Aboriginal people of Australia inhabit some of the most inhospitable country on the planet. For more than 50,000 years the indigenous tribes—originally numbering about 300—have maintained a full style of life in harmony with the fragile desert ecology. It has been suggested that this is due to their spiritual tradition. We now know that the Aborigines have an extremely rich and ancient culture, continually practiced, and based in ritual. They live close to the forces of nature. As we would expect, they possess an elaborate cosmography in which giants are vitally important and very much alive.

In the beginning, it is said, the original Great Ancestor dreamt the world. Then voices were given to the Dream Beings and they became real. The Aborigines refer to this creation as the "Dreamtime." This is a literal interpretation of the word. It is not what we mean by dreaming.

These legendary Ancestral Beings of the First Day were giants. Some were ancestors of the people. They sang the world into existence. In their journeys, the ancestors created the shape and nature of the landscape. They made rivers, hills, trees, billabongs (waterholes). They left footprints, buttock prints and other impressions. The shape of these features depended upon what speed they were traveling or how many legs they had or upon other traits. Where their paths or "Songlines" crossed the paths of the other creative spirit ancestors their interaction might result in a particularly unusual feature. The Great Rainbow Snake of the Northern Territories, for example, vomited up the bones of those he had swallowed to form an escarpment in Arnhem Land. Eventually, when all the land was sung into existence, the giants withdrew to the interior of the earth or the sky. The Snake Emianga of the Aranda is now coiled deep and not-to-be-disturbed in the final resting place of his "Eternal Home."[1]

Every feature of the landscape thus marks an episode in the story of the Dreamtime ancestors. The tribe whose territory is crossed by the ancestors knows the story, usually in the form of the song said to have been sung by them. Most songs are long sequences of territory-linked episodes, the beginnings and ends of which are known by adjacent tribes. The extent to which a tribe knows the songs of their neighbors marks the degree of kinship or allegiance they

*The songline or storyline of a Dreamtime ancestor, Arnhem Land. Each spiral is a specific place in the landscape and is a scene of key episodes in the story of the ancestor. The ancestors journeyed along the line from the place of emergence to where they went "back in." The side lines may show the creative paths of offspring or of other creative spirits. This pattern may be drawn in the sand while the person who has the dreaming tells the story in song*

enjoy with the neighbors. Not knowing the end of the "story-line" means one people does not know the other people or their territory.[2]

The Dreamtime or the Dreaming is the eternal time of creation, the time in the past-present-now. The Dreamtime and the Songlines are not fixed and unchanging but dynamic and responsive. Study has revealed that the songs are subtly changing as the world and society changes. New Dreamings are constantly coming into being. They are the mode through which congruence and meaning are established between the inner and the outer world.

To remain in communication with the ancestors of the Dreamtime is to ensure that this world conforms to the spiritual world that was in the original dream of the Great Ancestor. Communication with the creative Dreaming of the ancestor is established through the inner state achieved in ritual. Rituals at selected sites throughout the cycle of the year maintain the flow of *Kurunba* or life force along the lines of songs. Singing the Songlines keeps the life forces flowing and at "places of increase" amplifies their energies. Paintings on rocks at the Dreaming sites also stimulate the flow of natural forces that are present within them. Coroboree Rock and the great Ayers Rock, Uluru, in central Australia are places where many ancestral spirit paths cross and which are kept alive through ritual practices.

The Old Woman Dreaming is known as Gadjari, Kunappi or Karwadi. She is the fertility-bringing, nurturing, life-giving Mother. In the Northern Territory she is often combined with the Lightning Snake in dispensing these powers. The Snake Dreaming is known in the northwest as Ungud, the Rainbow Serpent, Kaleru in the Kimberley region, and Almudj, the Great Rainbow Snake in Arnhem Land. This snake lives in the billabongs, the rivers or underground. In the rainy season it goes up into the sky. It is often depicted in rock art or bark painting as a dual deity. The Rainbow Serpent can appear in the rainbows of the sky or of waterfalls. As the Rainbow Serpent of the Earth it appears in many-colored minerals, especially the opal. The Aboriginal people believe the Rainbow Serpent maintains the balance of life. If it were to depart then the earth would die. The dual Rainbow Serpent of earth and sky is the powerful spirit that we have already identified as the Plumed Serpent in America and the dragon in Europe.

In traditional Australian thought no dichotomy exists between spirit and matter, sacred and secular, supernatural and natural. Big Bill Neidjie of the Gagudju put it like this:

> Earth our mother, eagle our cousin. Tree, he is pumping our blood. Grass is growing. And water...we are all one.[3]

A person's soul is present in that person's *Tjuringa*, an oval plaque of wood or stone, in the same way as the Dreaming is present in the visible landscape. There is no

the ancient traditions of the world. The giant Ancestral Beings are to be found in the creative life force of the Dreaming and its inseparable interaction with humans and the world. Each one—the giants, the life force, the humans, the world—gives shape to the other. The ideas, the "dreaming" of humans are as important to the shape of giants as the "dreaming" of the giants is to the shape of humans. What they share in common is a life force, a spirit, which is represented as serpent or dragon. This spirit is visible in the physical forms of the world. Though originally created by the giant Ancestral Beings, the spirit of every physical form is maintained or increased through human actions which emulate the acts of the giants.

The songs and wisdom of the ancestors might eventually disappear if current trends continue. The native peoples of Australia have already lost much of their land. For each stretch of land certain songs tell the paths of the ancestors. If the songs are not sung, the land will die. If the land is not lived, the songs will die. If the young people continue to turn away from traditional customs, then the knowledge of the songs will be lost. This raises the question of whether the paths of the ancestors across the land will still be there, only waiting to be "remembered" when the songs are recovered by an interested future generation, or whether the songs, the ancestors, the Dreamings, the lines, die with the native culture.

The Aborigines say there is no difference between the songs and the land they describe. The songs are the land and all its features. The land is its song and all its features. The land spoke to the ancestors and gave its inherent sound and shape so the native people could always be connected to the earth and know where they are upon it.

separation between the two. There can be no world without the people, no rock without its song, just as there can be no dichotomy of "wilderness" as exterior and camps as interior space. It is difficult to get the Aborigines to live between walls where they cannot see and touch the land.

Through the living, though threatened, cosmological tradition of the native Australians we come close to an understanding of the original meaning of giants in

*The Rainbow Serpent, Arnhem Land. (Redrawn from an Aboriginal painting)*

There is a story given in Bruce Chatwin's *The Songlines*, that vividly illustrates the tie between song and land. An Aborigine was riding with some Westerners in a Land Cruiser across land that his tribe was claiming in a territorial dispute. He had the ancestors' Dreaming. He was asked to sing the songline belonging to that particular area. He emitted sounds so fast and run together that the Westerners thought it was gibberish. Then the driver figured it out, and slowed the vehicle a bit. The Aborigine's song tempered to a fast outpouring. The driver slowed more, and the song slowed more. At walking speed, the song could be heard at normal tempo. At last all the Westerners understood: each bit of the song correlated exactly to each bit of terrain and had to be "sung" while in that portion of land. This ancestral Songline had been established at a walking pace.

## GEOMYTHICS

It is here that the concept of "geomythics" can be introduced. This means that between humans and the external physical world there exists a resonance, whereby the forms of the landscape and the contours of the inner world are similar, if not one and the same. Language is the bridge. In Aboriginal geomythics, the song and the land that the songline refers to are one and the same. For Aborigines, the inner and outer resonance is gigantic, covering the whole Australian continent.

The "inner world" refers to everything contained in the minds of people: language, myths, beliefs, concepts, their worldview. People derive roots of words from the outer world and turn them into language. Language names things and names give order and thus meaning. These meanings are expressed and passed onto children in stories and myths which then shape their actions in the outer world. The "outer world" consists of animals, places, geography and topographical features. These provide the texture, contour, shape and signature of the landscape which forms sensory impressions in our mind. Language helps us to name, from the inner mental and emotional maps which we bring to every situation, the character or the "spirit" of places we find in the outer map. This interaction between the inner and outer landscapes is what is described by the concept of geomythics.

*Mythos* is the pattern of basic meanings, values and experiences of a people, translated through language and the arts. Myth embodies their cultural ideals and commonly felt emotions. Myth is the blueprint of where a people come from and who they are. It ultimately will determine where they are going. "Mythics" is a combination of these concepts revealed through storytelling, through the exact words and weaving of words chosen by a people.

Geomythics, then, is the connection between earth and culture, between place and placename. The names, words and myths preserved in a culture from ancient times give evidence of resonance between name and place. Geomythics is the symphony of correlations between our inner world of words and the outer world that the words describe and from which the words came. Since a placename tells what the original people thought or felt about a place, it is fascinating to note how often giants and dragons are named in ancient places. Apparently people formerly thought of land in terms of dynamic earth energy. They called on the giant or dragon of a place to channel that energy.

We said that language is the bridge between the inner world of the mind and the outer world of the physical planet. What many people do not realize is that language comes from the earth. In effect, we "earth speak." The origin of words lies in the shape of the land, the features of animals, water, hill, tree and stone. The *sound* of these earth features was imitated by early people, and these sounds became words. From deep in the earth comes a moan heard at the mouth of caves. From tree tops comes a message louder than all the swaying branches seemingly could produce. From animals come songs and warnings. From streams and oceans come unceasing choirs of water voices, some deep and some high. From avalanche, earthquake, tornado, hurricane and forest fire come the fearsome roars of giants.

When thinking geomythically, one is thinking the language of the earth. The body does this naturally and easily. Each language was shaped by its particular environment. That is why languages in a region sound similar, such as Spanish, Portuguese, French and Italian. Languages from different environments have little relation, such as Chinese and Arabic. Because language arises from the earth, it reflects what is important about the earth among a certain people. The Eskimos have many words for different qualities of snow. The Irish have many words for shades of green growth. Nomadic hunters have very different categories of words than agriculturalists.

Language is not just words. The sounds relay the contours of the earth. Language is used to create myths and stories that have actual resonance with the environment. There is a magical symphony of cause and effect. If one reads myths of another culture and they do not arouse this magical effect, the terrain of that culture probably is foreign to the reader.

*Ab origine* can be construed from the Latin to mean "from the beginning." Australian Aboriginal words have the ancient earth sounds of -ang, -ong and -ung. Boomerang and kangaroo have the first sound. Boomerang contains the word boomer which means a large male kangaroo. Billabong is a backwater and has the second sound; *billa* means river and *bong* means dead. *Yulunggul* has the third sound and is the great Rainbow Snake in his sacred waterhole. The one native Australian musical instrument is earth-based. The didgeridoo makes the droning sounds of animals and the earth. The instrument is formed by nature, from a long section of eucalyptus branch hollowed out by termites.

In all parts of the world, earth-based words form the root of language. Examples of sounds, babbles and grunts which became words are ma, og, and ur. Ma is the sound of life, the word that babies all over the world use for mother; it is found in the name Mary. Og is the sound of giants, such as Gogmagog, or Og, the only giant to survive the Flood. Ogham is an alphabet, given by the giant Ogma Sunface to the Irish 1500 years ago.

Every continent has ancient place names beginning with ur, which means proto or first. Places include Uruguay and Urubamba in South America; Urundi in Africa; Urfa in Turkey; Urga in Mongolia; Urumchi in China. Ur itself was an ancient Sumerian city. Mythology also contains this basic sound. Uraeus is the figure of the serpent sacred to ancient Egyptians; *uro* means asp in Egyptian. *Ouranos* is the Greek word for heaven; Urania is the Muse of astronomy. Uranus is the earliest god to personify the sky, the son and consort of the Earth Mother Gaia. A planet was named for him. *Ouroboros* is a dragon biting its own tail. In this alchemical symbol the circle represents endless sacred time and inner space. The dragon represents the life force in every living thing, balancing in itself the cosmic male and female. In psychology, Ouroboros has come to mean the primeval, undifferentiated mind. *Oro* means gold in Spanish. In alchemy, gold was the goal of the refinement of the psyche.

Forming a word to sound like what it refers to is called onomatopoeia (Greek: to coin names). Examples are buzz, crack and cuckoo. In geomythics, words sound like their place in the earth. Crooked water is a creek; prominent or elevated land sounds like hiiilll; rrrrock sounds hard. The word tree derives from *deru* meaning solid, firm, enduring. Deruid or Druid means knower of trees.

From these examples we can see how language developed in the natural environment. Human interaction with animals, trees, stones and water provided us with words and categories. It is through the act of naming that we understand more of what and who we are. Through naming an animal we understand that the meanings we associate with the animal can exist in us. For example, the name "deer" gives us associations of grace, agility, speed, shyness and peacefulness. The key is resonance. The name for something soft would become the word for everything that had the attribute of softness.

The capacity for conceptual thought is the marked difference between human and animal species. The making and decorating of tools by 200,000 BCE is a clear indication of conceptual thought. The roots of the words which shape the movement of conceptual thought are the context in which the mind thinks.[4] A result of our conceptualizing ability, and eventually of writing, is that language developed to a point where it apparently divorced itself from the object and the context of the environment. Language has become a tool of planning, of negotiating, of trading, of specialization, of metaphorical and allegorical thought which allows abstract contemplation of the universe and the place of things within it. The Druids of Europe recognized the distancing from the earth that written language would create and therefore forbade others to write. They carved runes and writings such as Ogham only for their own magical purposes.

One of the main principles of thinking is analogy, of like resonating with like. Through analogy, language becomes a means of magical cause and effect between the people and their native land. It provides order and connectedness in an otherwise apparently chaotic universe. Each racial or genetic lineage in the land of its arising generates a unique language which is embedded in the matrix of the land. This language becomes encoded in the minds of the people. As the language evolves over vast periods of time, it shapes the culture and the order of the inner world. This in turn, feeds back out to shape the order of the outer world.

Language embedded in its geographical context provides an enormous sense of identity and belonging for its speaker. Words have power. They are both meaning and the meaningful context they arose from. The sound of the spoken word itself provides a map to the surrounding world. The contours are the same. The movement, texture, quality, shape, feeling in the mouth, and mental picture of the words are all part of its meaning. A person who is speaking a language in its environmental context might sense this. The shape, texture and feel of the song of the giant Dreamtime ancestor are the shape, texture and feel of the land. A person who knows the song of the land can never be lost.

In such a resonant cosmos, like that of the Australian Aborigine, objects have power. Everything is infused with its own spiritual essence. Each creature, stone, tree or place is not separate from the perception that the user of the geomythical language has of it. When the Druids did write using magical alphabets such as ogham, the letters themselves had power. The thing was present, such as *tree, giant* or *halt*, that was named in the word.

Geomythical resonances are found in surprising places. It is often the case that entirely unbeknown to them, dwellers in a place have given the same names to landscape features or told stories equivalent to those the earlier dwellers told. Or sometimes the original name of a place, even though its meaning may be unknown and the features which gave rise to it have disappeared, has continued to affect the thinking and actions of subsequent inhabitants. If you were a child living near Giant's Leap or Serpent Lake or Dragon Hill, what mental pictures would you have?

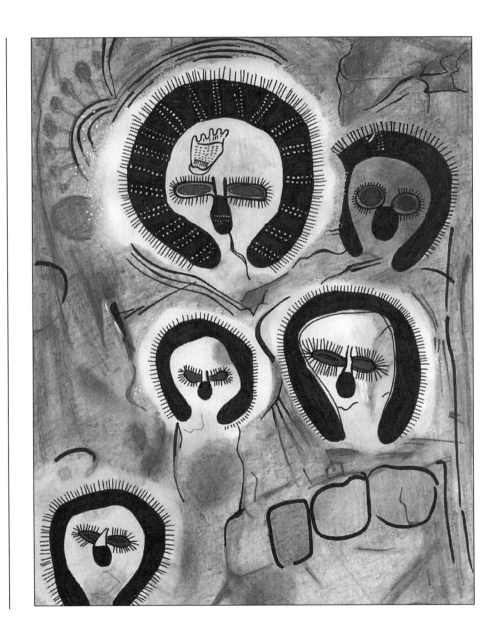

*The Wandjina, rock painting from the —imberleys. The Wandjina are awesome giant spirits who live in storms and whirlwinds. In the wet season they can be seen striding around the landscape on long, silvery legs*

The meaning of names and local myths, especially when they include topographical features, are therefore clues to the essential signature, character or "spirit of place." Meaning is the key point here. Geomythics defines and locates us as meaningful beings in a meaningful cosmos. Geomythics allows us to think in terms of what unites the apparent randomness of the external world. Thinking in terms of giants creates meaning. Geomythics is the spirit of the world in which human beings can participate through naming. The Songlines of Australia are a perfect illustration of this.

In Western society, language, meaning and landscape are apparently not so inextricably intertwined, but the tie is still there. The filters of our present cosmology are only a few thousand years old. They can separate us but not sever us from the immanent experience of life. Out in nature where the full sensory capacity of our bodies operates, we can still feel the subtle yet powerful connections between earth and spirit. Many of us feel the pull of the land during times of extreme stress. Or we may realize the communion of life when inspired by seeing an exquisite sunset, being in love or having a meditative experience.

## A COSMOLOGICAL TYPOLOGY

It will be useful at this point to present a cosmological typology in order to describe the essential differences between the modern and the tribal world. The human condition, culture and cosmology are in a constant state of flux. The process of human culture can be said to go through a typical cycle which is as follows:

※ *A phase of coalescence.* People are united in common belief. Cosmology is collective, alive, and made meaningful through connectedness with natural forces.

※ *A phase of manifestation.* People are willing to labor in external expression of their beliefs. Construction is intuitive and symbolic. Cosmology is collective, alive and made meaningful through correlation of natural and cultural forces.

※ *A phase of disintegration.* Loss of meaning and struggle for control of the externalized system brings about hierarchy, oppression and dissent. This may take the form of a massive increase in externalization, construction of formulaic sacred and secular works, and huge ritual displays before the final collapse. Cosmology is fragmented and mostly manipulates cultural forces.

In America, examples of these stages may be characterized by the early effigy mounds, followed by the huge ritual mounds, followed by the massive sacrifices at the Aztec pyramids. A similar cycle may account for the stupendous growth of Chaco Canyon, the building of the ceremonial ways, then the mysterious collapse and the "disappearance" of the Anasazi. Straight lines do seem to indicate that a culture is in a state of frozen ideology rather than in a responsive and fluid state based upon the creativity of nature. Lines may suggest that a culture is on the verge of collapse. We can witness this in the awesome but rigidly straight ceremonial ways built by the Maya, Chaco and Inca peoples. These may have been attempts to retrieve a power felt to be slipping away rather than an expression, from the people, of their beliefs in the earth spirit.

In Europe, the Neolithic people went through a similar cycle. They shared similar beliefs, expressed them collectively and joyfully in the early megalithic sites, and finally collapsed after the massive and enforced undertakings at Stonehenge and the long straight rows of stones at Carnac in Brittany.

A feature of the cycle is that in the final stage, although created from the flux of human ideas, the externalized world becomes the fixed and manifest proof of the "rightness" of those ideas. As the culture socially stratifies and increasingly specializes, its forms become more concrete. As interest groups try and consolidate their power, their structures become more pervasive and predominant. As the culture urbanizes and separates from nature, its forms become more rigid. As it experiences loss of connectedness to the natural world—and therefore loss of meaning—greater control and more laws are needed to maintain the world order. An example of this in recent times was Hitler's Third Reich. The Nazi Movement appealed to atavistic archetypal powers and structured itself and its architecture in the image of a divine cosmology. The result in this case, as well as in the other examples, was an escalation of meaningless rituals, sacrifice and manipulation of individuals and subsequently collapse.

Meaning derives from a sense of relatedness. Meaning arises from connectedness to the creativity and flux of nature. The organic diversity and wandering lines of nature are in direct contrast to an imposed geometric or disciplined order. This could account for why the Celtic Druids insisted on no externalization of their spiritual forms. They went "back to nature." They honored the natural sacred sites at grove and spring, built no temples and maintained a living oral tradition. The Aboriginal people of Australia never went beyond the first stage of the cycle. They never externalized their beliefs with construction. They represent the paths of the ancestors as wavy, meandering lines and maintain a living, earth-rooted cosmography. The Ancestral Beings of the Aborigines are quite likely the best living example of what we mean in this book by the "Giants of Gaia." ▨

## CONCLUSION TO PART ONE

A culture may locate shrines, pyramids, sacred objects, carvings and paintings in certain places, or conduct rituals at them, to maintain the earth spirit and the vision of the cosmic pattern in the material world. In order to do this the forms created by humans are conceived on a giant scale. Through resonance with the giants of creation the world order is maintained. The Songlines criss-crossing the continent of Australia find their parallels in the *ceques* of Peru, the *sacbes* of the Maya, the ceremonial ways of Chaco Canyon, the linear and effigy mounds of America, the pyramids of Mexico and the alignments and avenues of European megalithic mounds and circles. All these were conceived and carried out on a gigantic scale.

The Neolithic people, the Anasazi, the Hopewell and the Mayans manifested their cosmographies in physical form. Originally their constructions might have spanned continents but in the form we have today little remains. The Aborigines did not choose to physically manifest their cosmography, but their conti-

nent-spanning dreamings are still alive in the magnificent ritualistic, mythological, spatial dimensions of the Songlines.

# ENERGIES AND PATTERNS

# OF GIANTS

C H A P T E R   S I X

# EARTH SPIRIT

Once upon a time, a young woman called Jane was walking upon the strange hill in Avalon known as Glastonbury Tor, when an entranceway mysteriously opened up in the earth before her. Being the curious sort, she went inside and down a steep passageway. She soon reached a cavern. It was empty except for a bronze bowl with a hammer beside it. Jane could not resist and struck the bowl. The cavern reverberated with sound and a spinning ball of colors appeared. It slowed down enough for Jane to make out that it was a figure which was human, but not quite human. It seemed to have difficulty in stopping itself, for it spun in the opposite direction before returning to focus. "Yes?" it asked querulously. "Yes?"

It seemed in a hurry, so Jane plunged straight in without any formal introductions. "Can you please direct me to the Castle of Gwynn ap Nudd?" Jane tried to sound confident.

"Hah! A bold question indeed! You have quite the nerve to divert me. A minute of idle conversation here is an hour in your world. Besides, others have come here and the few who went back to your world, such as it is, were not heeded and were considered mad!"

Jane was alarmed, but again asked the fairy how to reach the castle. Grumbling, the fairy led the way down until they reached an enormous cavern full of hazy, green light. There were tables laid out with platters of leaves. Fairies everywhere were busy spinning and weaving. In the middle of the cave

was a huge golden throne where a giant figure of a man was seated. It was Gwynn ap Nudd, King of Faery, who conducts souls to the Celtic Otherworld. He rose to greet Jane in a most hospitable manner.

"Welcome," Gwynn said in an extremely loud voice. He invited Jane to be seated and join the festivities. Jane obliged and, cheered by the friendliness, soon got up enough courage to ask Gwynn why he was no longer seen in the outside world.

"That is a long tale, but one worth the telling. In the old days the people honored me and my twin. We worked together to increase the power of the trees, the animals, the grasses on the plains. The people held festivals to honor us. In return, we let our spirit swell in them and make them glad with life. Here in Avalon they would gather on May Day to watch the struggle between me and my twin. For you see, without polarity, without dark and light, without unfolding and enfolding, without male and female, nothing could be born and there would be no life.

"Yes, we had it nicely arranged." Gwynn chuckled and had a faraway look in his eye. "I was the Red Dragon and ruled the dark half of the year. My twin the Star Serpent ruled the bright half. That was how it had been given from the beginning by the Goddess in whom we both live. As time went by the folk dramatized and elaborated the whole thing a bit. They said I ruled over the Underworld and the dead, which is just the other side of life.

"But after a long while the newfangled ways took over and a very strange thing happened. In place of our dance honoring the polarity of life, they cut us in half and ruined the balance. They banished me from their world and made the Star Serpent the supreme deity. Whoever heard of a sky god ruling over all! And in that hopeless confusion, the Goddess became a passive daughter of a Lord of Light, meekly following him into his domain.

"Can you believe it? And do you know what they did?" Jane shook her head. Gwynn seemed to be getting rather irritated. "They stopped the honoring of the turning points of the year. They said I was a demon of evil, to be locked away forever!

*As if the disruption of the balance of dark and light could bring fortune to the world!" Gwynn sat back in his throne and clasped his great hands thoughtfully beneath his chin. "Now what we have instead of polarity is a false division of things into good and evil. Now there is an abstract god who is nowhere rather than right here in the Earth. Now male and female do not get along, the dark time is feared instead of honored, and this good earthly life is despised."*

*Gwynn lapsed into silence and Jane was afraid to speak. But after what felt like a polite interval she asked: "Who is the Goddess?"*

*"Who is your mother? Who is Earth? Honor life and you will honor her. Remember, it would be as mad to make a religion out of the Goddess as it has been to make one out of the God."*

*"But then, who are you, if you are not a God?"*

*Gwynn laughed, deep and long. The leaf spinners turned to look. "Who is the forest? Who is born and who dies? What is the secret of the wind? Of Jenny Wren and Cock Robin? Of the oak, the yew, the mistletoe and old John Barleycorn? I was made by your grandfathers and grandmothers to remind you of the eternal flux of life."*

*Jane shook herself and stared as she saw the deep tones of Gwynn's voice enter into the forms the fairies were spinning. She saw Gwynn's hair rise up and pass into the roots of trees. She saw his limbs enter stones and his blood become lava. Finally Gwynn's breath became the roar of the red dragon moving through the earth.*

*The spinning ball of a fairy guided Jane from the Underworld. Soon she was back, standing alone on the green surface of the land.*

---

he purpose of this chapter is to provide a background on ideas about those forces which are said to sustain life. They are present in nature and the earth in a subtle way. Such ideas are intrinsic to a culture's cosmology. We will show how these ideas change as cosmologies themselves undergo transformation. Ideas about giants, dragons, earth spirit and life forces are vital and meaningful in an earth-honoring cosmology, where they empower the people's reality, but these ideas may make no sense at all in the reality of another culture. What kind of a world do giants live in?

## THE SEARCH FOR INVISIBLE ENERGY

Ever since the time of Plato and his school we have records of the search for a force, an invisible energy, which was felt to mysteriously pervade and sustain all things. A fifth element, sometimes called "ether," has been postulated as an all-pervading massless medium of energy. It would benefit life if only it could be discovered and controlled. Alchemists such as Paracelsus (1490–1541) and Robert Fludd (1574–1637) pursued the "Divine Essence" in the relationships between the elemental forces and the human soul. Mesmer called a similar principle animal magnetism. In this century Dr. Wilhelm Reich pursued it in his ideas of a constantly flowing, pervasive energy he called orgone. And scientists today search on a quantum level for the constituent parts of the atom which oscillate on the boundary between material substance and pure energy.

The Hindus call this invisible life energy *prana*. It is present in all things. Copious amounts of it may be tapped in the human body from the kundalini energy which lies coiled like a serpent at the base of the spine. This energy is often depicted in spiral form. It has an inward and an outward turning path. It is thus like the breath, constantly flowing, invisible, yet life-sustaining.

If we were to think about it, what is life? What exactly makes the difference between being alive and being dead? Medically we say it is when the heart stops beating and the brainwaves cease. But what makes the heart and brain go in the first place, and then stop? Is it because the angels blow the heavenly wind through that body and then withdraw it? Is it because the universe unfolds a unique spark of life into a visible form and then enfolds it back into its infinite order? Is it because Gaia the Earth Goddess creates the planet's life forms like offspring, fills them with earth energies like milk, and guides their well-being as carefully as any mother? Is it possible that the power which we humans use—political, magical, electrical, physical—comes from the greater, self-regulating, living organism that we know as Earth?

## LEY LINES, DOWSING AND EARTH MYSTERIES

Geomancy means "divining the earth spirit." Chinese geomancers are extremely interested in tracking the currents of subtle energy called *chi* or *ki* as it moves in its many forms across the landscape. This geomantic practice is known in China as *feng-shui*. It literally means "wind-water." The power of the breath is fundamental to the feng-shui of a place. For perfect chi to be present, and not the undesirable *sha*—literally "noxious breath"—there must be the correct balance of *yin* and *yang*. This force, known as the dragon current, is represented by the white tiger, which is yin, and the blue dragon which is yang. The lines of the dragon current, the *lung-mei*, carry yin and yang forces across the countryside. The geomancer's task is to find and identify these currents. Then, like the balance of inbreath and outbreath, the geomancer brings them into harmony for the well-being of life.

The idea of balance between complementary polarities permeates the subject of earth energies. We find it in myth, especially in the duality of earth and sky—the red and white dragons of the Celtic tradition. We find it in science in electricity and magnetism. The flow of subtle magnetic forces between two poles, like the flow of the vitalizing breath, has always been a concern of those who pursue the earth spirit.

The whole surface of the earth is flowing with magnetic current. This is produced by the inner core of the earth. The flow is not uniform. Considerable variation is caused by the geological composition of the ground over which the current passes. Over faults, mineral deposits and rocky country a compass needle can spin wildly. Planetary and solar forces also affect the earth's magnetic field. This is most dramatic in the northern polar region where it produces the aurora borealis. It is unlikely that magnetic currents alone qualify as the life energy sought by philosophers, alchemists and scientists. But being able to predict an eclipse, when magnetic disturbances can be most dramatic, was a concern of the peoples who have developed geomantic systems. This kind of earth energy was important to the maintenance of their vision of cosmological harmony in life on earth. One of the geomancer's primary tools is the magnetic compass. It is used not only to orient a site auspiciously, but also to accurately determine the flow of local magnetic energy.

Many mystics and diviners have developed systems where different kinds of subtle energy can be detected through dowsing. Dowsing is a skill where, usually through the use of a tool like a wand or a pendulum, a person becomes sensitized to the reaction of his or her body to impressions beyond the range of the usual five senses. It is, in effect, a sixth sense. Experiments have shown that the body can detect variations in the local magnetic field produced, for example, by an underground pipe or cable.

Some of the dowsable energy patterns are said to be due to underground water, some are due to subterranean geology, some are due to planetary influences and some to the deliberate placement in the landscape of features such as standing stones. Many of the anomalies of life, such as sightings of ghosts; vanishing black dogs; moving lights; crop circles; auras around objects or living beings, are claimed by dowsers to be created by energy patterns which they can detect through the use of their divining skill.

Considerable public interest arose around these anomalies, which have become known as the field of "Earth Mysteries." Their pursuit was intensified by the discovery of straight lines through the English countryside. In 1921, after surveying parts of Britain, Alfred Watkins made a remarkable discovery which he later described in the book *The Old Straight Track*. He saw that in some bygone age a network of exact alignments lay across the surface of the land. The network was formed by lining up mounds, cairns, stone circles, roads, crossroads, fords, standing stones and eventually churches with notches in ridges, hilltops and other natural features. Since then, much work has gone into discovering what Mr. Watkins called "ley lines." An example is the St. Michael Line described in Chapter 3. But what really attracted interest was the idea that these were lines of some subtle energy which could be detected through dowsing.

By ley lines Mr. Watkins meant the alignment of natural and human-built sites, such as stones and mounds, across the land. He thought of them as being primarily trackways. But other ideas about their nature and about sacred sites in general soon came into print. Guy Underwood's *The Pattern of the Past* provided remarkable correlation between subterranean sources of energy, mostly produced by water, and the location and shape of ancient and comparatively recent surface features such as old tracks, stone circles and churches. "Blind springs," strong sources of aquatic underground energy, were deciding factors in the location of stone circles such as Stonehenge. It appeared that the builders of the megalithic sites were working with the subtle energies of the earth in ways that we now do not understand. It was a bit of a chicken and egg situation though. The patterns Mr. Underwood found could just as easily have been produced by the surface features as by underground water, though he did not think so.

Tom Graves attempted to define a more rigorous approach to dowsing. His book *Needles of Stone* remains one of the best on the subject. He suggested an equivalence between standing stones erected by Neolithic people and acupuncture needles, hence the title of his book. In the same way as the meridians of the human body are treated in acupuncture, megalithic stone "needles" were used to balance, focus, disperse and direct natural energies along the meridians of the "body" of the earth. He distinguished between lines created by the simple alignments of sites, and lines carrying dowsable energy.

He startled Earth Mysteries people and scientists by opening up the idea of dowsable "thoughtforms" or "place memories." He proposed that emotions or ideas could be stored by certain characteristics of a site. At that point all pandemonium broke loose. If dowsers had been asked to gather at a site to determine the pattern of its energies, there would be as many interpretations as there were dowsers. If thoughts and emotions could be picked up, whose thoughtform was creating whose pattern? Were people dowsing Neolithic thoughts and memories, or those of the dowser standing next to them? The results would be unverifiable.

Despite this subjectivity, writers like John Michell, Nigel Pennick and Janet and Colin Bord continued to present the beguiling case for earth energies. At its simplest it runs as follows: at some points in time people developed a method for working with the subtle energies of the earth. Through a technology now lost they could modify these forces for the enhancement of life. The Bords write:

> The earth currents were manipulated by the men who raised the standing stones, the routes of the current being guided and marked by these standing stones and other structures, and at these points the currents could also be released and controlled at certain times. This was an exact procedure, the stones, circles and earth mounds being positioned on precise sites so that the current could be used to the benefit of all....The mode of operation of these influences and emanations is as incomprehensible to us as are the workings of telepathy, poltergeists, psychokinesis, and all other forms of psychic phenomenon, but it is not valid reasoning to deny or ignore the existence of the phenomenon simply because it appears to be illogical and cannot be fitted into our conventional frame of reference.[1]

The academic and scientific establishment meanwhile was more than happy to deny and ignore what it felt to be worse than illogical. In fact it considered Earth Mysteries to be sheer nonsense. Scientists continued the analysis of stone circles and earth mounds in terms of the archaeological evidence. Here wonderful things were being found. It became possible to gain glimpses of the elaborate rituals which had gone on around the sites. Archaeology revealed what people had been wearing, what they hunted and ate, what their society may have looked like and, to an extent, where their cosmological interests lay.

Ancient people were certainly interested in the earth, sky and the seasonal cycle. They certainly aligned their structures to notches in hills and calendar events. But there was no evidence that they approached these matters in the way modern astronomers do, nor that their sacred sites were conduits for any energy understood in modern scientific terms. Even the "precise" alignments are questionable. They may be better described as wandering lines conforming to aesthetic and cosmological standards—just as we may align civic buildings along a line of sight—rather than possessing any energy-carrying purpose known to physics.[2]

Dismayed by this, other researchers in the field of Earth Mysteries made systematic attempts to discover exactly what earth energies were being worked with at the ancient sites. Most notable of these attempts is the Dragon Project in Britain. Under the guidance of Paul Devereux, the project has tried to measure scientifically the energies which were reported to be present at the sites. What was of particular interest were the ley lines, which were intuitively felt to be conduits of special power. But the nature and purpose of the leys could not be determined conclusively. Dowsing tests, ultrasound tests, radiation tests, magnetic and infra-red experiments were applied to the sites. Ley lines were statistically analyzed. To this day it must be said, that while some anomalies and synchronicities are definitely worth further investigation, conclusive results have yet to be obtained.

Mr. Devereux is now attempting subjective methods of determining the purposes of the ancient sacred sites. Dream work and other practices of shamanism are being explored. This is unlikely to lead to scientific results. Like the wind and water of feng-shui, definitions will continue to slip away from the methods of empirical investigation. However, such work will continue to reveal the wonders of the vitally subjective inner world. Perhaps Tom Graves' thoughtforms were right on the money.[3]

## THE EARTH SPIRIT

hen what remains? If subjective investigation can provide no consensus on earth energies and scientific research draws a blank, should we conclude that no subtle life forces exist in the earth? Should we conclude that geomancy and feng-shui are manipulations of superstitious minds and that orgone, animal magnetism, chi, place-memories, ley lines, and blind springs are psychic mumbo-jumbo? Or should we remind ourselves that electricity, gravity, sub-atomic particles, light and magnetism are poorly understood, yet no one denies the existence of these mostly invisible forces? Science is beginning to acknowledge its own subjectivity and the role of the mind in its research. The Bords were quite right in that ancient practice would not fit "into our conventional frame of reference." And, as Tom Graves delights in pointing out, what we call "technology" the ancients would probably call "magic," and what we today call "magic" the ancients, or tribal peoples, are quite likely to think of as "technology."

The point is that what humans think is very important. The ideas we hold in our minds, the meaning they have and the language we use to give voice to them is very powerful. Developments in science and technology are now recognized as being a result not so much of the objective gathering of data and information—although that is important—but of the way that information is held in our minds. Quantum leaps occur when we see through the limits of the way we hold information about the world in our minds and arrive at a new synthesis, an expanded picture.

What has this to do with giants? In the previous chapter we wrote of language and culture as emerging out of the interaction between the human mind and the world. In the same way as the Aborigines conceived the giant Ancestral Beings giving birth to the world by giving voice to it, so humans give birth to the world of the ancestors by giving voice to that. The ancestors may have originally created the world, the tribe, the hills, forests and billabongs in their songs, but it is their descendants who create the giant ancestors with their songs. This subjective interaction has maintained the Aborigine very successfully. It provides a way of thinking about the world that is conducive for life in the harsh Australian environment. Put in another way, the Aborigines

create, make sense of and order their world through their language and cosmology, and in that world giant creative spirit ancestors make perfect sense.

It has been estimated that over 300 different languages existed in Australia before the colonial invasion, as many as there were tribes. Each tribe maintained a vocabulary and a mythology made up of songs and stories of extreme complexity and size. A similar situation exists among Native Americans in North America. A rich oral culture also once existed in prehistoric Europe. The Celts actually forbade the recording of their mythical tradition. Their Druids had to undergo up to two decades of rigorous training in order to memorize songs, history and stories before they became initiated.

The *Book of Genesis* starts with: "In the beginning was the Word..." A people's cosmology defines their physical world and predisposes them to view it in a particular way. A cosmology is very powerful. It is formed by the people's pattern of thought. Thought is formed by the structure and categories of language. Language is formed by words, which are formed by the world around the people. The language with which we think determines the way in which we see and relate to the world.

The Aborigines, the Native Americans and the Druids maintained complex and fluid oral traditions of stories, myths, songs and teachings. The cosmologies of these peoples provide perfect conceptual tools for dealing with the changing complexities of their environment. Subtle forces, giants and dragons provide the language for understanding natural forces and cultural relations.

The concept of the earth spirit is not accessible to scientific instruments because the earth energies of nature-cultures do not operate within the mechanistic paradigm of science. The "magical" world of the Aboriginal people cannot be accessed from the technological world of the scientist and vice versa. Each possesses an entirely different vocabulary and thus dwells in an entirely different reality.

Earth energies at a certain site have to be measured within their total socio-political, mythopoeic, environmental context. From this perspective it would be true to say that feng-shui will not work outside of China. Only the Chinese relate to their landscape in the total cosmological terms that make feng-shui work. Likewise, the songlines stop at the borders not of the Australian continent but of the Aboriginal mind. It could also be said that the energies the megalithic people worked with at their sacred sites died with them, long ago. While those forces cannot be empirically detected, thousands of people today sense them or perhaps re-create them when they visit the sacred stones. The interaction of new human presence with the site, plus the potency of knowing that the site has geomythical congruency and that people have worshipped there before is very stimulating. There are instances of Native Americans employing European stone circles as medicine wheels.

The Dreamings of the Aborigines and the medicine wheel teachings provide a complete cosmology that arises from the interaction of the native people with the landscape. This process has evolved over thousands of years. The informing power of the Dreamings or of the medicine wheels cannot be taken out of their cosmological context. All native people have developed a geomythical language with profound synchronistic and synergistic resonances between mind and matter. Such language—and its meaning—arises within a specific geographical location. The first "alphabet" of the Celts, a forest people, had its origins in the trees. Each phoneme, the unit of sound, in the tree alphabet had a host of associated meanings and sympathetic magical resonances which allowed their forms to provide a complete map of the order of the cosmos. In such worlds giants can live.

So it is, that in another place, another time, people and their neighbors, and their neighbors' neighbors, lit fires on the hilltops to secure the blessings of the Giant Ancestral Spirits. They created sites which enhanced and guaranteed the securing of this power. Stones and mounds marking the position of the sun at this time assisted in this. Alignments to the stones increased their evocative power. The people gathered on the hills at the appropriate moment to congregate the energies from tree, fire, hill, giants, stones, mound and sun. In this way, people, landscape, time and spirits were brought into a symphony of correlating harmonies. The energy created in this total mind-body-spirit reality was vitally necessary for the well-being of its creators. They felt it. It sustained them. It turned the cycle of life.

## INTERACTION WITH THE EARTH SPIRIT

When the ancient philosophers, the alchemists and the Earth Mystery researchers sought the subtle energies of the earth spirit they were right in some ways but they overlooked some other very important things. They were right in that these forces are invisible, capable of interacting with humans, and difficult to comprehend, but they failed to see that these forces arose precisely in the interaction between humans and the world.

First, the earth spirit is found moving in the often invisible yet hugely powerful elemental forces present right before our eyes: winds, tides, currents, electricity, magnetism, gravity, heat, light and growth, to name a few. These immanent forces are part of the miraculous gift of life.

Second, the earth spirit is found moving in the invisible and unquantifiable vastness of the worldview which people carry within. The mind and its cosmology are very powerful and determine the character of the world. A characteristic of this huge inner dimension, shaped over time, is that it contains what Jungian psychologists call the archetypes. These have extraordinary informing power upon individual consciousness. Let us look at this idea for a moment.

The archetypes, such as the dragon, wise woman, giant, animal ancestor, goddess, warrior, queen and emperor exist in the realm of the collective unconsciousness. No one, least of all Jung, is suggesting that they have a real, nuts-and-bolts existence. They are patterns, which although uniquely held in every mind, repeat themselves on a cultural scale. They then find expression in the works of a people's cosmology, and by repetition and agreement they have the power to imprint themselves upon the world. The world, being user-friendly, obliges and arranges itself in the order being projected upon it. Eventually the external world is actually made in the image of the inner "word" with laws, buildings, palaces, temples, roads and other cosmos-defining institutions.

In this world, depending where the culture is in the stages of its cosmology, the energies of the earth spirit are perceived and felt to flow. It seems the Chinese through the art of feng-shui were able to move the energy of the earth spirit—for quite long periods of time—through the manifestation of the cosmic order upon earth. This energy centered upon the emperor's palace in the "Celestial City." The lung-mei or dragon lines, focused on the palace, collected and dispersed the subtle forces of the earth spirit and so maintained terrestrial harmony. Louis XIV, the "Sun King," briefly achieved similar cosmological congruency through the establishment of his throne at the quasi-geomantic palace of Versailles. Similar designs were created for the capital cities, Canberra, Moscow and Washington.

In order to discover the earth spirit, something has to happen which honors and synchronizes the creative power of the imagination and the natural forces of the world. Then, in the interaction of the creative power of the mind and the creative power of the world, the giants are born, the songs are sung, the myths are told, the dragons fly. When the spirit of the earth is dreamed, it shakes off its chains and soars.

Yes, people did gather at sacred sites to concentrate and disperse energy. Yes, people did construct "dragon lines" along which this energy could flow. Yes, people did invoke giants and spirits to conduct this energy. They did call upon heavenly and subterranean beings. They did more than most of us today can possibly imagine. But their cosmos was different than ours, their mythology was not our mythology, their power lines were not our power lines. If people today wish to invoke and reawaken the Earth Spirit, what is needed is a view of the universe where "earth" and "spirit" are again one and the same. ✖

# GIANTS AS DRAGONS

I called out in great need, petitioning my power animal—whatever that was—to come. Through a swirl of colors and mist, the dragon came in its serpent form and gave me a vision.

At first I saw myself huge and dominating, looking down on a small snake from above. The more I looked down, the more uncomfortable became the thoughts which slithered into my mind. Was I falsely trying to hold on to superiority, pretense, outward behavior that did not match my inner urgings for change? No. My life was perfect. I had it all together...or, was that pretense also? The thoughts piled on top of each other. But if the life I have built up is false, then what's left? How can I face changing everything? How would I explain to others? "Face?" "Explain to others?" Even the words sounded pretentious. Help me, dragon. Show me your wisdom.

With frightening speed, the vision switched. Now the serpent was huge and loomed above me. I was a minuscule human. No! I recoiled. I hate being dominated! I feel crushed in this position. Don't do this to me! Don't use your power this way!

The image disappeared, leaving a blank. "Now do you see?" came a voice from the void. "No, I don't see! What are you? Where are you?" I asked in confusion.

Instantly the vision switched again and my breath left me. Now I was lying on the ground, staring straight into the glowing, slanted, hooded eyes of a serpent. It was the same size as I. Frightened, intim-

idated, I explored the energies shooting out at me. I found them benign but enormously powerful. I was quivering with attention. The snake slipped out of its old skin as easily as flipping channels on a television set. Did this mean I could change my life so easily? If my present life channel felt false and outdated, could I simply replace it at will?

Immersed in this realization, I almost missed what the dragon said next. It was an answer to my plea for wisdom. It said, "Get down. Get real. Get genuine. Here you are on the ground, on the earth. No pretense here. Nothing between you and me. Here you can use my energy. Whenever you are in doubt, get down here."

hildren believe in dragons. The heroes of mythology battle them. Druids, alchemists and royalty used dragons as their chief symbol. The father of King Arthur was called Pendragon, "head dragon." Yet modern adults think of dragons as mere fantasy. If dragons are only a fiction, why then do they persist? Why do fighter pilots put decals of dragons on the sides of their war planes? Why are dragons so popular in jewelry and sculpture? How is it that each of us can easily describe our own image of the fabled beast? The reason must lie in symbology.

## DRAGONS AS GIGANTIC SYMBOLS

Dragons symbolize power, pure energy. With no need for life support systems, dragons can fly, live under water, breathe fire and travel underground. They are the most powerful creature that people can conceive of. Dragon power can be used to transition between the material and the non-material worlds. "Dragons are the outer aspect of an inner knowledge."[1] The inner image of dragons is power.

The outer image is earth spirit, currents that move through every dimension. People need a meaningful way to deal with life and death, spirituality and mysteries. Dragons have symbolized each of these and by venerating the symbol, people can invoke its meaning and power.

In Classical mythology, the Giants were born of Gaia as a result of the mutilation of her lover the sky god, Ouranos. This was done by the jealous Titan, Cronos. The Giants had the heads of humans and the bodies of serpents. After they and the Titans were defeated by the Olympians, they made their dwelling in the elemental and subterranean realms. Gaia, in rage at their defeat, created an even more formidable opponent to the gods, the monstrous Typhon. This giant being was said to have wings, the arms and legs of serpents and eyes of fire. He was only defeated when the mountains he hurled rebounded upon him. His fire still belches from the earth to this day.[2]

Not surprisingly, therefore, the major characteristics of giants that we have presented in this book also apply to dragons: they are large, powerful, magical, earthy and difficult to kill. Despite all attempts to suppress giants and dragons, they cannot be made to disappear. There is a saying: "For who can confine Dragons, for their thunder will come through the walls."[3]

In all the mythologies of the world, dragons are the preferred way of representing the raw power of the elements. They are the supreme rulers of elemental energy. Most everything in the next chapter concerning elementals can be translated as "dragons." They also represent sexual power, fertility, instincts and the animal world.

How is it that people in every culture, every era, chose the exact same symbol? The Chinese built carefully so as to not disrupt the dragon currents called lung mei. To help a current on its way they would place dragons under eaves or on roof lines or wrapped around columns. The Babylonians and Egyptians, Hindus and Tibetans, Mayans and Aztecs, native Europeans and Native Americans all had dragon deities. Did all these people have ways of communicating with each other across the planet that we do not know about? Or did the symbol arise out of inner, mental pictures that were encoded in the brains of our ancestors? Are they archaic remnants, as Jung describes, the images of the collective unconscious? Did the symbol come from a once-real creature?

Although humans did not co-exist with dinosaurs, many mammals did. The dinosaurs dominated the planet for an incredibly long time—140 million years. Reconstructions of the *Stegosaurus* show it to be an ideal prototype for the dragon. Perhaps the dinosaur/dragon continues to live in the depths of what has been called our "reptilian brain."

Whatever the explanation, the appearance of dragons around the world is amazingly similar. They are gigantic winged reptiles. They differ from snakes by having horns, scales, claws, wings, legs and sometimes ears. In the Han Dynasty (206 BCE—221 CE), the philosopher Wang Fu first described the requisites for a Chinese dragon as: horns of a stag, head of a camel, eyes of a demon, neck of a snake, scales of a carp, claws of an eagle, ears of a bull, and long whiskers. In Medieval Europe, some dragons had the throat and legs of an eagle, the body of a huge serpent, the wings of a bat, and a tail that twisted back on itself. The eagle represented celestial power and vision. The serpent contributed secret and subterranean characteristics. The wings stood for intellectual elevation. The tail shape, coming from the sign for Leo in the zodiac, stood for reason.[4]

All these varied attributes suggest that the dragon is the connecting link between levels or dimensions. It has traits which give it power below ground, on the surface, in water, in air and in fire. It can mediate between two extremes of cosmic forces. We saw in Chapter 4 how the Plumed Serpent, Quetzalcoatl, joins "Those Above" with "Those Below." And in Chapter 5 we saw how the Australian Rainbow Serpents connect earth and sky. The Chinese say "The earth joins up with the dragon" when it is raining.[5] The dragon can move between the symbolic worlds of the spirit, ordinary life, and the telluric forces within the earth. It speaks the energy-language of minerals, plants, animals, humans, giants and deities.

Why do people need agents or external forces such as dragons and giants? There are several reasons. They provide explanations for the way people see the world. "We see what we need to see," said an Irish witch recently. The Celts see beings with serpent shapes, just as Native Americans see power animals. These images and forms occur among people who have a spiritual heritage that does not make brittle separations between real and unreal, animate and inanimate. People need them to carry out accomplishments that are not attributed to humans, tasks that only giants and dragons can do. The earth mounds and stone circles of megalithic Europe were reportedly

*Chinese dragons*

As the opening tale of Chapter 6 relates, Celtic legend has it that Glastonbury Tor is the home of Gwynn ap Nudd, Lord of the Underworld. Every May Day he would fight a celestial opponent for the hand of the solar goddess. Here we have the fundamental imagery of the Great Goddess and dragon. The energy of the cosmos is manifested by the dynamic polarity of earth and sky represented as yin and yang dragons or Gwynn ap Nudd and his twin opponent. Their telluric dragon coils are wrapped around a powerful unified source, the spiral hill of the beautiful solar goddess. In art and mythology this is typically represented as a circle, fiery disk, sun or egg wrapped around by the cosmic serpent. An egg with a serpent around it is one of the most complete symbols of the earth spirit. The egg is a symbol of wholeness and unity, with the potential to generate and be fertile. The serpent is a symbol of energy and movement, which actualizes the fertile potential of the egg. The Ohio Serpent Mound is a perfect symbolic expression of this cosmology on the North American continent.

Our focus is on dragons as gigantic symbols. Dragons represented two of the most powerful and mystical life forces in nature-cultures: energy and rebirth. Each is of gigantic importance. We will first look at the meanings surrounding energy.

Much like a dog can sniff the exact trail of its master, early people noticed traces of energy and attributed them to the presence of dragons. They noticed that this force gathered at springs, at openings, cracks and fissures in the earth. It flowed in streams and rivers and blew in the wind down valleys. It came in storms and lightning. When outraged it emerged in torrents of fire.

Nature-oriented people pictured dragons as currents of the earth spirit, gliding in serpentine channels

built by dragon-powered giants, as were the pyramids in Egypt and the Great Wall of China. People need them to explain the awesome powers of nature and to animate the stuff of the planet: earth, stones, water, trees. Indeed, dragons can be defined as the life force of giants.

As a symbol, the dragon is interchangeable with the serpent or snake. In *The Mists of Avalon*, Marion Zimmer Bradley says "The dragon is the same as the serpent...A symbol of wisdom; a Druidical symbol."[6] The Druid name for a wise person, *Naddair*, meant serpent and is the source for our word adder. The ancient Maya and the Sioux also referred to wise people with words meaning serpent.[7]

Dragons and serpents are sacred emblems of the old devotion to earth spirit, and perhaps to the Great Goddess. If we journey far back in time we find records of these beliefs. A simplified form of the coiled serpent, the spiral, is found frequently on ancient worked stones. The oldest spirals, dating from 20,000 BCE, are found in the cave art of northern Spain. In Ireland, the massive entrance stone at New Grange, carved around 3300 BCE, is covered with spirals. Carvings of spirals made a thousand years ago are visible upon the rocks of Chaco Canyon. Many petroglyphs in the Southwest show dragon-like serpents with their bodies ending in a spiral, representing the natural energies of the earth.

dragon energy gave life to the crops and to the people living on the surface of the land. When angered it could hurt or destroy. In Celtic mythology such forces were called Afancs or Adancs. They were manifestations of one great dragon that surrounded the earth and was sometimes visible moving in its depths.

Evidence indicates that the earliest people cooperated with dragon forces and honored them. Their shrines are often situated upon or near openings into the earth. The oracle at Delphi was situated beside a deep chasm. Over this chasm the Pythoness, the priestess, would receive her prophecies from Gaia or Ge, the earth goddess. The earth goddess had many places of oracle around the world.

Later, people attempted to control the earth spirit or "fix" its fertility in a certain spot, as a result of settlement and the development of agriculture. At that point, the dragon either had to be killed or staked. The name of St. George, a famous dragon killer, comes from the Greek *ge-orgos,* meaning "tiller of the earth." The St. Michael line across England shows the route of the dragon which is now dominated by churches named after St. Michael.

The second life force that serpents represent is rebirth because they are rejuvenated when they shed their skins. A milky substance is secreted between the old and new skin, even over the eyes, until the snake can slip out of the old skin. Snakes also lay copious numbers of eggs. A connection with the feminine principle of transformation is shown by ancient representations of goddesses such as Artemis, Hecate and Persephone carrying a snake in their hands. Every new moon was thought to be the dragon's gift to people on earth. It allowed them to be reborn monthly and to make new wishes for the direction of their lives. The Druids celebrated the spring equinox as a time when a throng of snakes came together and laid a world-egg from the Milky Way. This act perpetuated the cycle of the year on earth.

Neolithic people attributed dragon characteristics to patterns they noticed in nature. The earth's rebirth in spring and the return of the snakes from hibernation was said to be the dragon awakening. Underground water courses were said to be the path of a dragon. Where the dragon surfaced at a spring was considered to be a location of special power and an ideal site for a shrine. Hot springs were especially powerful. The goddess Sulis Minerva, "sun wisdom in the earth," had for centuries a sanctuary at the hot springs in Bath, England. Pagan rites conducted there included rebirth through immersion in the scalding, mineral-rich water. The Chinese say the dragon owns the "pearl that grants all desires," which controls moon phases, tides, rain, thunder and lightning, and the cycle of birth, death, and rebirth."[8]

Place names give us a clue as to the ancient haunts of dragons. The Anglo-Saxon word "drakan" probably comes from the Greek *drakon,* meaning serpent, and from the verb *derkein,* meaning to see clearly or foretell the future. Drakelow in Britain means dragon's barrow. The name Drakeford indicates that Neolithic people associated the earth goddess with water, whereas Dragon's Hill possibly shows her association with high places. A swath of Celtic settlements keeps dragons alive in placenames in Germany, such as Drachenfels and Drakensber. In southeastern Europe one can find Dracha, Draga, Draconis and Dragashani.[9]

## EARTH, AIR, FIRE, WATER

Because the dragon is an eclectic combination of animals that are equipped to live in every environment, it can be found in all four of the traditional elements: earth, air, fire and water. The dragon is a way of explaining the awesome basic power of the elements below ground, on the earth's surface, in water, in fire, and in the space above the earth. The Chinese say dragons are gods because they can transform without limit, ascend or descend outside of Time. If a dragon desires to become small it shape-changes into an earthworm. To become gigantic it lies hidden in the world. To ascend it becomes clouds. To descend it enters deep wells. These powers of transformation make it the divine mother of all living things.[10]

Regarding the element Earth, its dragons travel on and below ground. Those under the earth are sometimes held responsible for earthquakes, but more benevolently for currents of earth energy. Early psychologists envisioned non-rational human behavior as being like deeply buried dragons. Freud called this the *id* and Jung the collective unconscious. In the Christian cosmology, underground forces were changed to demons and their lair was changed to Hell.[11] The science fiction writer Frank Herbert resurrected these forces as giant worms in his *Dune* books. In Norse, dragon is *ormr*, meaning worm. Traditions of earth dragon-worms can be found through placenames such as Ormskirk or Wormingford.

Sir Walter Scott wrote of Wormeston in the Scottish Lowlands, now called Linton Hill, where the local lord "Slew the wode [angry] worm of Wormistoune." The "serpent, dragoune, or worme" had her den in a hollow piece of ground. Many had attempted to destroy her but, as with giants, ordinary measures failed. Finally the local lord attached a fiery wheel atop his lance and thrust it down the throat of the dragon, mortally wounding the monster. For this the lord was knighted by King William.[12] According to legend, this is the deed preserved in sculpture over the door of the old parish church.

In the Wormeston legend all of the later, Christian dragon symbology is wrapped into one tale: female, monster, super-human, devil, worm, chivalry, impaling lance and St. Michael-like hero. However, the legend also reveals symbols characteristic of the earlier time when dragons were perceived as good. The fiery wheel is the ubiquitous symbol of dragon energy, originating in epochs when cultures honored the earth spirit. And, in its death throes, the dragon coiled around the hill and contracted its folds, imprinting the spiral path which Wormeston hill shows to this day. The hill, like the Ohio Serpent and Glastonbury Tor, is an earth-sculpted gigantic representation of the cosmic egg with its encoiling serpent.

On the surface of the earth, dragon currents have directed Orientals and Occidentals alike to build in auspicious places. The veins of the dragon are often marked by features, such as pagodas, in the landscape of China. The churches of the St. Michael ley line trace a major dragon current across Britain. Naturally occurring dragon-like features are revered as power sites, such as the Devil's Spine at Galisteo, New Mexico. This is an undulating volcanic dike, about three miles in length, looking just like the back of a dragon "swimming" through the earth. The Anasazi covered this "dragon" with petroglyphs approximately one thousand years ago. A recent appearance of dragon signs on the landscape are the crop circles which abundantly and enigmatically appear mostly in southern Britain each summer. Since a circle represents the Ouroboros, the crop formations are based on the most ancient and fundamental symbol for eternal time and sacred space.

Regarding the element Air, it is a sphere that dragons, being winged, enjoy. Aerial dragons are particularly auspicious at sunrise and sunset. In Britain, they reportedly fly along lines between ancient sacred sites, seeming to follow the ley lines from above.[13] A report from 1787 tells of a dragon flying between the hill fort of Cadbury Castle, legendary site of King Arthur's Camelot, near Glastonbury, and the nearby hill of Dolbury:

*Here you may see some fyve myle distant, to the south-east...another down, called Dolbury-hill, between these two hills (you may be pleased to hear a pretty tale) is*

*said...That a fiery dragon...hath bynne often seene to flye between these hills, komming from the one to the other in the night season, whereby it is supposed ther is a great treasure hydd in each of them, and that the dragon is the trusty treasurer and sure keeper thereof.*[14]

Dragons take to the air to reveal their power. They can be seen at sunset when the wind paints them in fiery patterns across the palette of the sky. The dragon is the legendary guardian of barrows in Britain. A few tales report that when people plundered sacred mounds, an immediate, violent thunderstorm occurred. As guardian, the dragon could terrify intruders and local inhabitants by such powerful displays. The dragon at Longwitten in Yorkshire could change into a whirlwind. One at Torrylin in Arran became a tornado which struck the house of a barrow plunderer. An Aztec sign for weather maker shows it living in "Dragon-Mouth Cave" and causing rain when it releases mist-laden breath. In the Caribbean, Huracan is the dragon responsible for both hurricanes and earthquakes.

Chinese descriptions of aerial dragons are poetic:

*When rain is to be expected, the dragons scream and their voices are like the sound made by striking copper basins. Their saliva can produce all kinds of perfumes. Their breath becomes clouds, and they avail themselves of the clouds to cover their bodies. In summer the dragons divide the regions amongst themselves and each of them has his territory. This is the reason why within a distance of a couple of acres there may be quite different weather: rain and a clear sky. Violent rain is dragon rain.*[15]

Regarding the element Fire, dragons are depicted as breathing fire and able to live in it. Fire can be a sign of destruction and devouring. When fire pours from the nose or mouth it indicates that anything in the dragon's path can be inhaled and swallowed. Yet dragons typically used fire-breathing for warning or some purpose other than offense. Their fire can indicate the blaze of enlightenment, the power of magic, the heat of the sun. Fiery breath is a way to envision pure spirit, since spirit means breath in Latin. But the primary reason that dragons associate with fire is to show transformation. Ancient people realized that rather than destroying it, fire changes what it touches. Just as the reptile form of dragon shows transformation by shedding its skin, the fiery form of dragon shows transformation through creative energy and divine power. Gnostics believed the fiery dragon was like a universal solvent, the way through all things, the spirit in all things.[16]

Dragons are basically helpful to humans. But if humans try to harm them, dragons might be forced to use fire to destroy crops and houses. Fire-breathing dragons are credited in legends in many parts of the world with bringing fire to earth. Snakes, salamanders and reptiles are credited with keeping fire in their bodies. Throughout Central America the iguana *Itzam Na* is a fire god, a two-headed monster with the sun in its mouth.

The salamander is a common symbol of fire dragons. In myth, the salamander is a lizard-like creature that can withstand fire. The Romans thought asbestos was the wool of this creature. In alchemy, the salamander was equated with "Prime Matter," and fire with purification. The salamander was part of the complex process of metaphorically turning lead into gold. The salamander served as a temperature gauge, leaping into the coals when the fire was hot enough to start the transmuting process. Alchemists worked to transmute dragon "firewater" into the liquor called elixir of life.[17]

Regarding the element Water, a 1919 author said it is the "fundamental element in the dragon's powers."[18] Underwater dragons live in the mythology of every culture, and are to be found there to this very day. In Lake Tele in the Congolese jungle, a brontosaurish creature 35 feet long called Mokele Mbembe was "seen" as recently as 1981. The Loch Ness monster is possibly Scotland's most famous inhabitant. Dragons' daughters are called mermaids, which some sailors claim to see. In Iceland, *nykers* are sea goblins, and in Anglo-Saxon, *nicor* means any strange beast in the water.[19] Very ancient stories in India tell us that dragons guarded wells. Macedonians call wells "dragon-springs." The Chinese say that "a dragon in the water covers himself with five colors" making itself a rainbow deity.[20] Beneficent water dragons controlled early irrigation systems and the fertilizing overflow of rivers. Most of the Rivers of Europe have or had names derived from words for serpents.

The Greeks had many stories of water dragons. Phorcys was a Greek sea monster, which became *Orcus* in Latin and the root for our word *ogre*. This is an example of a sea dragon turning into a fabled man-eating giant. Hydra (from the Greek *hudra*, water serpent), was a many-headed monster that grew two heads for each one cut off. Hercules killed it by cutting off each head and cauterizing each neck, but the golden and immortal ninth head Hercules buried, still hissing, beneath a rock. The constellation in the southern sky called Hydra is also known as the Snake.

In British mythology, red and white dragons appear frequently. When Merlin was called in to solve the mystery of Vortigern's collapsing castle, he revealed that this was due to two dragons, one red and the other white. They were locked in conflict in a deep pool beneath the castle. At the ancient pagan center of Glastonbury, two springs rise side by side. One is calciferous white and the other is carboniferous red. They are called the White Spring and the Blood Spring.[21] They rise from below the landmark hill called Glastonbury Tor, which at some ancient time had been sculpted with spiral terraces resembling the coils of a dragon.

## OUROBOROS

Myths tell us that the dragon is so ancient that it was spawned before the elements existed, when all was chaos and flux. The flux was a female abyss of water stirred by a fiery male spirit whose light allowed it to see. Since nothing was as yet created, all that the fiery eye could see was its own reflection in the abyss.

The chief trait of dragons worldwide is their acute vision. Yet when actual snakes rebirth themselves, the milky substance between their skins covers their eyes and for several days the snakes cannot see. So the dragon both creates itself and engulfs itself.

The dragon is Two in One, containing both sexes, involved in the cycle of birth and death. It is at the beginning and the end of the universe. This is the famous Ouroboros or Tail-eater.

Alchemists saw this death-birth process as self-fertilization. This represented the magical power of transmuting one thing to another. The ouroboric dragon became the most recurrent symbol in alchemy. In devouring its own tail the dragon swallows the past until the same point in the time cycle comes around again. Prehistoric people saw Time as being cyclical. Their world was a complete unit composed of interacting cycles which they knew, and which they expected to recur. For them, the past did not disappear, but rather went inside the earth.

Alchemy had several levels of significance. At a deeper level than Time, the dragon's circle represented the image of inner Space where the soul resided. Where Space and Time crossed, the innermost mystery of alchemy occurred: the curative power of Mercury. Mercury, the winged dragon, the messenger moving like quicksilver between the worlds, represented mystical healing power which could make a person whole. This was what alchemists meant by baptism: initiation into a new world of being. Wholeness meant knowledge of the inner and outer worlds. Only the initiated possessed the secrets of these realms.

The Hindus have a dragon-goddess called Kundalini. She is symbolized by a coiled snake in the form of a spiral or a ring, representing inner strength. As a Yogi performs spiritual exercises, the snake uncoils and stretches up through *chakras*, literally "wheels," corresponding to ascending areas in the body. When it reaches the forehead area the scales of illusion fall from the inner eye. The wisdom achieved by linking female and male forces is represented by this third eye of Shiva. Shiva is the androgynous Hindu deity of destruction and rebirth. The coiled snake is a circle, rebirth is a circle, the ouroboros is a circle and the wheeled chakras are circles. The circle implies the qualities of timelessness, completeness and perfection.

Nearly every dragon myth we have examined contains the image of a circle. Whether it is an orb, an egg, a fiery disk, an eye, a pearl, a round barrow, a spiral hill, ball lightning, an omphalos or the sun, the serpent and the circle are inextricably connected. At Avebury, the mile-long avenues wind like serpents off the huge central circle. Galaxies reveal a turning core with spiralling, serpent-like arms. In the Tantric tradition, the serpent is depicted as two opposing currents turning around the central pearl. Once awakened, this energy passes up the *axis mundi*, the world axis, around which is coiled the serpent of wisdom.

In Chinese art, the dragon is invariably shown beside a circle of solar or dynamic energy. This is the "golden flower," the resplendent energy body awakened by the

---

*Pictish symbol stone, Newton, Aberdeenshire. Serpent, Z-rod and Double Disc with unusual notch*

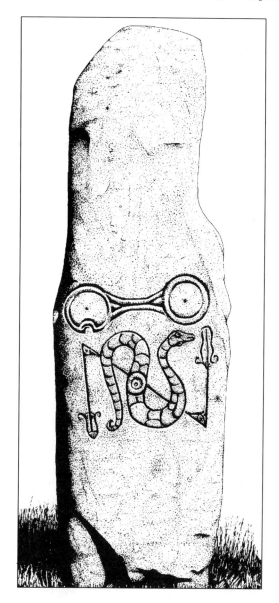

correct balance of polarized dragon forces. In China, dragons are associated with the cycle of life and death. The Chinese version of the Ouroboros is the yang-yin symbol which contains all aspects of cyclical life: dry/wet, constructive/destructive, active/passive, masculine/feminine, light/dark, affirmative/negative/, matter/energy. The yang-yin symbol is half white and half black to symbolize that the world is made from the energy of polarities. So too, the Egyptian Ouroboros of 1600 BCE had a black half of the dragon to symbolize the dark and a white half to symbolize the light.

## THE BENEVOLENT DRAGON

The Chinese have used the dragon symbol since antiquity. Chinese dragons, unlike their Western counterparts, are almost always depicted as helpful and beneficial. They are the symbol of good fortune and luck. Chinese dragons are called upon to influence the elements of water and air, thereby bringing rain, directing rivers, and circulating the wind. Dragons supervise branches of activities such as music, literature, bridge building and law. They are involved intimately with human and cosmic affairs.

In the Orient and in non-moral religions of antiquity in the West, dragons characterized positive power. Dragons were sent as messengers to the gods who owned fire. As did Prometheus, the dragons brought the gift of fire back to humans. Dragons, like giants, were guardians of temples and magnificent treasures. Sometimes dragons were associated with death, in the sense of helping to transition from life in the outer world to life in the underworld. Dragons were close to sovereignty, as in Phoenician, Saxon and Manchu drawings which show the dragon enthroned.

Dragons were strong, vigilant, protective and wise enough to be prophetic. This reflects back on the Greek root derkein, which means "seeing clearly." Later the unusual vision of dragons was distorted into the "evil eye."

## THE EVIL DRAGON

The status of dragons parallels that of giants, who at first were good and later were depicted as evil. Dragons and snakes became associated with evil in the period when the ancient earth-goddess or Great Round cosmology was suppressed and replaced by sky-god religions. That which we call the feminine principle in both females and males—the intuitive, non-rational side—was labeled primordial and demonic. The serpent, especially the horned serpent, represented sexual power. That which pertained to reproductive and sexual processes was demoted in favor of heavenly spirits. Beliefs in the Great Goddess and earth deities were deeply embedded and persistent, however. People were forbidden to practice these beliefs but never stopped holding them in reverence. The seasons of the year, the earthy attraction of sex among males and females, the cycle of birth, death and rebirth were too obvious and important to be discarded.

The West shifted to religions with a single male god and developed law-giving, urban, pragmatic, militaristic states. At that time, the religion of the *paganus*—the "country dweller"—went underground. This happened literally as well as figuratively. From that time on, the earth goddess or the snake was represented as a lowly, vain and evil female attempting to corrupt the elevated and noble male. A few examples of this portrayal in Western writing include the temptation of Adam by Eve, Jason by Medea, Hercules by Omphale, and Caesar by Cleopatra. Since writing *per se* did not exist when the Great Goddess was revered, her cosmos has no advocates in literature, although many examples exist in mythology.

The Great Goddess and Great Round cosmology had made the entire planet sacred. People received from the earth only what the spirits put there. Their rites and ceremonies asked for and gave thanks for what the earth spirit provided naturally.

With the shift to settlements and agriculture between 5,0 00 and 0 BCE, depending on the location, this worldview changed. One goal of the new cosmology was to increase the productivity of specific places on the earth by artificially stimulating their fertility. Another new occurrence—perhaps due to competition for resources—was war. For the first time on the planet, signs of killing other humans occurred. Besides agriculture and war, a third major change left its mark, namely the erection of great temples. These proclaimed the domination of the sky god over the earth energy. Towers, spires and megaliths checked the wandering serpentine energy and fixed it in one location, creating or enhancing power spots. Many of these power spots were turned into observatories of solar, stellar and lunar phenomena—the interests of the sky-god worshippers.

The male deities and mythological heroes achieved status by victory over dragons or serpents, the sacred emblems of the ancient goddess cosmology. Hercules slew the Hydra. Jason killed Medea. Zeus killed Typhon. The sanctuary of the goddess at Delphi was taken over by the sun god Apollo. The serpents of the Pythoness were killed, and she became Apollo's oracular servant.

Christianity began in a world which was already transitioning to transcendental and solar gods. Here the chthonian goddesses, giants and dragons had to be mastered, controlled, sublimated and ordered for the purposes of urban-culture and the rational mind. The triumph of linear logic over cyclical mystery was impressed upon the people. The triumph of heaven over earth was emphasized by showing the earth spirit as an evil dragon being conquered.

During the early centuries of Christianity, dragons were represented as the devil. They were incarnations of sin that needed to be destroyed. Images of dragon-killers appeared in stained glass windows.[22] Dragon-hunting became a chivalrous, if frustrating venture for knights. In the crusades of the eleventh to thirteenth centuries, knights were charged with conquering infidels, whether these were Moslems in Jerusalem, Cathars in France, or Celts in the British Isles. The righteousness of battling the devil allowed people to rationalize the looting of non-Christian sacred places. Dragon lairs such as Neolithic mounds were plundered and their pagan treasure seized. These actions were termed "purification" and "killing the dragon."

By building Christian churches dedicated to a dragon slayer over many sites formerly revered for their earth spirit, the new religion erected what it thought would be powerful deterrents to pagan celebrations. In the American Southwest, large mission churches were built near or over the circular, subterranean kivas of the Pueblo Indians. It is likely that some spiritual practitioners entered the new temples in order to gain access to the old deities.

In Europe, Christianity provided two male dragon slayers in the form of St. George and St. Michael. They were the patron saints of knighthood. Most churches named for St. Michael indicate there had been an ancient sacred place at that site, and that the earth spirit in the form of giant, dragon or goddess was forced underground there. On St. Michael's Mount, the giant was tumbled down a well. On Glastonbury Tor, the giant/dragon Gwynn ap Nudd was exorcised. The goddess became identified with Mother Mary, but her full nature was suppressed. In most dragon legends she became the meek and helpless maid in need of rescue.

St. Michael the Archangel, a Christian version of the Celts' sky god, took over hilltop shrines after slaying their dragons. Tradition says that St. George killed his beast on Dragon Hill. This is within sight of a gigantic dragon-like figure carved into a chalky hillside at Uffington, England. A humorous view of St. George and the dragon was given by John Aubrey 300 years ago:

> *To save a mayd St. George the Dragon slew -*
> *A pretty tale, if all is told be true.*
> *Most say there are no dragons, and 'tis sayd*
> *There was no George, pray God there was a*
> *mayd.*[23]

Another threat to dragons was missionaries. St. Patrick was credited with "driving the snakes out of Ireland." The climate of Ireland was never a tropical playground for snakes. Rather, this claim means that the Pope directed Patrick to destroy the earth goddess religion and remove its Druidical "snake" priests and priestesses. We know from the few instances where the Druids did represent their knowledge—for example, the Pictish Symbol Stones—that a chief symbol was the snake or dragon.

Below the surface of the earth and of consciousness however, the old ways went on. The Pueblo people continue with their ancient traditions such as snake dances, right alongside Christian traditions such as Easter services. In Europe, pagan customs continue within Christianity, manifesting as May Day processions and adoration of the goddess as the Black Virgin.

In summary, dragons originally represented the life force and the balance of male-female principles as depicted in the circular Ouroboros. From Paleolithic to Neolithic times, they represented positive power, sexuality and nature-honoring spirituality. The symbolism was routed through the cosmology of the Great Goddess. Attributes included rebirth through the skin-shedding snake, purification through fire, energy through polarity, fertility through placing her image in the form of an egg, circle or spiral at sacred sites. Reproduction through the union of male and female was depicted as a snake around the Tree of Life. The dragon's traits of wisdom and inner knowledge, associated with wells and water, can be seen as baptism and unlocking the "unconscious" in modern usage.

In the later sun-god cosmologies, the dragon-snake came to represent evil, temptation, seduction, irrationality, the unconscious, chaos and danger. All of these traits were abundant in the feminine-identified forces of nature. The dragon was conquered by a male god by means of lances, columns, pillars of stone and other fixed and rigid forms. The dragon killer then controlled the earth's flow of energy which became focused in one location instead of flowing freely. Acquiring dragon treasure was part of the spoils of battle. War, agriculture and monumental sacred places are signs that dragon power has been conquered.

Giants were perceived as the matter through which the earth energy of the dragons moved. If the giants were the natural elements of life then the dragons were the forces which stirred them. If the giants represent earth then the dragons represent spirit, but in truth they cannot be separated. In the ancient myth of Gaia, their forces were combined. The loss of one is the loss of the other.

We humans have ancient images in our minds which we use to explain the universe. People seek outside of themselves those spirits or guides which best match their inner pictures. For the Celts, who are reverent about water and wells, trees, mounds and stones, the spirit of place takes the form of fairies, dragons and giants. When power is needed, one of these forms is invoked to supply it. Then the people get

on with the task at hand. We will see in the following chapters that many people attribute beautiful forms in the landscape to the work of elementals, dragons and giants.

*The Uffington White Horse, Oxfordshire, Britain. This figure is over 350 feet long and 1000 – 2000 years old. It may once have been a dragon*

# ELEMENTAL GIANTS

Jane had lain down in the grass for a short nap when she became aware that someone was watching her. Whoever it was, a hole was being bored into her back. Jane drew a deep breath, turned, and with the vision you have when you are four years old and the world is full of wonderful things, saw the watcher. Straight and very tall, shaggy and leafy green, the watcher stood poised like a heron on one leg. He had one unblinking eye in the middle of his forehead. In his one arm he carried an extremely large club. But due to some trick of appearances Jane could never work out which side of the body the one arm and leg were on.

"Gruagach...?" Jane began.

"No. Gog to you," came the solemn reply. Jane felt she really should have known and was about to apologize when a bell-like tone sounded. It went off and upwards in an ever-increasing pitch. The next thing Jane knew she was sitting in the crown of an oak tree. Gog was beside her, his one huge foot up on the branch, looking exactly like he was part of the tree. Jane was full of questions, but was distracted by the peculiar mixture of leaves and hair that grew around the knotty crevices of Gog's face.

"Do you know that I once covered these hills farther than the eye can see?" Gog didn't seem to be addressing his remarks to anyone in particular but Jane nodded enthusiastically. "All life turned around me. The beasts ate of me. They buried and hatched themselves within me. They nested in me. The plants grew on me and below me. And the people honored my strength and power."

As Gog slowly spoke, Jane saw the great oak forests, thousands of years in the making. She saw the trees cover the land, part of a world of life which was supported by the oak trees and which supported them. "Now look at me. Soon I will be nothing but a tale in the mouths of children."

"Tell me, my friend," Jane said. "Tell me how you were honored."

"Ah, the life of it! The beat of it!" Gog replied, filling his massive chest so deeply his skin crackled. "In spring the people came and blessed the power stirring in every seed, every nut, pip and acorn. And after the hawthorn awakened and the handfastings were made, I would burst into leaf! Then the augurs came and told, from the shape of my leaves, what the year would bring. I would teach them. Yes, I would. They who call themselves Druids, I taught. They would hang on the tree until they grasped the secrets. For none can understand life until they can understand the trees.

"The Christians misunderstood. They made the tree a place of death. But no, it is life! We are the inexhaustible source of every need people could ever have. They say he walked three days in hell, but he walked with us. They forget. Yes, so they do...

"Then, in summer, the people came and climbed me and looked through my crown. They lit fires and added old bark from my trunk to honor me. And when the smoke curled up they saw me dance. I set the forests ringing with my dance! And they saw the golden winged dragon of the sovereign sun held in my crown. And they knew that to be blessed they could cut the golden mistletoe but it must not touch the ground. To the very few, I gave an oak dragon from my limbs.

"Then they shouted my name. And smeared themselves with juices from the berries and covered themselves with leaves. And not a few mated on the bed of last year's leaves and mast. It was good. And now..." Gog's voice trailed off. Jane squirmed un-

*comfortably in her perch. "...They do not know me. I am the last of the old race... the forest which is only a memory...*
*"Where now lies the forest of healing, of nourishment, of life? Where now lies the gateway to the forgotten forest?"*

iants most happily reside in the natural elemental realm. They are at their finest in nature. Giants from every tradition are at home in water, with fire, under mountains, with the animals, with wind and frost, with gold, iron, stone, trees and the forest. No giant tale is complete without its underground cave, its stone castle, its golden treasure or clubs made from whole trees.

In the traditions of elemental spirits that have come down to us, or are present in nature-cultures, we find a good way of thinking about the world. W. B. Yeats lifts the veil to this magic realm:

> *Many poets, and all mystic and occult writers, in all ages and countries, have declared that behind the visible are chains on chains of conscious beings, who are not of heaven but of the earth, who have no inherent form, but change according to their whim, or the mind that sees them. You cannot lift your hand without influencing and being influenced by hordes. The visible world is merely their skin.* [1]

Nature spirits are called elementals because each spirit inhabits one of the four "elements:" earth, air, fire, water. They are guides that instruct us about the essence of that element. They are ways of letting us see and feel nature through direct experience. They are the animating forces in nature. They embody the intelligence and wisdom of the realm where they reside. They trace the inner landscape of that element. They are usually invisible except for the effects of their energy.

*Glendalough in the Wicklow Mountains, Ireland*

Nature spirits take whatever form the cosmology of a people suggests. They are guides that match the inner images we use to explain the universe. When wisdom or power is needed, one of these forms is invoked to supply it. Nature-cultures honor the nature spirits through ritual. In the words of the poet Kathleen Raine, elementals represent "the unchanging nature of things visible and invisible common to all traditions. In all times and places, with the sole exception of our own machine-made world, the universe is held to be living. The visible is but the outer aspect of the one life, diversified into spiritual beings, energies and agencies of many kinds."[2]

In his remarkable book *Talking With Nature*, Michael Roads describes how the elementals broke through his disbelief and spoke to him inside his thoughts. He learned to approach every natural form—river, rock, tree, animal, blossom—and interact with its elemental. He was not going to write the truth about how he spoke to Nature directly until the elementals convinced him to be open about his experience:

> *For a long time I stared across the river, trying to pretend it was not happening this way....The rock beneath me was very patient. In a physical sense it had not moved in a very long time, but I could feel a surge of conscious activity. This is ridiculous. I cannot just write that I listen to trees and rocks and rivers, that I talk to them and they talk back into my mind. I squirmed and fidgeted, pretending I could not hear the river chuckling as it flowed smoothly past my rock. "Okay, I'll do it your way, but...please help it to become credible." The energy of river, coiled in an almost serpentine formlessness around me, was suddenly in motion...expanding outward....It said "Go now."*[3]

For all the wonders of science and technology, we cannot *make* earth or air, fire or water, trees or stone. We can utilize them but we cannot originate or fabricate them. They are part of the mystery of life. We can take stone and work it together till it builds a wall or church, but the Irish know that if the elementals and fairies do not want it built they will undo it during the night until the project is abandoned. Who is in charge here?

All the "building blocks" used for sacred sites—the four elements plus stones, mounds and trees—are enspirited or animated by the helpful guides and non-material agents called elementals. We will briefly describe the qualities of each elemental.

## EARTH ELEMENTALS

he elementals in earth can be seen as giant spirits or dragons spreading their currents of energy in ways that were felt by Stone Age people and are being recreated by earth mystery "dragon hunters" today. A giant network of earth elementals animates the whole region inhabited by each culture. It is their "Holy Land." The myths of Europe tell us that dragons, giants and fairies inhabited mounds and other megalithic sites until they were killed off by knights, or exorcized by monks, in the Middle Ages. Many other cultures have built mounds, not because their technology was too "primitive" to construct something more complicated than a child's sand castle, but because the circle is the perfect form and the earth is the home of elemental spirits and the sacred source of life.

Trees give us the model for the cyclical nature and connection of all things. Our myths describe this in the symbol of the Tree of Life. Trees connect the Below and the Above, the continuity of past and present. The Norse World Tree, Yggdrasil, connected all the worlds made from the body of the frost giant Ymir.

Trees of one kind seem to speak to each other around the world in a phylogenetic communion. Once a year they inhale and exhale together as the seasons change and the greening comes and goes. Druid colleges were located in groves of oaks so initiates could live among the tree-teachers. The Druids received the alphabet, calendar and healing essences from trees. On the small end of a magical telescope, trees are the habitat of fairies and elves, and on the large end, giants live in trees and are trees, as is the case with Gog and Magog in Glastonbury.

Trees are givers of wisdom to anyone who has ears to hear. The tree elemental beckons you over. You rub the bark, smell the sap, pick a leaf and look at its veins. You admire a blossom, crack a nut, collect dead twigs for the campfire, climb the branches, sit on the roots and meditate. You lie in its shade to rest, listen to the birds, hear the chant of the swaying branches, open yourself and receive instruction.

Besides mounds and trees, a third home of earth elementals is in stones. As far back as magic can be traced, stones were invested with mystical powers. People with this belief think that rocks know everything that has ever happened on earth. Stones have a character which looks into eternity. Clear stones, like quartz, have scrying (crystal gazing) and other powers. Stones can only be moved by cooperation with the giant spirit, as legend tells us happened at the great pyramids of Egypt, the cities of ancient Greece and the Great Wall of China. When people are in harmony with this elemental, stones move effortlessly into their correct place. Stones have been present in almost every structure of the human spiritual journey, ranging from the decorated walls of Paleolithic caves to Neolithic circles of standing stones, to pyramids in Egypt and Mexico, to Asian temples to medieval cathedrals.

Certain single stones are thought to be the center of the universe. The Rock of Jerusalem is sacred to Jews, Christians and Moslems alike. Christ said "Thou art Peter and upon this Rock I will build my church." The cosmological center for Moslems is the black meteorite housed in the Kaaba. The Greeks revered the omphalos at Delphi as the navel of the universe. Alchemists sought the magic of the Philosopher's Stone. And there are many examples in myth and legend of enspirited stones. The future of the sovereignty of Britain lay in the stone which held the sword Excalibur. The Lia Fail stone at the Hill of Tara in Ireland and the Stone of Scone in Westminster Abbey are reputed to tell if a person is worthy to be crowned monarch.

*Yggdrasil, the World Tree*

## AIR, FIRE AND WATER ELEMENTALS

Air elementals have the qualities of movement and quickness—so quick that adjacent areas can be affected by different air elementals at the same instant. Wind, clouds, thunder and storms are favorite, and sometimes alarming, expressions of the air elementals. Formations of flying birds have leagues of admirers among bird watchers; the unison of their formations has taught humans how individual creatures can work together in harmony. In the upper canopy of air, the stars in their animated shapes are credited with influencing our very lives, as every known culture has developed an astrological science.

Fire has the qualities of transformation and change. It contains the birth-death-rebirth cycle, demonstrating that destruction is necessary for creation. Fire mesmerizes and fascinates. It offers life-giving warmth. It transforms raw food into a variety of possibilities for nourishment. Fire gives light like a nighttime sun. Fire giants can be seen in lightning, particularly the ball lightning found around sacred sites and ley lines. Fire giants are also seen in forest fires, volcanos, lava and hot springs. The sun itself is a fire giant that spreads its glowing greeting across the morning sky. It spreads its parting magnificence in sunsets, which act as a flint from which to light our campfires and tell stories.

Very old magical sites were located around water, particularly holy wells where benevolent elementals caused positive feelings and healings. Water giants are found in river deltas, oases, waterspouts, waterfalls, white water, floods, rainstorms, and in water dragons such as at Loch Ness. Giant ocean elementals, guardians of certain watery passages, have been reported from as long ago as Odysseus to as recently as single-handed sailors near Tierra del Fuego, Easter Island and the Bermuda triangle. Water is a favored element of dragons. In Africa the giant rainbow serpent helped the supreme being Mawu to create the world. It then coiled itself under the ocean to support the weight of the earth. The movement of its coils can be seen in the rippling of the ocean surface.

In the following sections we will look at stories that connect giants with each of the elemental forces. Perhaps your grandparents told you similar stories from their native land, and you can see how they would fit here.

## EARTH, STONE AND SMITH GIANTS

In Germanic mythology the megalithic circles and standing stones are giants who have been turned to stone, usually for dancing on Sunday or some such thing. Similar traditions are found in Britain at Stonehenge, Callanish, Stanton Drew and the Merry Maidens stone circles. The traditions preserve the ancient association between stones, giants, music and dance. It is the giants who built the stone walls of mythical cities such as Elysium, Babel and Asgard, and the actual cities of Sacsayhuaman and Tiryns, as well as many ring forts and castles in Europe.

One tradition from North Yorkshire concerns a helpful giant called Wade and a giantess called Bell. They built Mulgrave and Pickering castles but only had one hammer between them, so they would throw it back and forth, giving a shout to warn the other when it was coming. The ancient road between the two castles, known as Wade's Causeway, was built in a trice by the two giants. On a few occasions the apron strings of Bell broke, leaving the stones she was carrying in great heaps nearby.

The giants worked not only stone but also earth. The giant Grim, who was the Norse god Woden, gave his name to many sites in northern Europe. Most spectacular of these is Wansdyke, "Wodens Dike." This is a defensive ditch and bank which runs through three counties in southern Britain. The giants also worked the minerals of the earth. They were reckoned to have dug the prehistoric flint mines at Grimes' Grave in Norfolk.

The giant underworld serpent of the Native Australians was visible in the rainbow of the many-colored minerals. The mineral deities of the Native Americans were also conceived as lying in the earth on a gigantic scale. Sometimes the giants are associated with the dwarfs, the archetypal miners and earth elementals. Sometimes they are associated with the larger elves, the best smiths and craft workers. Most often they are smiths in their own right.

Hephaistos, the lame smith god of the Greeks, had a parthenogenetic origin from the Great Mother. He was taught his craft by elemental goddesses of the earth and sea, Eurynome and Thetis. Thus he has an origin in the chthonian realm from which came the Giants. The Giants are said to have assisted Hephaistos as the forgers of thunderbolts.

Another giant smith is the Norse Völundr. He is known in Britain as Weland or Wayland, and his parents Wade and Bell are mentioned above. His dwelling is a Neolithic chambered mound known as Wayland's Smithy on the ancient Ridgeway in Oxfordshire. If a traveller's horse had lost a shoe, all he had to do was leave the horse and some money at the smithy. The next day the horse would be newly shod. The practice seems to have been long standing for when the site was excavated in this century, offerings from various periods were found to have been deposited there. Völundr, Wayland and their Germanic equivalent, Alberich, are connected with the elves and dwarves of the "Hollow Hills"—magical smiths who live in the elemental realm of earth.[4]

## TREE GIANTS

J. R. R. Tolkien immortalized the tree elementals in *The Lord of the Rings* when he created the Ents. Just when the action is becoming too fast and desperate, the introduction of the slow-moving, deeply pondering tree people is a welcome relief. Tolkien shows them, correctly, as giants with considerable power. Ponder they might, but when they decide to act they are not ponderous. This is a welcome respite from the sentimental images of Dryads and other nymph-like tree spirits that had been created in the Victorian era.

The older stories and legends of the tree giants also reveal powerful beings. The concept of woods and forests being fearful places inhabited by ugly and stupid creatures was created by urban-cultures. But when that overlay is removed, there are some wonderful remnants in the Native European Tradition of the wise and giantic nature of the trees. One such remnant is found in the Bachlach. He is an axe-carrying shaggy giant, from whom comes the legend of Gawain and the Green Knight.

The stories of the Bachlach and the Green Knight turn around a beheading game. In this the hero can chop off the giant's head as long as the hero has the courage to submit to the same. The giant, of course, cheerfully picks up his head and departs, saying where and when he can be found for the reciprocal blow. Few have the courage to play, but Gawain in the Arthurian epics and Cuchulainn in the Irish tale fulfill the terms of the game after passing various tests involving the directing of their sexual energy. Eventually Gawain meets the Green Knight on a mound described as the Green Chapel. There he bows his head to the giant, who mearly scratches his neck with the blow.

In the Celtic tradition there is another being closely associated with the trees. He is the Green Man from whose mouth, and sometimes eyes, ears, cheeks, brow and nose, emerges leafy vegetation. The story of the Green Knight connects with the Green Man at this point. He teaches the correct channeling of the sexual energy so that it can enter the head—the seat of consciousness to the Celts—and emerge from the mouth as words, poetry, story-telling, music or some other form of creativity and inspiration. The Celts rated skill in these arts above all else.

The giant Bachlach presented as the archetypal Wild Man of the woods and the Green Knight on his green mound were not simply playing violent games.

They were initiating men into the mysteries of the trees. The result was the accumulated wisdom—in the head—of the complete cosmology of the culture. Memories of this tradition found expression in sculpted heads of the Green Man disgorging vegetation. This was a much-used motif of later ecclesiastical architecture.[5] We can see from all these early traditions of earth and tree elementals that enormous intelligence was perceived to lie in the forms of the world and that humans were not separate from it.

Trees and their giant elementals were thus much more than simply inanimate objects. The Celts credited the trees as the source of the original phonemes from which words were formed. A complete cosmology was woven around the tree-provided "alphabet," the *Beth-Luis-Nion* (birch-rowan-ash). Such alphabets were magical and were not written down. The trees were associated with times in the calendar of the year, with animals, minerals and deities. They were the source not only of food, of material, and of fire but of inspiration and the names which created and ordered the world.

## FIRE GIANTS

The Christian cosmos confined the chthonian deities of other cultures to the subterranean depths where, it was taught, the fires of hell ensured their torment. The confinement was somewhat misconceived, however, as giants take to fire as easily as angels take to thrones. Perhaps greater torture could have been devised by denying the giants their home fires and banishing them to the ranks of those eternally singing in choirs around the ethereal godhead.

As we saw above and in Chapter 7 on dragons, the power of the fire giants is that of transformation and change. The primordial cells which evolved in the elemental soup billions of years ago grew in the warmth which ultimately derived from the sun. Since then they have combined to create ever more complex organisms. What if the mythical gift of fire and light from the Titan Prometheus is actually a cellular memory of an ancient epoch in the evolution of life on earth?

The fire dragons, the salamanders, are huge beings who can quickly get out of hand. They become visible in lightning, molten lava and raging blazes. They can leap from place to place, and travel underground. They can be guided in furnaces, forges and crucibles, where alchemists, engineers and scientists seek new elements, some of which still cannot be controlled. In Australia, some Dreamings tell of the ancestral spirits who live in the "yellow earth"—uranium—and how they must never be disturbed. If they are disturbed, then their proliferation will eventually swallow the entire earth. Thinking of such powerful elements in terms of giant beings seems to be an excellent way of maintaining the respect they deserve.

## AIR, THUNDER AND WIND GIANTS

Giants are very much at home in the air and are often represented in the form of a winged animal. The Thunderbird of the Northwestern American peoples is so powerful it can pick up whales in its mighty talons. It is often given the topmost place on the elaborately carved totem poles. The Thunderbird brings the rain so necessary for life in the interior of the continent, where the Sun Dance is celebrated in its honor. An Eastern equivalent are the Rukhs (Rocs) who dwell on islands in the Indian Ocean. They carry off elephants as their prey. In Europe the eventual task of the winged horse Pegasus was to carry the thunderbolts of Olympus. In Australia, the giant Dreamtime ancestor Irria, associated with the black cockatoo, brings the rain and thunder of the wet season. The Wandjina live in storms and whirlwinds.

The giants hurl storms, create winds, whip up hurricanes and tornados and otherwise control the weather. The wind giant Boreas, son of the Titan Astareus and Eos the Dawn Maiden, would come rushing down from his northern caves. It was he who mated with the mares to produce the multitudes of breezes that are visible racing across the oceans and over fields of grass. Halcyon, daughter of the Titan Aeolus, Lord of the Winds, married Ceyx, son of Atlas. During the War in Heaven, Zeus changed them into waterbirds. The sea goddess Thetis caused the sea to remain calm while their eggs hatched in floating nests. Now they are the kingfishers of the world.

Among the Iroquois nation, Ga-oh the Wind Giant is the single capricious controller of the winds. Through his smaller relatives, human needs are mandated and ministered to. In China and Japan there are many deities of the winds and rain. Each has its own domain. The Aztec Quetzalcoatl, as the deity uniting earth and sky, not only shows the people where to hunt for the precious minerals of the earth, but is responsible for the winds of heaven. In this Quetzalcoatl is like the dragon, the supreme ruler of the energy of the elements.

## WATER GIANTS

Water giants are closely associated with those of the wind and air. In the Australian Aboriginal traditions, the watercourses, lakes and billabongs are the dwelling places of the Rainbow Serpent ancestors of the Dreamtime. Every summer in the northern regions the ancestor Wala-Undayua emerges from the river which is his home and goes to live among the clouds. There he can be seen walking among the thunderstorms on his long, silvery legs. The giant horned serpent of the Native American tradition also dwells in the rivers, but is capable of lifting itself up into the sky. In the Celtic tradition almost every river was named after a serpent deity. In Tibet the rivers and waters were the home of the serpent deities known as the Klu. All these deities were naturally huge, sometimes dangerous and required the utmost respect.

Possibly more Celtic artifacts have been found in water, where they had been placed or thrown as votive offerings, than in any other Iron Age archaeological source. Some rivers, it was said, could never have a bridge put across them. When they did it was necessary to placate the bridge trolls who grumbled underneath. Some rivers had spirits—the "Kelpie" in Scotland—who would not rest until they had taken a human life. The Dart River in Devon required a life every year. In the *Iliad* the Scamander river would rise up as a wrathful god to wash away its foes.

Waters represent the primeval state of the world. In ancient Mesopotamia the waters of the earth came from the first beings: the giant Apsu gave the fresh water and Tiamat gave the oceans. From this duality the gods and goddesses came forth. In Japan the creation myth tells us the world was a chaotic mass, egg-shaped, but without limits. The waters separated from the Above. Then the churning of the waters by the original couple Izanagi and Izanami allowed them to give birth to the land. The Yavapai people first originated from the circular sink hole in Arizona known as Montezuma Well. The Inca people came from Lake Titicaca. In nearly every tradition, water is the source of life. The lake or ocean from which the people come is invariably round or egg-shaped. This is the image of the womb of the primordial giant—the undifferentiated, "chaotic," male and female, ever-changing and creative Great Goddess.

Is it extraordinary that there is so much similarity between the origin of life as described in the churning waters of so many creation myths and the scientific description? Here life emerges in the element-laden watery soup, warmed by the sun, that allows cells to move, join, divide, multiply and so evolve. With the advent of quantum theory it is now known that these cells did not combine by lucky chance or by mere accident. They evolved through the working of universal orders of information, intelligence, relationship and mind. The giants of our creation mythologies may ultimately be the information held in the cells, bacteria, DNA and RNA of our bodies. More on this in the following chapters.

How the elementals combine to produce all life, knowledge and power is depicted in a poem by the Irish mystic known as "A.E." who saw radiant visions of the old deities of Ireland.

> A cabin on the mountain-side hid in a grassy nook,
> With door and window open wide, where friendly stars may look;
> The rabbit shy may patter in, the winds may enter free
> Who roam around the mountain throne in living ecstasy.
> And when the sun sets dimmed in eve, and purple fills the air,
> I think the sacred hazel tree is dropping berries there,
> From starry fruitage, waved aloft where Connia's Well o'erflows;
> For sure, the immortal waters run through every wind that blows.
> I think when Night towers up aloft and shakes the trembling dew,
> How every high and lonely thought that thrills my spirit through
> Is but a shining berry dropped down through the purple air,
> And from the magic tree of life the fruit falls everywhere. [6] ▨

# PRINCIPLES OF

# CONSTRUCTION

# AND ORDER

H anyiko, frog, said, "Build me a shelter." So the people went and cut four posts and put a roof over them. And he said, "No, not like that." They leaned three posts together. He said, "No, not like that." He showed them how to do it. Then they went and got a cottonwood and set it up in the middle of the camp. Hanyiko said, "Yes, that's the way to do it."

He sat in its shade and every time the sun moved around he moved with it. In each place he sat he told the people about that place. He told them the time to plant the corn and when to harvest it. He told them when to go south to pick the saguaro fruit, and when it was good to get the agave. He told them the names of each direction and the star that went with it.

Hanyiko was the first elder, the first shaman. When he died the world was destroyed by water. But before the place of Hanyiko's people was flooded, corn grew from his heart in the place where he was buried. The people climbed up the cornstalks to enter the next world. He showed the Yavapai many good things.[1]

I f the giants and the forces they embody are to be found in the reality which results from the interaction of our inner and outer worlds then examples of their nature can be studied. In the many and varied cosmologies of the people of the earth, giants have always been "good to think." And if the reader wants to know more about how cultures have created and worked with giants, it will be helpful to sketch out the principles which underlie the nature of giants, wherever they occur.

It is not the intention of this book to provide an analysis of giants in myth and literature. It is our intention to illustrate the patterns giants have made in the landscape. Through interaction with these patterns it may be possible to find a way "back in"—a way to "remember" the earth-spirit consciousness. The next few chapters will go into structural details of various places where giant forms in the landscape are to be found.

## GEOMANCY

G eo is the Greek root meaning "earth." The suffix -mancy comes from the Greek verb "to prophesy." It signifies the power of divination by a specific means or in a particular manner. So geomancy literally means "divining the earth," or "predicting by means of knowing earth forces." It is very relevant for our study of landscape giants. It is a holistic discipline in which mind and body, spirit and matter are seen as one.

The "spirit of place" or *genius loci* is an important geomantic concept. By knowing the character of a place, it is possible to tell how auspicious it is for a specific purpose. Is the spirit of place conducive for the founding of a city? Will it favor a farm, a temple, a bank or a tomb? These are the kinds of questions asked of geomancers in Asia today. It is their task to assess not only the subtle influences which prevail upon a site but the practical ones as well. Of course, to a mind not thinking in terms of dualism between spirit and matter these influences are the same. The fact that a pure and constant water source flows into a site is a blessing from the spirits. It makes sense to cooperate with these forces and not offend them.

Where the wind blows not too strongly, but enough to provide a circulating current of fresh air; where the earth is fertile, with plenty of water, but well drained; where sunlight is plentiful but not scorching; where trees provide resources and animals thrive; where the view is varied, looking out to hills and mountains; where snow, hail and flood do not ruin crops; where the seas are navigable and good harbors present; where stones do not cover the ground, but are ample for building; where every element is favorable and harmonious, then it could be said the spirits of the place smile kindly upon the inhabitants. Conditions can, of course, be influenced and altered by human intervention and building. In these situations the geomancer has to determine what action is appropriate and what is not.

Geomancers have to bring to bear upon the situation not only their knowledge of the land: its water, weather, flora and fauna, but the cosmology held in the minds of the people. This determines the way in which the land is seen. Geomancers cannot stand outside the situation. They too are structuring the land in terms of the cosmology of which they are a part. A belief held at one place and in one time might not apply in another place and time. This means that geomantic concepts are fluid and changing, and each situation is unique. Yet certain principles do seem to stand out over time. Let us examine some examples of sites from different peoples, especially where giants are present, to clarify common geomantic themes.

## THE CENTER AND THE CIRCUMFERENCE

The fundamental geomantic act—from nomads making camp to priests laying out a temple—is a spatial one. It is the establishment of the center or the axis around which the world turns, and the establishment of the circumference. Which comes first is impossible to say. Without the surround there cannot be a center and vice versa. This generates the spatial qualities of unity or the circle and center, the line and the plane, which yield volume. It also generates the numerical stages of 1 which corresponds to center and unity; 2 is the line, the axis dividing the above and the below; 3 is the middle plane or surface; and then 4 is the cardinal directions, the world. Five appears in most cosmologies as the number pertaining to the world of organic life, and 6 to the total expression of above, below and center.

Every known cosmology in its manifest expressions—the camp, the town and the temple—invariably begins with these fundamental spatial acts. These are expressed in the creation mythology. Whether the temple is large or small, a shrine or a simple stone, its establishment creates the area within, the area without and the gateways or portals between the two. This sacred space is defined by its *temenos*, Greek for a ritual boundary. It is the "template" for all sacred space and time. The Latin for time is *tempus*.

The *axis mundi* in the center of the sacred space generates the symmetry of the middle, the above and the below. We have seen how the Native American cosmos distinguished between the Sky Beings, the Thunderbirds, and the Underworld Beings, usually represented by the Giant Horned Snake. These powers were unified in the Middleworld by the Plumed Serpent. The Mound Builders centered the world axis and the sacred directions on their mounds. Among the Maya and the Aztecs this tradition found its fulfillment in the pyramids and Quetzalcoatl. In Christian cosmology this three-fold division is represented by the realms of earth, heaven and hell.

Establishing the sacred template is one of the purposes of mythology, ritual and ceremony. According to Mircea Eliade, through the re-telling of myth, especially the myths of creation, the order of the cosmos is renewed. Ritual ensures participation within it.[2] Through the re-enactment of the sacred drama of creation the cosmos is maintained in its perfect form and humans can participate in every part of it. Details are important, such as the placement of ritual objects in certain directions, the counting out of precise numbers in measures, movements or objects, the walking and singing of the paths of the Dreamtime ancestors. This repeated construction of sacred space according to the cosmic template ensures that all the universal elements and patterns are maintained in their rightful order. The cosmology is not separate from its creators.

Mimi Lobell puts forward the case that in the earliest societies the cosmos was not divided in any way. Before the "Great Round" Neolithic cultures with their circular structures and cyclical views of space, there existed a stage she calls the "Sensitive Chaos." Here space is an "immediate flowing topological continuum with little geometric order." The landscape is a living "organism with lines and nodes of energy depending on human care for vitality." Humans were merged with their environment. The predominant symbol is the spiral.[3] This is a useful idea and certainly applies to early human experience. But the Paleolithic cave artists and shamans, even as they represented the world in the undifferentiated form of the Great Goddess, still drew upon basic spatial concepts such as center, before, behind, above and below.

Returning to the fundamental geomantic act, it is probable that the simple *gnomon*—an upright post or pillar—provided the first step in establishing the sacred template. Placed in the center, the gnomon entered the earth below and reached to the sky above. Around it turned a shadow, forming a circumference. From the movement of the shadow could be determined daily and seasonal time, direction and measure. Many traditions have myths to illustrate this. At the beginning of this chapter we gave one from the Yavapai of Arizona.

In many creation myths the world is spatially conceived in terms of giant forms. The Yavapai live on the breast of their Mother and were shown how to reach new levels on the world axis by climbing the corn which grew out of their first shaman's heart. In Scandinavian mythology the enormous world tree, Yggdrasil, unites Utgard the Underworld, with Mitgard the Middleworld, with Asgard the Upperworld. The world is made from the body of a giant. In America, Indonesia and India the world is upheld by a giant turtle. These themes, as well as that of the world being surrounded by the great serpent Ouroboros devouring its own tail, are found in many traditions. Our modern minds may scoff at these conceptions, but the point is that they convey a felt connection with the world.

The Big Bang and entropic theories of science separate us from living directly in an enspirited world that the geomorphic, geocentric creation myth inspires. Science is correct, as far as the purely mechanical material universe goes, the earth is not at the center of the universe. Things do appear to be winding down. But those who put the earth at the center of creation are right as far as the growing, living universe goes. To illustrate the difference between these two radically different paradigms, we give the following story, which was told to us by Father Charles Moore.

*An old lady attended a talk on the solar system given by a professor at the local university. He explained the orbit of the planets around the sun and the forces of gravity. At the end of the talk, the old lady approached the professor. She said had enjoyed the talk but he had gotten one thing wrong.*

*"Oh, and what might that be?" the professor inquired. "The earth is not held up in space by its orbit around the sun," the lady replied. "It's held up on the back of a giant turtle!" The professor politely hid his surprise and asked, "Well, if that is the case, what is it that supports the turtle?" "It's standing on the back of a second giant turtle," came the prompt reply.*

*The professor, thinking he now had the better of the old woman, then asked her what she thought supported that turtle. She hesitated for a moment before rounding on him firmly with, "What you say is no good, you know. It's turtles all the way down!"[4]*

## SACRED GEOMETRY

Geomancy involves *geo-metry*, which means "the measure of the earth." It is important to keep in mind that the combination of eye and brain works geometrically. Long before people consciously employed geometry and number, the intelligence of the body-mind could precisely calculate the niceties of the trajectory through space of an arrow, spear or stone toward a moving target. It has long been appreciated that all life forms, from the visible to the microscopic realms, contain and are differentiated by their geometric patterns. Robert Lawlor writes:

*All our sense organs function in response to the geometrical or proportional—not quantitative—differences inherent in the stimuli they receive. For example, when we smell a rose we are not responding to the chemical substances of its perfume, but instead to the geometry of their molecular construction. That is to say, any chemical substance that is bonded together in the same geometry as that of the rose will smell sweet.[5]*

Sacred geometry attempts to discover the principles underlying the order of the world and then work with them to maintain harmonious relations in the world. Geometric principles are found to be universally present in organic and inorganic forms and these can be expressed as certain relationships, ratios or proportions.

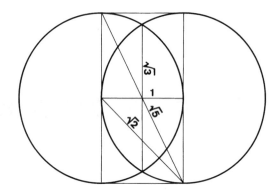

Traditions of sacred geometry from around the world are responsible for establishing what are known as the "canons" of proportion. These are universal ratios at the root of all mathematics and science. For example, canonical proportions are present in the square roots of 2, 3 and 5. All these are present in the figure known as the *Vesica Piscis*. The Vesica Piscis in its proportional geometry creates root 2, which governs the expansion of planes; root 3 which governs the expansion of volumes; and root 5 which leads to the Golden Proportion. This is also known as the Golden Mean or Section.

*Some of the geometric ratios underlying the world of form are shown here being generated by the Vesica Piscis. This figure is formed by the circumference of two equal circles passing through the center of each other. The Vesica Piscis leads to the square roots of 2, 3 and 5*

The two overlapping circles of the Vesica Piscis are supremely generative; that is, every basic geometric form can be derived from the figure. It is expressive of where unity, in the form of a circle, multiplies by two, and so creates the exemplary pattern for the succession of polygons: the equilateral triangle, the square, the pentagram, the hexagram, the octagon, the decagon and the dodecagon. In India the vesica at its center is known as the *yoni*, the female genitals. It was used in laying out the directions and for "opening" the ground plan of a temple. In the Christian cathedrals the vesica was used to frame sculptures of Christ or his mother. It also determined the proportions of the building.

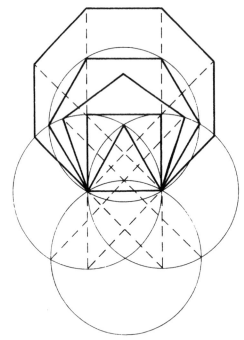

The Golden Proportion or *phi* (Ø) is not a number. It is a relationship. It is present in the spatial intervals of growth in many organic forms. It is to be found in the arrangement of leaves on a tree, in flowers and spiral shells and in the proportions of the human body. Its ratios are present in the pentagram or pentacle. Architects employ its proportions so that their buildings are in harmony with natural patterns of growth and regeneration.

Phi is the ratio where the smaller is to the larger as the larger is to the sum of the two, or A:B::B:A+B. It can be numerically expressed in the ratio of 1 to 1.61818 or its reciprocal 1 to 0.618. It can also be numerically expressed in the Fibonacci series. Here the result of adding two numbers, say 1 and 2, is continued by adding the resultant, in this case 3, to the last number. So 2 plus 3 equals 5; 3 plus 5 equals 8; 5 plus 8 equals 13; 8 plus 13 equals 21 and so on. As the numbers increase the proportion between them comes closer and closer to phi. For example, 8 over 5 equals 1.6, but 21 over 13 equals 1.615.

The Vesica Piscis can also take us to a geometrical concept known as the "Squaring of the Circle." This is where a square is constructed whose perimeter is

*The Vesica Piscis and the succession of polygons*

equal to the circumference of a circle. Another solution is where the enclosed areas of the square and the circle are the same.[6] Squaring the circle is a metaphor for resolving contradiction or accommodating apparently incompatible opposites. In this case, the immeasurable, spiritual, primary, unified and irrational qualities of the symbol of a circle are resolved with the measurable, physical, secondary, multiple and rational qualities of the symbol of a square. This has often been expressed architecturally through the placing of a dome on the square form of a temple. The Great Pyramid in Egypt offers a solution to the squaring of the circle in the ratio of its height to its perimeter. That is, if a circle were drawn using the height of the pyramid as its radius, its circumference would be equal to the perimeter of the square base of the pyramid.

Finally, the practice of sacred geometry by geomancers includes the study of number and measure. By basing their ideas upon geometry—the measure of the earth—they thought in vast and sacred terms. Through the use of standard measurements that are in an exact ratio to terrestrial and heavenly orders the architects of the ancient temples could achieve cosmic harmony. It is known for example, that the ancient geomancers of Egypt, Greece, Rome, Maya, China and India based their numbers upon the movement of the heavenly bodies and their measurements upon the size of the earth. For example, the base perimeter of the Great Pyramid is 3,041.28 feet, exactly half the shorter nautical mile, or half a minute of the meridian circumference of the earth. The nautical mile is one minute of one degree of the circumference of the earth. So if someone were to take the circle created by using the

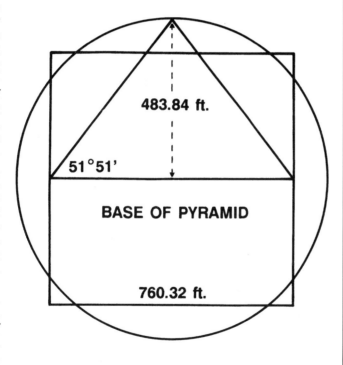

483.84 ft.

51°51'

BASE OF PYRAMID

760.32 ft.

height of the Great Pyramid as radius and roll it around the earth, it would be an exact fraction of the earth's meridian circumference.

What has this thumbnail sketch of sacred geometry got to do with giants? The point is this: the canonical proportions and with them the sacred numbers and the geodetic units of measure are bridges between the different dimensions. The ratios and their measures not only go down into smaller and smaller fractions and atomic and sub-atomic forms, but up into ever-increasing figures and gigantic forms. Sacred geometry is like a ladder between them all. If the wish is, as it often has been, to converse with the angels, then giants can be included in this too. We will find that people everywhere possessed an intuitive grasp of the spatial concepts of sacred geometry. They used these principles in the landscapes of the giants which we are examining. ▧

---

*The solution offered by the Great Pyramid to the problem of the "squaring of the circle." The circumference of a circle made using the height of the pyramid as its radius is equal to the perimeter of the pyramid base. Base = 3,041.28 feet. Height = 483.84. Height x 2 x pi = 3,041.22 feet*

# GIANTS AS LANDSCAPE TEMPLES

Jane was now in an extremely tricky situation. She had done what she thought the Giant had said but she was making a real mess of it. It seemed no matter what she did her friend, the dragon, was becoming more and more tangled up in itself. "Bother!" Jane said, as with a last great heave the dragon finally jammed itself together into one intractable knot.

Just then, up the path came none other than Rewald the Magician. "Oh, oh sir!" Jane called. "Would you be so kind as to help me untangle this knot?" Rewald fingered his long beard for a moment and nodded. He then got out a book of magic spells, spun round a few times, and a puff of smoke appeared on a nearby hillside. He looked disconcerted for a moment, then got out another book. Soon Jane was busy with ropes and pulleys and levers while Rewald bent over complicated equations. "Now!" Rewald called. Jane sweated and heaved, and heaved and sweated, and landed in a pile as a rope snapped. The dragon hadn't come undone an inch.

"What now?" asked Jane, who was beginning to wish she hadn't asked. Rewald tried another spell. Nothing happened. Then another book came out. He did more equations which looked awfully impressive but the dragon remained in its knot.

Rewald suddenly looked up with a gleam in his eye. Jane hoped it wasn't another plan with ropes and pulleys. She became dismayed when the magician rushed at the dragon waving a great sword. "Sir! No! Stop! Stop!" The sword went back over the shoulder of the magician, but it never came down. The Giant had appeared, as if from nowhere, and had caught it in his hand.

"Thank goodness you're here," said Jane breathlessly. "I've got myself into a bit of a tangle..." The Giant picked up Rewald by the collar and sat him down on top of the hill. He turned to Jane and asked her if she had tried the beans.

"The beans! What could they do?"

The Giant helped Jane make a bed for them beneath the dragon. Then they sat back. While the Giant took a nap Jane watched the beans begin to grow. Soon they were climbing all over the dragon who, it must be said, was thoroughly miffed by this time. Jane started to help the bean stalks get in every nook and cranny of the folds between the dragon's body. Soon, with a bit of clever maneuvering, the dragon started coming undone. By the time the giant was yawning and stretching himself awake, the dragon was off, happily snorting and blowing across the landscape like before.

"Thank you, sir!" Jane called out. The giant looked bemused for a moment then said: "Thank yourself. Remember, go with the grain not against it. Let your hands and tools work for you, not you for them. Let the river carry you in its own way. And when you come to rapids go with them, not against them. The best teacher is one who enables the pupil to say..."

"I know," smiled Jane. "I did it myself!"

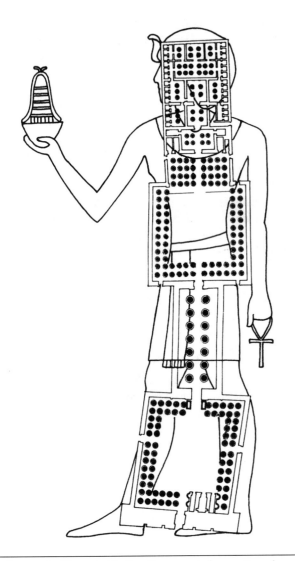

*The Temple of Luxor in the Egyptian canonical proportions of a man. (After R.A. Schwaller de Lubicz)*

## THE COSMIC TEMPLE

n the search for common themes which unite the giants of the world we find the idea that either the giants made the world, as in the Dreaming of the Australian giant Ancestral Beings, or that the world was made from giants. For example, in the Norse myth of the creation, as recorded by Snorri Sturlusson about 1220 CE, the world is shaped from the body of the frost giant Ymir. The seas and lakes were made from rivers of his blood, his flesh became the earth and his bones the mountains. Ymir's eyebrows made an enclosure around Midgard where humans could live, and his skull was lifted up and placed on four corners to form the canopy of the sky. For the Chinese, the giant P'an Ku named the features of heaven and earth. His breath was the wind, his speech the thunder. On his death the rivers and mountains as well as the sun and moon were made from his body.

The body is the pattern, the metaphor for describing that which is gigantic in the world. Using bodily terms such as "mouth of the river" makes the natural world accessible, immediate and comprehensible. The summit of Mont Blanc is known as *La Dent du Géant*, the tooth of the giant. Some Nordic giants sprout bushes and trees. In most traditions, giants are merged with the natural world.

The giant as the natural world, however, may be contrary, capricious and destructive, causing storms, avalanches, floods and whirlwinds. This aspect of the giants is emphasized in the Western world. In many stories of giants this is characterized by a preoccupation with their voracious appetites. The Cyclops for example are cannibals. The Danish giant Grendel will eat fifteen humans at a sitting. Gargantua and Pantagruel of Rabelais, accidentally swallow armies. In Western cosmology the chaotic forces of nature must be controlled.

Among cultures that do not make the strong distinction between humans and nature a more organic conception of the cosmos prevails. Nature achieves order through the action of its forces as they find balance between themselves. We know from ecology what an accurate picture of nature this is. Here the giant forces of nature are seen as living beings who can be cooperated with but not controlled. The concern for working with the giants may be seen from the ritual practices of such cultures.

The Native Americans offered tobacco ties or prayers to the river spirit when crossing it. They made pilgrimages across a landscape that was alive because they identified it with the body of a giant. The Yavapai of Arizona clearly describe the giant figure of their founding deity spread across the landscape. The Native Australians speak in terms of the giant bones, feet or arms of ancestors in the landscape in their practice of making ritual journeys along the Songlines of the Ancestral Beings. When the whole body of a giant describes a "temple" in the landscape we find dramatically visible expression of how people ritually work with this conception of the sacred cosmos.

In Chapter 9 we said that the word temple derives from the Latin for time, tempus, and from the Greek for a sacred enclosure, temenos. The temple is the template for all sacred time and space. The temple mirrors the cosmic order through its practices: ritual, spatial, architectural. It attempts to bring the human world through these practices into harmony with the divine. For example, the sweat lodge of the Native Americans is modeled upon the giant turtle which forms the American continent. Every detail of the structure evokes the comparison. The first sacred enclosures may have been circular spaces—maybe dance floors—mirroring the body of the Great Goddess. The temples of the goddess on Malta, which we shall look at in a moment, were built in the shape of her body.

The analogy between the human body and the divine is also found when a large area is held as sacred. In ancient Egypt the Kingdom was perceived as a huge body lain down the length of the River Nile. The feet of the gigantic figure spread out into the tributaries of central Africa. The fan of the Nile delta, with the sacred site of the Sphinx and the pyramids at Giza as its center, was the head. Much of the ritual calendar and honoring of the deities of the Egyptians was devoted to the Nile, especially to the seasonal flood which secured the fertility of the fields and the prosperity of the people. Originally this was conceived in terms of the fertility cycle of the Great Goddess, but the Pharaoh King eventually became the means by which intercession between the human, the physical and the divine worlds was effected. At the Temple of Luxor the geometry inherent in the ground plan is simultaneously based upon the proportion of phi, the body of the Pharaoh King, and the body of the Cosmic Giant. The huge execution of the architectural design is based upon the canons of proportion for a gigantic figure.

Building the temple in the form of the body automatically ensures the presence of the geometric proportions of the universe. The ratio of phi or the Golden Mean is found throughout the human body. It is in evidence, for example, in the proportion of the forearm to the hand, the hand to the fingers, the fingers to the first knuckle and so on. The Hindus built their temples to this proportion, saying it revealed the presence of *Purusha* or the Cosmic Man. His body connected heaven, sky and earth. We have just seen that the Egyptians built the Temple of Luxor on the proportions of the human figure. This is also the case for the Greek temples, notably the Parthenon, and is also true for the Christian cathedrals. Here the design was patterned on Christ upon the cross of creation. Not only does the Golden Mean define the ground plan of these temples but in many cases it is employed in the elevation.

*The human figure as ground plan for the temple. The 'Purusha' from a Hindu architectural manual*

Clearly all these cultures with widely differing cosmologies felt it important to include the proportions of the cosmic human figure in the manifestation of their most sacred templates. Conceiving the temple as a giant figure brought resonance through proportion with the creation. Eventually the Hindus, the Egyptians, the Greeks, the Christians and other temple-building cultures arrived at a canon of sacred proportions for number and geometry. This was conceived as originating from outside and "above" the physical world.

According to Plato and his school, the closer to the realm of ideas the form became the more perfect it would become. The Greek philosophers conceived the Divine City in the geometrical patterns that underlay nature but which never quite perfectly manifested *in* nature. With the discovery of mathematics the world could be measured, and, unlike the chaotic and dynamic world of the Great Goddess, mathematics was perfect. It presented a cosmos of fixed rules, of perfect

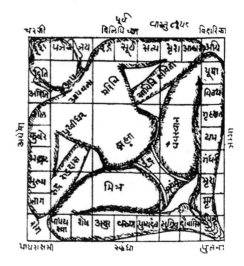

unchanging order. From there it was an easy step for Plato to say the world was but a shadow and that our physical senses deceived us. Only in the realm of pure ideas lay the perfectly ordered, geometrically structured world. All the chaos of the world could be reduced to this underlying, invisible canonical order.

At this point the forms of the temple departed from nature and began to be constructed in direct contrast to it. The canon was said to be sacred as its symmetrical and unchanging order succeeded in manifesting the perfect form. Given the human tendency to think in spatial terms of the divine as being bigger, greater and higher it also made sense to increase this power and perfection by creating sacred space on an ever-increasing scale.

*(Above) The body of Christ describing the ground plan for a cathedral. (After Francesco di Giorgio Martini)*
*(Right) Neolithic stone from Scotland. Carved with tetrahedral geometry*

## INTUITED VERSUS INTENDED GEOMETRY

The builders of the megalithic sites demonstrated geometrical ideas they were not supposed to know. There are spheres carved from the hardest stone found in megalithic contexts, circa 3,000 BCE, which reveal the universal building blocks that we know as the Platonic Solids. Measurement of the stone circles reveals 3,4,5 and other Pythagorean Triangles. All this was achieved several millennia before Plato and Pythagoras! Were the Neolithic people intentionally applying the abstract principles of perfect form and measure? Although later examples of megalithic sites do seem to be theoretical experiments—for example Woodhenge in Wiltshire—most of the sites cannot unequivocally demonstrate application of geometrical principles. They are best understood as intuitive expressions-from-within. New Grange, for example, is primarily symbolic. It represents giant powers coupling. Only secondarily is it geometric. Geometric ratios are there, but they are too haphazardly produced to be intentional and systematic.

The same holds true for the design of the megalithic temples on the small island of Malta in the Mediterranean. The temple complexes were either built underground, sometimes by carving directly into the bedrock, or were covered by earth and stone. The classic example of Ggantija, "Tower of the Giants," is surrounded by massive walls giving little indication of the interior. The subterranean temples take a bulbous, five-fold form, reminiscent of the Paleolithic, squatting, fertility goddesses. We identified the same five-fold feminine form in West Kennet Long Barrow. The Neolithic Maltese temples were conceived as an expression of the cosmic giant as Great Goddess. At other temples, such as Al Tarxien. there are spiral carvings on the stones. On occasion, there are statues of the goddess herself exhibiting the same form as the temple. The ratios of sacred geometry are present in the proportions of the temples. But the impression is that they were not executed to a grand idea or design. It is rather that the design was arrived at organically. Indeed Ggantija grew through many stages in the third millennium BCE before it arrived at its final form.

Eventually the megalithic sites do begin to exhibit signs of systematic application of geometric principles. The final stage of Stonehenge appears to have been executed to a complex plan. Its neighbor, Woodhenge, mentioned above, was a theoretical attempt to reconcile radius and circumference to come up with a value for *pi*.[1] Some megalithic experiments literally went to extraordinary lengths. The stone rows at Carnac in Brittany, stretching for miles, appear in the landscape like scales on the back of an enormous dragon. But careful surveying has revealed geometric intentions.[2]

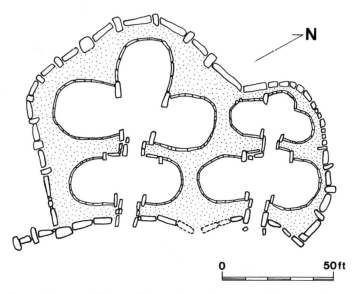

0        50 ft

Some cultures have not labored to produce huge sacred or secular spaces. Even so they have demonstrated a natural inclination toward selecting as sacred sites those places which reveal the universal ratios in the proportions of their natural geometry. This creates the interesting idea that nature-cultures work intuitively in the creation of sacred sites rather than from the application of geometrical theory. They arrive at the cosmic template as it emerges from within rather than from an idea outside and above the world. It somehow makes sense that a people closely involved with the wisdom of their own and other natural bodies would intuitively express the ratios they experienced every day in their creative acts. The cave art of the Ice Ages is a case in point. The Paleolithic artists achieved a realism barely repeated until the twentieth century. They echoed the realism of the world as they saw it rather than attempting to express themselves in contrast to it.

So, taking one more step into the nature-cultures, what examples of sacred landscapes exist which naturally exhibit the principles which the late megalithic culture

and urban-cultures deliberately built into their temples?

Turning to the American Southwest the first example which comes to mind is the four-direction principle for defining sacred space. The Navajo, Hopi and the Pueblo people speak of their land as being the "Middle Place." It is between the above and the below and the four directions represented in their cosmography by sacred mountains. The world order is maintained by regular pilgrimages to the shrines on the four sacred mountains. This four-fold principle is found in the laying out of the temples of all the urban-cultures mentioned above. They employ the Vesica Piscis to lay out the quadrature of the temple.

A further example from the Southwest comes from the Pima and Tohono O'odam tribes of southern Arizona. Their cosmography turns around the sacred mountain of Baboquivari. In their creation mythology the Earthmaker placed Iitoi, the Elder Brother, upon the mountain. From its summit he would come down and visit the people. The path he takes around the mountain is described by the labyrinth design used in basket weaving for which the Pima and Tohono O'odam are famous. The labyrinth design shows Iito—the "Man in the Maze"—as well as the sacred directions, the center, and the meandering path between this world and the next.

The Hopi also speak of the labyrinth in cosmographical terms. One form of the labyrinth shows the sun, the four directions and the path to follow through

(*Left*) Ggantija, Malta. *Third millennium* BCE *complex.*
(*Above*) The "Classical Labyrinth." *A motif found across the world*

life. Another form depicts the Mother Earth with a child in her womb.[3] The sacred mountain, the path around it and the space it encloses invariably find expression among urban-cultures in the form of the temple. The Mayan pyramids such as those at Tikal, the ziggurats of Mesopotamia, the temples of Java, India, Egypt, Thailand, Bali, Greece and medieval Europe, all echo the form of the sacred mountain. Nearly all these cultures also possess a labyrinth tradition.

The Hopi speak of their original emergence place from the first world being situated in the Grand Canyon. So gigantic is this natural feature that even the Anglo-Americans created a giant origin for it in the story of the folk-giant Paul Bunyan. A feature so huge had to have a cosmological "explanation." It made sense to think of it as the primordial origin place of the people. The Grand Canyon shares with Canyon de Chelly of the Navajo Nation the distinction of being the home of Grandmother Spider Woman, the Great Goddess, the original giant.

Canyon and mountain, cave and mound, these are the basic forms emulated in the sacred architecture of both nature- and urban-cultures. The pueblos of the Southwest echo the mesas and mountains around them. The circular kivas echo the circular springs and lakes which are the emergence places of the people. All such architecture employs the canonical proportions of geometry. These proportions are not arrived at abstractly. They are derived from the world and are used intuitively. It would be hard to discover the proportions of sacred geometry at the Grand Canyon, although they would be there in the forms created by the flow patterns of water. But another nearby, similar sacred site in the smaller Red Rock Country displays them readily enough in its natural formations.

## THE SEDONA LANDSCAPE TEMPLE

The beautiful landscape in Red Rock Country around Sedona, made famous in many movies, is best known by the red rock buttes known as Courthouse Rock, Bell Rock and Cathedral Rock. Other formations in this area include the Twin Buttes and the Madonna Rock beside the Chapel of the Holy Cross, the Seven Warriors, Camel Head and the Airport Mesa. The latter, as well as Cathedral and Courthouse/Bell Rocks, have achieved notoriety in recent years as "vortex" centers.

What is not so well known is that this area is considered to be the place where the First Woman of the Yavapai and the Apache Nations "emerged" after the flood which destroyed the first world. It is also not well known that all but one of the sites mentioned above fall on the circumference of a circle. The exception is the Twin Buttes whose Madonna Rock is at the center of the circle. Moreover, the three "vortex" sites—Cathedral Rock, Courthouse/Bell Rock and Airport Mesa—lie on the circle in such a way as to divide it into five parts. The crest of Lee Mountain is the highest point in the area. It and the buttes behind Camel Head form the remaining two points.

From such natural geometry in the landscape it is possible to create a pentagram or pentacle about 5 miles across. Upon this can be superimposed a human figure. Whichever way the human figure lies, the sexual organs will be in the center, in the area of the Madonna Rock. The pentagram contains the geometrical ratios of growth and generation in that its lines are divided according to the proportion of the Golden Mean or phi. Of course the presence of the giant geometrical figure in the landscape is only coincidence, a simulacrum. But where it becomes extraordinary is that it coincides with the principles expressed in the creation mythology of the native peoples. (The mythology is given in Chapters 4 and 12.) Is it "only coincidence" that sacred geometry, sexual organs, local names and the creation myth of the Great Goddess, all referring to growth and generation, should come together at one place in the landscape?

If this was all, it would be enough to see that the same principles are at work in a nature-culture's sacred site as those present in an urban-culture's temple. But there are even more geometrical figures present in the Red Rock Country.

To the northwest of the pentagram in the Dry Creek area lies a hexagram, a six-sided or a six-pointed figure. Its lines are defined by primary features in the landscape: Steamboat (Thunderbird) Rock at the head of Oak Creek Canyon, Lost Wilson Mountain, Isis Rock in Long Canyon, Doe Mountain, Gray Mountain or Capital Butte at its center. It also has, in common with the pentagram, the "vortex" center on the

Airport Mesa. The native name for the string of peaks at the center of the hexagram is Thunder Mountain. Looked at from above, as mentioned in Chapter 4, these peaks form a serpent.

Coincidence or not, the center of the serpent falls on a natural arch known as Devil's Bridge. The association between the serpent and the Devil is common in the Christian world. If the serpent were to be extended it would be 6 miles in length, the diameter of the surrounding hexagram. If the feature called Lizard Head is taken for the head of the giant serpent it would be rather small. If Chimney Rock is taken as the head then the serpent has some rather splendid horns. The triangles which interpenetrate in the hexagram are present on the backs of many snakes. The "Star of David" is associated with King Solomon who was proverbial for his wisdom. In many native traditions the serpent is renowned for its wisdom, the word for serpent often being synonomous for "wise." Horns are signs of wisdom, sexual energy and power. The connection between serpents and lightning is also common, which takes us back to the native name for the mountain.

Where the coincidences between the natural landscape and the native tradition in the case of the hexagram become extraordinary is when the Hopi tradition is considered. According to the *Book of the Hopi* the Snake Clan constructed six equidistant, radiating shrines across the landscape wherever it went in its migrations. The shrines would be placed some distance away from the central kiva. This would form a hexagram on the scale of that in the Sedona landscape. The Red Rock Country could have been one of the places the Snake Clan journeyed through in their migrations. The Hopi tradition often mentions a place known as Palatkwapi, the "Red City of the South." Horned serpent pictographs are common in the Dry Creek, Secret/Bear Mountain area.

The geometry inherent in the serpent hexagram is complex and contains many of the ratios and proportions found in the practice of sacred geometry. In *The Dimensions of Paradise*, John Michell elaborates greatly on the hexagram showing its use in the geometric practice of "squaring the circle." When the landscape hexagram is compared to the pentagram it is found that they are in proportion to each other in the

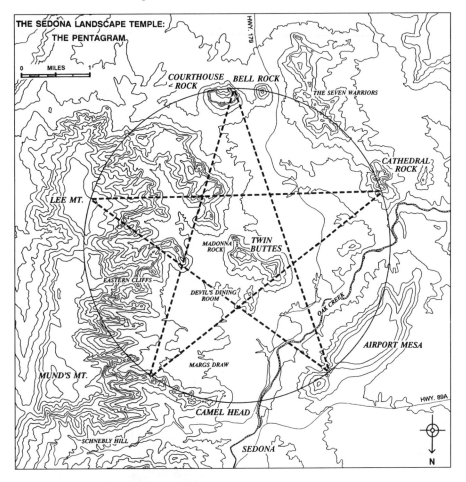

The pentagram in the Sedona landscape

order of the square root of 2. Put in another way, if a square were to be drawn around the circle of the pentagram then the circle of the hexagram would contain that square. This produces a figure identical to those Mr. Michell uses to demonstrate the construction of Stonehenge and St. Mary's Chapel in the Abbey Church at Glastonbury. Root 2 governs the expansion of area, the power of multiplicity in the universe. So it is closely related to the generative principle of phi.[4]

We have seen how a giant figure five miles in length can be superimposed upon the pentagram. This ties in very nicely with the story of the First Woman's grandson, Sakaraka'amche. He ascended into the heavens and received medicine power from his fathers, Sun and Cloud. He came back down to earth on the lightning flashes and pressed himself into the Red Rock Country from one end to the other. In this way sacred power was given to the people. Sedona became a place where healing, visions and other forms of power could be found.

Still further sacred geometry exists in the natural landscape of Sedona. If the pentagram and the hexagram which extend across the Red Rock Country are seen as a whole, then another giant figure emerges. This giant is eleven miles long. Many prominent features of the landscape fall on the common axis of the two geometrical figures. They create an alignment where not only do the features possess several remarkable lines of sight, but they are equidistant from each other. In the diagram on page 106 it can be seen that the square root proportion between the pentagram and the hexagram creates seven equidistant centers in the natural landscape which can be taken as the axis of the giant body of Sakaraka'amche. Or is it the body of the First Woman as Grandmother Spider Woman? The line runs from the area of the Madonna Rock with its generative properties, through the Airport Mesa and Thunder

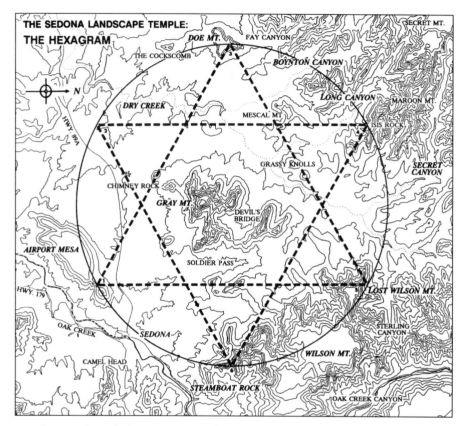

*The hexagram in the Sedona landscape*

Mountain to a pinnacle in Long Canyon known as Isis Rock. This is near many ancient dwelling sites, including the cave honored by the Yavapai-Apache as the home of the First Woman.

In the natural landscape of the area we thus find giant figures, geometrical figures and the canonical ratios of sacred geometry which have geomythical resonances with the sacred places and traditions of the area. It is not possible to prove that the Hopi or Yavapai were aware of the sacred geometry inherent in the area. That is not our case. We set out to show that nature-cultures are working with the principles of sacred geometry on the intuitive level. Only in urban-cultures are these principles codified and removed to the realm of pure ideas. The Sedona landscape temple reveals in its natural forms the geometric and other principles that we find in built temples around the world.

The Yavapai and Hopi traditions show that giants—human or animal—are a good way of thinking about landscape which is held sacred. This is not "primitive" thinking but rather holistic thinking where there is a remarkable felt connection with the external world. It is also non-intrusive. Nature-cultures find where geomythical resonances lie, they honor them and do not attempt to manipulate them.

## GIANTS AS CHAKRA SYSTEMS

In the preceding section we described the presence in the Sedona landscape of a giant figure formed by the combination of hexagram and pentagram. This figure in the analytical terms of sacred geometry yields seven equidistant landscape features along the length of its body. This may be the body of the culture-hero Sakaraka'amche described in the myths as pressed into the landscape. Or it may be the giant figure of the First Woman, Komwidapukwia. Both their actions gave shape to many of the features of *Wipuk*, the Red Rock Country. Their "footsteps" are said to be found there. Both grandmother and grandson taught the people many things and gave them medicine powers. For this reason the land is sacred and visited for the purpose of prayer or for seeking power.

Whichever giant it is in the landscape, Eastern traditions have credited the human body with seven energy centers or *chakras*. If this idea can be translated from one tradition to another, then the seven centers along the line of Sakaraka'amche's or Spider Woman's body are places where energy analogous to that chakra in the body can be accessed. Isis Rock for example will be the crown chakra, the doorway to the spirit world. The Airport will be the solar plexus, concerned with the movement of will, as well as physical, mental and emotional energy. The area around the Madonna Rock—the center of the pentagram—will be the root chakra, concerned with basic issues of security, rootedness and raw earth energy.

This idea is not unique to the tradition of India where the name, chakras, originates. It is also present in other esoteric systems such as the Kabbalistic "Tree of Life." It may be only coincidence, once again, that the Sedona landscape yields a good representation of the Tree of Life in its juxtaposition of a pentagram and a hexagram.

The chakras are centers of subtle energy which may be understood as graded frequencies of cosmic energy manifesting in the physical spectrum. Indeed, the colors of the rainbow and the vibrational qualities of sound are attributed to them. It is said that it is not the breath and the beating of the heart which maintains the health and the life of every living being, it is the energy emanating from the chakras or vital centers that maintains the breath, the heart, the circulation of blood and every other system. In the same way as ideas from acupuncture can easily be translated from the human to the planetary body, so concepts of energy centers analogous to those in the human body can be applied to centers of energy in the landscape. The concept of a gigantic body applied to the landscape as a means of making it comprehensible must include the idea of the invisible energy body.

Chakras, like giants, are useful conceptual tools for working with the external world once the realm of subtle energies is accepted. The ancient philosophers and architects sought to manifest in the outer world the perfect principles of divine form which they perceived as being present in the archetypal inner world. They did this through an understanding of sacred geometry. In the same way, geomancers attempt to conceive the outer landscape as being underlain by a perfect inner realm of universal energy. Great Round cultures would have perceived these energies in terms of dragons; the description of the root chakra is often given as a serpent. The way in which this is perceived all lies in the cosmology of the beholder. Modern science entered this century believing that energy and matter, like mind and body, were quite separate. Einstein irrefutably showed that energy and matter were different manifestations of the same thing.[5] Whatever the tools or principles employed, we find the idea of giants as energy systems to be extremely useful when it comes to the scale of the natural world.

Vital energy centers in the landscape analogous to those in the human body have been described in many traditions. For a time, this concept has been latent. But people are again talking about the landscape in terms of chakras systems, Gaia Theory, devas, angels, energy patterns, temples, or—and here we submit our case—giants.

It has been suggested that any discrete area such as a hill, an island, a peninsula, a town, has energy

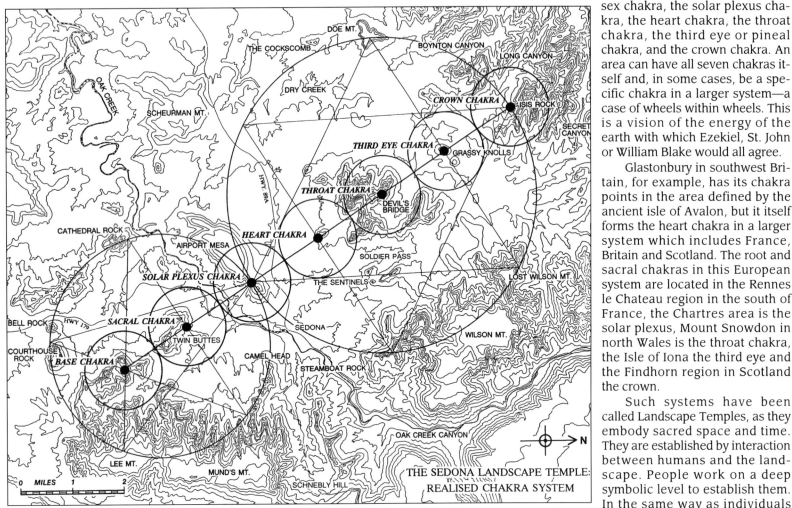

THE SEDONA LANDSCAPE TEMPLE:
REALISED CHAKRA SYSTEM

*Chakras found in the Sedona landscape*

sex chakra, the solar plexus chakra, the heart chakra, the throat chakra, the third eye or pineal chakra, and the crown chakra. An area can have all seven chakras itself and, in some cases, be a specific chakra in a larger system—a case of wheels within wheels. This is a vision of the energy of the earth with which Ezekiel, St. John or William Blake would all agree.

Glastonbury in southwest Britain, for example, has its chakra points in the area defined by the ancient isle of Avalon, but it itself forms the heart chakra in a larger system which includes France, Britain and Scotland. The root and sacral chakras in this European system are located in the Rennes le Chateau region in the south of France, the Chartres area is the solar plexus, Mount Snowdon in north Wales is the throat chakra, the Isle of Iona the third eye and the Findhorn region in Scotland the crown.

Such systems have been called Landscape Temples, as they embody sacred space and time. They are established by interaction between humans and the landscape. People work on a deep symbolic level to establish them. In the same way as individuals

centers which may be characterized in terms of the seven chakras: the root or base chakra, the sacral or

may choose to delve into their own personal unconscious to heal trauma which leads to the retrieval of inner power, so working with energy from a collective level of the unconscious may lead to healing and power on a transpersonal, national or racial scale. The temples derive from cosmographical mapping with an aim to restoring or creating the sacred landscape. Perhaps it is here that ancient conflicts, for example that between the Irish and the English, can be dealt with. By thinking in terms which operate on a cosmological scale, the old wounds in the collective unconscious archetypal realm—irreparable by any other means—can be healed.

Landscape temples are really classic examples of thinking in terms of giants. The concept can be applied to any landmass. Mountain chains, such as the Pyrenees, are often described in local lore as the body and bones of a giant. The Isle of Man, a small island in the Irish Sea, has ancient sacred sites along its axis which naturally lend themselves to the analogy of the body of a giant. It also has a folklore rich in support of such an idea. Stories range from the island's namesake the sea god Manannan, who often played tricks of shape-shifting, to the Fynnoderee, a huge, hairy, naked wildman whose help may be enlisted in farm and field.

In the United States it is possible to think of mountain ranges, valleys, plains and rivers, or at least discrete sections of them, in terms of landscape temples. In southwest Colorado, Sleeping Ute Mountain resembles a prone chieftain with an eagle feather headdress. Perhaps there is a myth that one day he will awaken, and, like King Arthur in Britain, finally restore his country. Where the authors currently live in Albuquerque, New Mexico, it has proved rewarding to think of the Indian Pueblos along the Rio Grande valley as chakras, or the natural features of the valley itself as chakras. The mountain rising a mile above the city was conceived of and originally named after the turtle in Pueblo mythology. The pattern of shrines on the back of the turtle mountain could be thought of in terms of a chakra system.

It is also interesting to ask what relationship do the States and cities of the United States have to the whole? Is the federal capital a microcosm of the whole? The founders of the city went to great lengths to create a precise geomancy. As the heart, what effect does the geomancy of Washington D.C. have on the body of the nation? Or is New York the heart of the nation and D.C. the head? What is Chicago? Los Angeles? What effect does the network of Interstate highways have? Do they serve as arteries for the life-blood of the nation or do they structure it in a less positive way?

Landscape giants or temples can be conceived of in terms other than chakras. Sometimes the area is far too complex to be so defined. In the next chapter we turn to examples of other kinds of giantic systems. ✶

CHAPTER ELEVEN

# THE SCIENCE
# OF GIANTS

"*So you're saying giants never really existed?*"
"*No. They did exist. But it was in a world where the boundaries between body and mind are very different from ours.*"
"*Oh, I get it. They only existed in the mind.*"
"*I can see I haven't made myself clear. The mind may turn out to share a common origin with substance, form and being.*"
"*Yes, but the giants never actually existed in bodies like ours.*"
"*Actually, to borrow your words, only giants ever really exist. Mind and body are only particular realizations of the world of giants.*"
"*Wow! You believe in giants!*"
"*Yes, if I believe in the wind, the hills, the atoms, the sun, moon and tides, the intelligence and information which makes every part of life on earth breathe and act together as a whole.*"
"*Are they the giants?*"
"*If you want them to be.*"
"*O.K. I want them to be. What next?*"

"*Well, think of the giants next time you shop for food, cook a meal, light a fire, dig the garden, run water, build a house, plan a journey, cross a river, write a song, a report or a poem. They will be there to help...*"
"*Like, they relate everything to the whole?*"
"*Exactly.*"
"*Giants unite!*"

---

## GIANTS AS ZODIACS

 n about 1580, Dr. John Dee, the scholar and physician to Queen Elizabeth I, visited Somerset in south-west Britain and recorded in drawings and in notes what he called "Merlin's Secret." He wrote:

*...the starres which agree with their reproductions on the ground do lye onlie on the celestial path of the Sonne, moon and planets... all the greater starres of Sagittarius fall in the hinde quarters of the horse, while Altiar, Tarazes and Alsschain from Auilla do fall on its cheste... thus is astrologie and astronomie carefullie and exactley married and measured in a scientific reconstruction of the heavens...*

For several centuries no one was quite sure what Dr. Dee meant by any of this. He was dismissed as a maverick and a magician. Then in 1929 an artist, Kathryn Maltwood, published a book called *A Guide to Glastonbury's Temple of the Stars*. In this book she described a pattern on the ground which was a replica of the signs of the Zodiac in the sky.

The terrestrial zodiac around Glastonbury, Ms. Maltwood said, was formed by the combination of natural features such as rivers, streams, hills, hollows and contours, and human-made features such as field and wood boundaries, mounds, banks and causeways. The figure of Aquarius for example, was formed by the natural hills and boundaries of the Isle of Avalon, and perfected by the placement of earthen banks and roads. The 12 signs of the Zodiac cover an area whose circumference is 30 miles, and whose figures are many miles in length. Each figure approximates the stellar configuration it represents. Occasionally it differs from the standard pattern, making a phoenix out of Aquarius, a ship out of Cancer, a dove out of Libra. Some say Scorpio is an eagle and Capricorn a unicorn. It is a true collection of giants in the landscape.

The signs of the Zodiac appear to have been agreed upon, with only minor differences, from an extremely early date across the world. The similarity of the ancient Middle Eastern, Egyptian and Chinese Zodiacs either suggest extensive global communication at a time when it was not thought possible, or parallel but independent development. Carl Jung would have described this as an example of synchronicity.

It does appear that people throughout the ages have closely studied the stars. Perhaps it is here that we find the exemplary models for the configuration of giants. The stars give us giant beings, animal and human, which are eternal and powerful, progressive and orderly. Their occasional outbursts or planetary conjunctions suggest energy, a dynamic realm of spirit. The Milky Way or Draco may have been the original dragon, Virgo or Orion the prototype for all gi-

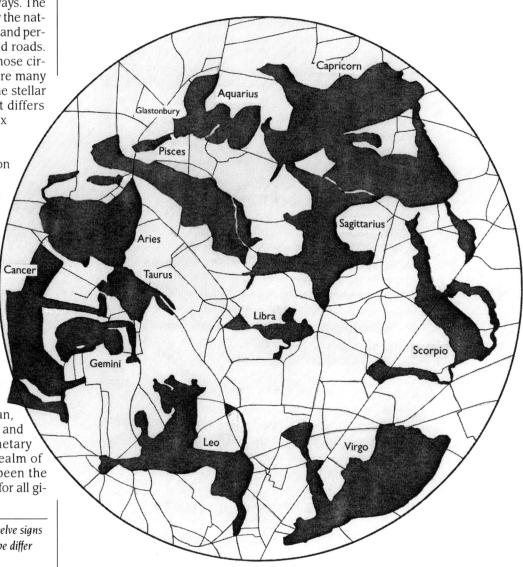

*The Glastonbury Zodiac. About 11 miles across, the twelve signs formed by natural and artificial features in the landscape differ somewhat from conventional zodiacs*

ants. Every culture recognizes the giant in the constellation of Orion. The Arabic name for him is al-Jabbar, "the giant." The Greeks say he is a descendant of the Titans. He was slain by his lover, the goddess Artemis. She in her grief made him the most beautiful of constellations. The Hebrews say that Orion is the giant Nimrod, builder of the Tower of Babel. His punishment was to be strapped to the dome of heaven.

In Britain in the late 1940's another Zodiac was found in Carmarthenshire. It was centered on the village of Pumpsaint. In the 1970's investigators of this claim discovered an even larger Zodiac in the landscape of Dyfed around the Prescelly Mountains. Both Zodiacs repeated the patterns of the Glastonbury Zodiac. Claims were made that the artificial features of them all originated in Neolithic times. Since then research has unearthed other places in the British landscape which yielded up Zodiacs when the pattern was applied. The most documented of these are the Nuthampstead Zodiac Temple discovered by Nigel Pennick and the Kingston Zodiac Temple discovered by Mary Caine.

Aerial photography opened the way for most of this research. Although Zodiacs seem plentiful, they are rare compared to the discovery of many huge individual figures in the landscape. These mostly take the form of dragons or other animals created by contours and perfected by the placement of earthworks or sacred sites. The Sedona Great Bird and Serpent would fall into this category. What about the Ohio Serpent or the Effigy Mounds?

The main difference between the Effigy Mounds and the giant figures of Sedona and the Zodiac temples is that the mounds are unequivocally intentional, while proof for the intentionality of the giant figures is disputable. Although the symbiosis between the Zodiac signs and the landscape is intriguing and at times incredible, most of the time it is only credible in the minds of the believers. Scorpio in the Glastonbury Zodiac differs according to which plan of the figure is being studied. The reflexive landscape happily accommodates all interpretations. The earthwork which makes a creature's horn, yes, can be seen in that light, but it also can have a perfectly mundane explanation as a defensive or boundary-marking outwork.

Let us look at the mind of the beholder. As we have seen in the preceding chapters, the mind is very powerful. To deny the existence of something as "only in the mind" is to deny the world-making power of the cosmologies which each of us carry in our minds. Nicholas R. Mann has lived in several places within the boundaries of the Glastonbury Zodiac for many years, and can only confirm that the Zodiac *does* exist. It informs and makes sense of the landscape. It makes it alive, intelligent and dynamic.

A very definite sense of place arises from living within each sign. The Zodiac begins to permeate actions, until walking, driving, building and naming new places achieve resonance within the greater context. It becomes meaningful to visit Taurus for its earthy qualities, to take a walk to the heart of Leo on a Sunday morning, to stand on the brow of Gemini, to meditate on the eye of Aries, to drink the water which gushes from the mouth of Aquarius. Even people who normally do not give esoteric matters a second thought find the quality of the giant on which they live permeating their thinking and informing their ideas.

The giant pattern of the Zodiac is as though an energy blueprint of the mind with its origin in the stars has become superimposed upon the natural landscape. As a result, the invisible archetypal forms of the Zodiacal giants will inevitably appear, gradually manifesting in physical reality what is being held in the cosmological realm. In this context it becomes superfluous to argue whether ancient peoples originally conceived and labored to create a Zodiac. This is attempting to achieve legitimation, based upon antiquity, for ideas and actions which need no such justification. The Zodiacs exist to the extent that people point out their boundaries, make pilgrimages around them, walk their paths, name their houses and businesses after them, hold them in their minds and, above all, feel that they are important to the world today. As their pattern is visible almost every night in the stars, the terrestrial Zodiacs are classic examples of giants rendering meaning, intelligence and dynamic order to the physical world. Giants are good to think.

## ASTRONOMY

A further example of celestial influence at work in the principles surrounding giants is the concern for correct astronomical orientation. It seems wherever people have gone they have watched the heavens and created temples upon the earth in harmony with the celestial order. The terrestrial Zodiacs are perhaps the most fantastic of these temples. There is no question that all the ancient peoples from whom examples of giantology have been drawn were astronomers and calendar keepers.

Through a simple method using a *gnomon*, a stick, set in the ground and watching its shadow, it is possible with a rope to precisely orientate oneself to the terrestrial axis, to the solar plane, to the cardinal directions, to the square, circle and the cycle of the year. A little more sophistication yields lunar cycles, even eclipses and planetary movements. We know the ancient peoples of the world watched these events and attached great significance to them. We have little evidence of day-to-day observation or record keeping, but what we do have lies in the monumental undertakings made by the ancient peoples. This is what links astronomy to the giants.

Stonehenge, the "Giants' Dance," is located at the only latitude in the northern hemisphere where its chosen astronomical axes cross at right angles. The axis oriented to the northern and southern major lunar extremes crosses the axis oriented to the summer and winter solstice to form a rectangle. The henge also incorporates cross-quarter day alignments. These mark the sun's position halfway between solstice and equinox.

The stone circle and avenues at Callanish in the Outer Hebrides comprise a megalithic site said in local tradition to be giants turned to stone. The legend of the "Shining One" walking along the main axis at Midsummer is enough to indicate its astronomical functions. But what is fascinating about Callanish is that its latitude places it so the moon at its major extreme, which occurs every 18.6 years, does not set but walks along the contours of the horizon. As it does so it highlights the recumbent figure of a giant woman.

Alexander Thom was impressed by the incidence of first magnitude star rises in the stone rows on

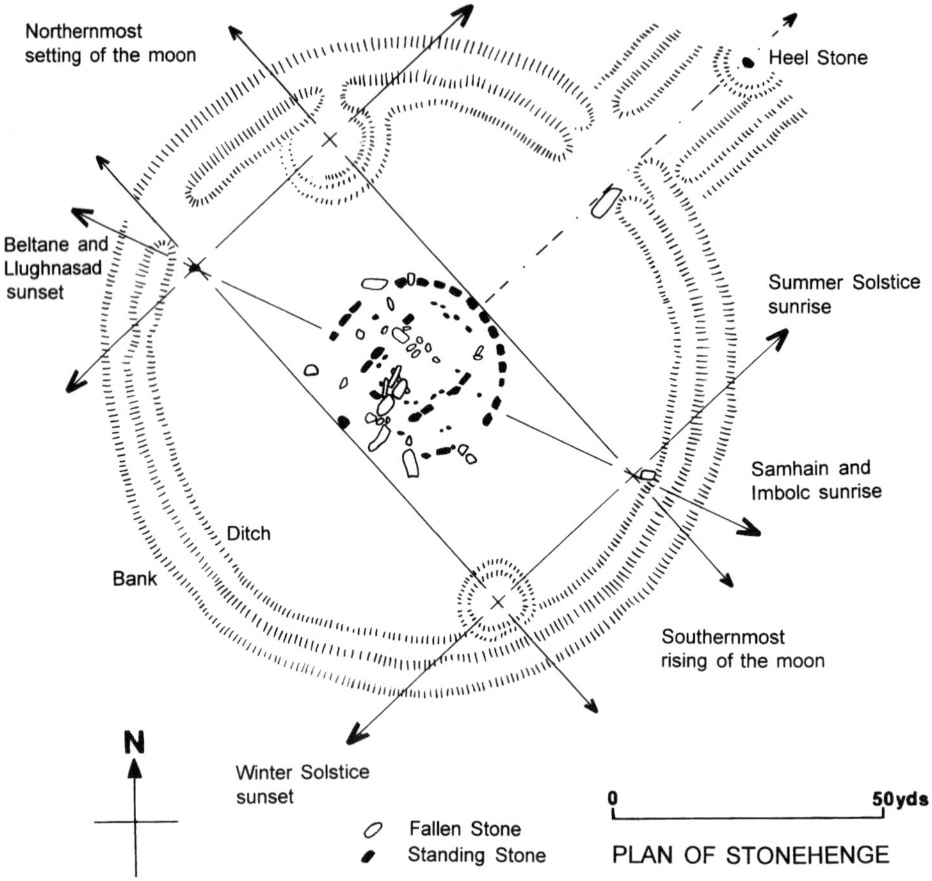

*Stonehenge astronomy*

Northernmost setting of the moon

Heel Stone

Beltane and Llughnasad sunset

Summer Solstice sunrise

Samhain and Imbolc sunrise

Ditch

Bank

Southernmost rising of the moon

N

Winter Solstice sunset

0        50yds

○ Fallen Stone
● Standing Stone

PLAN OF STONEHENGE

Dartmoor. The astronomical orientations of New Grange, West Kennet, Gavr'inis and Stoney Littleton chambered mounds have already been mentioned. It is from evidence like this that we can be certain almost every megalithic site is aligned—more or less precisely—to some significant celestial event. And it is likely that these alignments had intense cosmological significance for their makers, such as the legends associated with the giant Orion mentioned above.

Strictly verifiable astronomical findings have not been easily forthcoming in America or Australia. We know they are there from the stories of Star People, the giants who walk from horizon to horizon in the space of a single night. During the course of each year the movement of sun, moon and stars was observed. Patterns of light were made to move over sundial petroglyphs, as at Chaco Canyon and Holly near Hovenweep. Easier still, the solar path was marked by watching the movement of the sun across rugged horizons. Giants, the Hopi say, hold the quarters of the sky at the places marked by the four extreme rising and setting points of the solstices. Among the Maya the evidence is profound. The movement of the gods themselves is to be seen in the heavens. Astronomical lines have been demonstrated in the giant figures of the Chimu at Nazca in Peru. And although the evidence is not yet clear, it seems the giants who majestically sit on Rapa Nui, Easter Island, are also gazing at the skies.

## GIANTS: ORDER VERSUS CHAOS

In whatever form the megalithic people, the ancient Egyptians, the Yavapai and Hopi Indians, the cathedral architects, the Chimu, Pacific Islanders or the Zodiac builders were conceiving their temples, certain principles were present. First among them all is size. It made sense for the temple to be on a scale that was all inclusive. The ultimate model for this may have been the celestial bodies held within the cosmic body of the Great Goddess. Sacred places conceived on a vast scale brought the people closer to the divine. They suggested the entire world could become a mirror of the divine harmony.

Giants are not only huge, but as bodies they contain within themselves centers with specific functions such as head and heart. The idea of the chakras of landscape giants was discussed in the previous chapter. As bodies they also possess the divine proportions upon which all life is understood—through intuition or reason—to be based. Such inherent geometry is the second universal principle. It led, in some cases, to the creation of complex temples which based themselves upon the ideal proportions of the figure of the Cosmic Man.

At this point there is a schism between nature-cultures and most urban-cultures. Nature-cultures prefer to keep their cosmos peopled with giants who are complex, organic and diverse beings, quite capable of changing their minds, while urban-cultures prefer giants that are unchanging ideal principles based on fixed and simple geometric laws. The development of mathematics and geometry with their unchanging canonical principles gave rise to ideas like Plato's Atlantis and the New Jerusalem of St. John. In these utopias the entire landscape, natural and artificial, is in accordance with the underlying laws of the ideal cosmic template.

It was, alas, an idea taken too far. Urban-cultures' preoccupation with scale or with implementing numerology or proportion became a kind of geomantic fascism. Everything had to fit the plan and the eccentricities of nature had to be eliminated. In the attempt to resonate with the universal ratios in their perfect archetypal form, the fact that every expression in the world deviates from the pattern to produce its own unique form was forgotten or neglected. Indeed nature herself may manifest the universal ratios in her aberrations, in the degree of deviation from a random pattern, not in the pattern itself.

It must be remembered that in nature-cultures' cosmologies the primal unity was always expressed by the Great Goddess. Her cosmos was inclusive, transformative and always changing. The reader will have noticed that the urban-cultures with their sophisticated temples invariably spoke about them in terms of "man." Along with the split between spirit and matter, mind and body, reason and feeling, went the split between the Great Goddess and her son. Eventually he became dominant and his body replaced that of the goddess as the template for the cosmic order.

The new order of solar gods pinned down the wandering lines of the earth spirit with their lances, walls and temples. The urban spirit of the Greeks ended the chaos of nature with grid plans for their cities. Obelisks replaced the sacred groves. The son represented the rule of law imposed from without rather than order arrived at from within. The son represented the saviour who would step in and save humans from the consequences of their actions in the world. This is not true for many native peoples such as the Australians or American Indians who did not make the body-mind split. But we can see it in Europe at the megalithic sites, where after about 2600 BCE, the concern shifts from the body of the goddess to astronomical and mathematical experimentation.[1]

The recently developed realm of Chaos Theory—a product of super computers—has shown that it is irregularity and differences in the natural world which can be modelled. There is no absolute space and time, no controllable measure, no deterministic predictability. But on the boundary between the knowable and the unknowable, in the relationship between the quantifiable and the unquantifiable, in realms previously dismissed as "chaos" and "turbulence," there is order, pattern and beautiful, breath-taking symmetry. Even time, once thought to be so absolute and quantifiable, is now thought of by physicists as rate of change—a relative term similar to how people of nature-cultures think of time.

Western science is part of a cosmology which it helped to create. It seeks to reduce every level of reality to simpler and more fundamental laws. The image of this cosmos is a hierarchy, with one simple cause at the apex: the ultimate ideal law, God or the Big Bang. As science investigates the universe, however, the evidence indicates the exact opposite. Nature does not reveal reductionistic laws but regions of ever-increasing complexity. From the subatomic realm to every part of the universe, greater and greater complexity is revealed. The fractal geometry of chaos theory infinitely recedes, like the wheels within wheels of the chakras mentioned above. It is no accident that atoms

have been compared to galaxies. Whole new worlds may exist in grains of sand. In such a vibrant view of the world it is not surprising that zodiac patterns of the sky appear in microcosm upon the earth.

In a sense the older, rougher idea of giants was more accurate than the beautiful visions of the perfectly ordered and symmetrical cities of Plato and St. John. Eventually the geometric temples of the urban-cultures became too neat, too non-intuitive, too structured, too measured, and not in accord with the haphazard and capricious character of nature. The "sensitive chaos" of the Great Goddess was a better image of the universe than the "divine order" of that of her son. Gaia's giants, the builders of the natural order on earth, worked with change and with the dragon-like dynamic patterns of polarity on the earth, rather than by trying to impose a rigid order upon it. It is precisely nature's flexibility and irregularity which allows it to adapt to ever new arrangements in the ongoing process of life.

Plato's culture was a slave culture so we know who would have built the streets and canals of his beautiful city of Magnesia. The avenues stretching away from the homes of the aristocracy in Britain, France and America were also built on slaves, unequal trade, feudal relations and war, so they too were not an expression of the divine on earth. The straight lines at Carnac, the grid cities of the Greeks and Romans, the *sacbes* and pyramids of the Maya, the linear *ceques* of the Inca and the ceremonial roads of the Anasazi at Chaco Canyon eventually brought too much order, too much control. They were no longer in sympathetic resonance with the flux of the cosmos as held in the minds of the people. The reason for the ultimate collapse of these cultures is still a mystery, but it may lie in this area.

The Hopi Landscape Temple in the Grand Canyon or the Yavapai sacred land in the Red Rock Country may ultimately tell us more about the nature of the sacred than the Great Pyramid or a Gothic cathedral. The sacred groves where the Druids worshipped, Baboquivarai of the Pima, or the many unadorned but labyrinthine sacred mountains of the world may be among the best expressions of the divine on earth.[2] The sacred is not a heavenly city of the future. It is not a divine order imposed upon a profane world. It is not a hero who is going to step in and save humanity from the actions they are committing. The sacred world is the world we live in right now.

## QUANTUM GIANTS

Quantum theory has already been mentioned several times in this text. The theory evolved when certain phenomena of physics occurred which could not be explained by classical mechanics. We shall attempt a simple definition here. In physics, a quantum is the smallest, indivisible amount of energy by which a given system may change. The theory is about the nature of reality in which atoms and molecules are composed of even smaller elementary particles. Examples include neutrons, positrons, neutrinos and quarks. Such particles escape mechanical causality by virtue of their unpredictability and by the inseparability of the physicist from the act of observation. The scientists, their perceptive modes and bodies, are made of the same properties as the things they are trying to examine. It is probable that the nature of the elementary particles—whose numbers are proliferating wildly—is determined by information and relationship rather than by a material nature.

In the "quantum field" version of the theory the elementary particles are in a constant state of formation and dissolution within the background state of a universal quantum field. A field in this sense is a region of space characterized by a physical property. For example, a neutrino is continually oscillating between energy and matter, between manifest and unmanifest, between the "implicate order" of the whole and its own "explicate order." Attempts to measure this quantum state are conditioned by the observer who is in turn conditioned by the quantum level. In a sense, material processes are structured by the information impressed upon them, but the information itself is changing as the structures of the world impress themselves upon it. Quantum theory establishes a two-way flow between the previously considered separate orders of mind and matter.[3]

The strictly Newtonian, Cartesian view of the world saw mind as quite distinct from matter and had no room for elementals, giants and dragons. But science has since expanded its horizons and the current quantum theory of matter may yet find room for them. Through the ideas of scientists like Jean Charon, Rupert Sheldrake and David Bohm the world has been shown to reveal endless orders enfolded within each other. Bohm's idea of an implicate order applies equally to matter and consciousness. They cannot be treated separately. On a deeply formative level it can be said that both mind and matter are the explicate forms which emerge out of a common generative order.

The mind is capable on some deep quantum level of literally moving matter, and matter reveals the information and intelligence we impute to mind. Energy and matter are the same thing. Carl Jung died before he could prove his hunch that the unconscious psyche is the same phenomenon as matter, where one is observed from within and the other from without.[4] Indeed it may be that the gathering of bacteria and cells which form our bodies is human consciousness and intelligence. Every one of the microorganisms which form our body cells was developed millions if not billions of years ago in the earth's chemical soup. Through cooperation they found that they could make more efficient use of their environment. What could be better for a cell than to combine with other cells to form an organism that through the sum of their intelligences could give the cells locomotive abilities, constant ambient temperatures, food supply, longevity and protection?

Consciousness and intelligence are characteristics of everything on the planet and in the universe. These traits infuse and energize every single thing. Let us say that flicks of energy-matter, which exist only for a nanosecond and can never be recorded, have intelligence. If one does not choose to accept that, then the burden of proof shifts to the disbeliever to establish when exactly consciousness and intelligence *do* enter into matter and existence. What is the turning point, the critical mass, the miracle that accomplishes the presence of these qualities? Consciousness cannot simply be imposed—*deus ex machina*—on top and outside of life. Quantum theory indicates that all life—animal, vegetable and mineral—is in a sense, conscious. Whatever the elemental forces of life are, it makes sense not to separate them from the intelligence of mind. We are as much a part of the giant forms of life which surround us as those forms are a part of us. However we look at them through the filter of our cosmology—as giants, dragons, cells or quantum orders—we are all a part of the living, self-regulating organism called Gaia.[5]

Quantum theory is therefore a modern way to directly approach the subtle orders of a universe of energy, form, intelligence, interconnection and relationship. The ancient peoples achieved this with their concepts of giants and dragons. The world came to them as an immanent and revelatory experience in which they did not make mental category distinctions dividing the cosmos into "ideal" and "gross," "spiritual" and "material." They thought with what this text has been calling the "body-mind," the inherent intelligence of the total of a person's psychosomatic being. In this perceptive mode, a people's cosmology and language might distinguish a hundred kinds of snow, a hundred shades of green vegetation, but it will not make categorical distinctions between mind and matter. In this mode it is as impossible to make distinctions of "real" and "unreal" as it is to distinguish between the world "as it is" and the world "as perceived." Each conditions the other.

It is possible to be caught in our paradigms, our worldviews. In the Western world the dominant institutions treat mind and matter as quite separate. Mental filters, which are created to give order and meaning to the world, can actually prevent people from experiencing the world. As Einstein said, "It is the theory which decides what can be observed." Minds can become fascinated by the repetitive acts and fixed order created by a cosmology in order to locate and define the holders of that worldview. But going around and around in this way makes people unable to tap into the pure creative essence of the mind which could give a way out. The order says, "This is how it is," and people forget it was made by their own ideas.

Giants, circles and dragons suggest change, flux, interaction, complexity, connectedness, consciousness and creative force. Grids, blocks and pure geometry suggest rigidity, fixity, reductionism, separation and even stagnation. If the full implications of quantum theory permeated the Western mind, then there would be a radical shift toward holistic thinking and a living ecology of body, mind and spirit.

## GIANTS IN THE LANDSCAPE

Plato sought a canon of measure which could accurately reflect a standard believed to be present throughout creation. This measure would encodify the ideal celestial and terrestrial dimensions and could be represented in music, geometry and the proportions of the temple. It was the realm of pure *psyche* or mind. However, the numbers found underlying the world were not whole numbers, but "irrational" ones. These could be expressed only as a proportion or as a ratio in relation to something else. The human body—*soma*—was never perfectly expressive of the canonical proportions of the Cosmic Man. Neither was the flower, the tree or the spiral shell. The canons were ideals that never quite existed in the complexities of time and space.

But who are the giants if they are not forms given to the underlying patterns Plato was trying to grasp? Perhaps Plato and subsequently Western thought went in the wrong direction by insisting on mathematics and geometry as the *only* underlying pattern. What if a different emphasis had been made? What if a more organic and complex concept—one from biology rather than mechanics—had been accepted as the model for the new world-determining cosmology?

Such complexity is acknowledged in Chaos Theory when it comes to standardizing figures for the radius, diameter and the circumference of the earth. Geodesic measures have been found, but by what criteria? Chaos theory answers in its classic question: how long is the coastline of an island? If a large map is taken and the coastline measured say with string, one answer is arrived at. If a pedometer is pushed around the island, another answer is obtained. But should the measuring be done at high tide or low tide? If the surface of every boulder, stone or grain of sand which lies on the coastline is measured around—the snail's measure—another answer, far exceeding any of the above, is reached. Mean circumferences of the earth are thus obtained by a standard which hardly does justice to the contours which make the earth's surface the ideal place for the diversity of life which exists upon it.

In Chapter 6 on Earth Spirit we spoke of a group of dowsers suggesting as many different configurations for the pattern of energy in a place as there were dowsers. They were all right, just as all the answers to the length of a coastline are right. It all depends upon the dimensions selected. It all depends upon the cosmology. Plato was describing an inner state of mind in his canons patterned upon heaven, not a reality. The patterns he chose derived from philosophical and mathematical ideas that were going around in his day. Unlike the Milesian philosophers who thought about the cosmos in terms of an ever-changing, complex dynamic of natural forces, Plato and the Pythagoreans thought of the cosmos as being created by mathematically perfect underlying laws. It only remained to understand those laws, reduce them to their simplest expressions, and then through application of mechanics everything in the universe could be brought into the ideal cosmic order. Western science developed along these mechanistic lines until the advent of relativity and quantum theory.

Let us look at weather as an example of seeing something from different perspectives. The weather as a system of fronts and pressures is a science, but as the play of giants it is alive, immediate, predictable and unpredictable. Is this not the game meteorologists play? In Chaos Theory it is said the beating of a butterfly's wings in the

African savannah creates a hurricane in the Caribbean. The subtle variables and influences which create weather are so many that in the final analysis an unknown force, as capricious and unquantifiable as consciousness—a giant—could as well be making our weather. Nothing in meteorology can be reduced to simple, underlying laws. We can see patterns, but we can never know for certain if it will rain.

As they are, mathematics, mechanical and now quantum physics have taken us to the place where we are able to comprehend the marvelous complexities of the living organism in which we all live. Without them we would not have the scientific understanding of the world that we now possess. But each science is only one giant among many. We need them all: biological, elemental, geometrical, mathematical, celestial, chaotic, quantum, if we are to think about the cosmos as a whole, living and immanent presence.

Instead of reducing the world to simple parts, giants allow parts to unfold in all their beautiful uniqueness and splendid complexity. Wherever people have retained the cosmology of giants for describing the natural forces of the world, the same principles are at work as those present in the great temples, but without being set into fixed laws. The world of giants is active and dynamic. It is contextual, connected and conscious. It puts psyche and soma together. The giant lived on or under the sacred mountain, but the mountain did not need adornment nor a temple which made divine law explicit. The mountain itself contained and expressed all the complexities of the divine.

This does not prevent us from applying mechanistic and scientific understanding to the world. Newton was right, things will fall at a constant and quantifiable rate of acceleration. But the understanding must include all the variables, including the position of the observers and the contents of their minds. This is precisely the point which Western medicine is beginning to acknowledge, that the mind helps to heal the body. It is precisely the point quantum physics has reached as it moves into the unquantifiable relativity, interconnectedness and infinite possibilities of the sub-atomic realm. Environmental science tells us the same thing when it speaks of every system in the living biosphere balanced in an ever-changing but harmonious and cooperative interrelationship with one another.

We are not separate from life. We are always a part of the subtle web of interrelationships which make up life. We are never "merely an observer." Our cosmology determines our health, science, environment and every one of our relations. We now understand that the mind is not separate from the body. The mind *is* the body. The body is the mind. Spirit is not separate from the world. Spirit *is* the world. The world is spirit.

In Brittany there is, or was, scarcely a community that did not look on the sea with feelings of respect and dread. They had a giant, the *Bugul-Noz,* the Night Shepherd, tall and alarming, whose task it was to patrol the shore. He could hurt those who resisted his warnings of darkness and storm, but he would only strike them in their own

interest. This elemental giant knew how long the coastline of Brittany was. He knew how ferocious were its cliffs and rocky shores. He knew the distances of the seas and the time of day and night. For those in boats, giants were a good way of thinking about it all. Maps, weather forecasts, chronometers, sextants, compasses, the trappings of the temple, will never replace the hand that taps on the shoulder and says, "It's time to go home."[6]

## GIGANTIC THINKING

Giantic (*Gaian-tic:* "of the earth") thinking incorporates the sacred proportions and canonical laws naturally. They emerge from out of the process of life. They cannot be prescribed. An inspired musician will play the numbers of the sacred laws, an intuitive architect will build in canonical ratios, an instinctive dancer will naturally move with the "music of the spheres." If they were to play, build or dance to formulae, the result would be formal and contrived.

Giantic thinking allows for deviation, anomaly, idiosyncracy, capriciousness—the power which taps you on the shoulder, and says "go home." It allows for the differences prevailing in nature where nothing is repeated twice. Yet, giantic thinking recognizes that which unites. Nature constantly provides examples of co-ordination, symmetry, synchronicity, cooperation, distribution, networking, a regulation of self-interest and collective interest. Out of apparent chaos comes the new order. Out of polarity, plurality, flexibility and imbalance comes the new balance. The dynamic polarity of life is perfectly expressed in symbols as the eternal struggle of two dragons around a central circle or sphere.

Giantic thinking includes what each of us thinks about all of this. Our body-minds are flowing with new strategies for living just as the trees, the amoebas and the microbacteria are. The myths and beliefs of one's cosmology will define these somato-psychic strategies. Out of mind unfolds matter, and out of matter unfolds mind. What a person thinks will define the next move: will it be for integrated or destructive self-interest? Are people in the world to use it as they please, or do humans need to be in constant cooperation with it? Does nature really give humans a choice? The answer, ultimately, will not mean much for life on earth, but it will mean a lot for human life. Is nature in the image of a rigid, mental pattern—a god with a pair of compasses—or is it in the image of the womb and the ever-changing flux of the Great Cosmic Goddess of all?

Nature deviates constantly from any attempt of ours to mechanistically describe it. Newton created a perfectly workable model for observable matter in the universe when he composed his laws. Einstein found other elegant models which worked for more complex things. Chaos and quantum theory are doing the same for even more complex things. The Native Australian songlines work on these levels too. They include from the outset both intelligence and form, psyche and soma. Giants, as impulsive and inconsistent individuals working within the quantum orders of energy and matter, intelligence and form, are excellent ways to think about the world. They cannot be roped down, despite the efforts of Swift's Lilliputians.

Giants turn around the sky. Giants move in the currents of earth and sea. Giants live below the earth, shaping stone. Giants move in the wind and thunder. Giant forces live in the animals, the trees, the plants, the bacteria, the mitochondria and the chloroplasts. Giants move through the cells of our being. Giants are the generative order out of which unfolds the sublime play of energy and matter, mind and body, each unfolding and enfolding each other. On occasion, people are inspired to move with the dynamic of these powers and create something which expresses them. How is this done? If it cannot be imposed from without, how can it move us, move through us, and emerge from within? Answers to that question are offered in the third part of this book. ▓

### CHAPTER TWELVE

# THE SEXUAL FACE

# OF THE LANDSCAPE

In the beginning there was only the giant Grainya whose name means "Old Woman Sun Stone." She walked here, she walked over there and she grumbled about how bare the fields were. "Why, there's nothing growing here but rocks!" she would say. One day the wind got so tired of her grumbling it said, "You needn't complain, Grainya. I've made the perfect bed for you."

"What do you mean?" said Grainya. And the wind told her about a place where the fields were soft and billowing with all kinds of life. It sounded so good she walked over to the place. When she got there she said, "Huh, I don't think much of this. It's just a pile of old rocks!" There was nothing at the place except an entranceway to a cave. But it did look quite inviting. Grainya crept inside to sleep. Then the wind got busy.

Soon she was wide awake. "What's going on?" she cried. Outside, something was coming. It crept up over the land, getting brighter and brighter, until it burst over the horizon in a flash. It flooded the inside of the cave with light. Grainya was lying on her back with her legs open wide and the sun felt good on her insides. She rubbed herself. That felt pretty good too. So she rubbed herself some more, and soon the fields outside were getting green and standing up full of people.

Soon some of the people came up to the cave and said, "Thank you, Old Woman Sun Stone. We were tired of lying around in the darkness. To honor you, we shall make places all across the land where the sun can shine in to you and give us life." That stopped Old Woman Sun Stone from grumbling.

After a period of time spent creating some of the features of the Red Rock Country, the First Woman, Komwidapukwia, felt a longing and went to a cave where the water dripped all the time. This cave is honored today by the Yavapai and the Apache peoples. The name of their first deity means "old woman medicine stone." She entered the cave before dawn and lay down exposing herself. At the moment water dripping from the spring touched her, it was illuminated by a beam of light from the rising sun. That is how she became pregnant. Eventually she gave birth to a daughter.

When the daughter came of age Komwidapukwia told her to go to the cave before dawn and do what she had done. The daughter obeyed, but soon returned home saying that the water and the sun beams turned away from her. Komwidapukwia said she knew how to fix that and the next morning she went with her to the cave. She lay down on top of the young woman. At the moment the sun rose and the water dripped the old woman quickly moved aside. So sun and water entered the daughter thinking she was their wife. In this way the grandson, Sakaraka'amche, was born and he could claim Sun and Cloud as his father. The First Woman and her grandson were responsible for all the features of the Red Rock Country.[1]

It is very difficult to know from the mass of European folklore and tradition what has a truly ancient origin and what does not. It has been the practice to create an ancient origin for any new religion, custom or law in order to legitimate the needs of their proponents. As a result of all the overlays we do not know what the beliefs of the European Neolithic peoples were. But from examples of people who have maintained their indigenous myths and beliefs, as in the Yavapai story given above, it is possible to imagine what they may have been, and create the first story of the European giant Grainya.

*The dolmen and menhir at Les Pierres Plats, Locmariaquer, Brittany*

## PRE-CHRISTIAN SEXUALITY

An area which has been almost entirely obscured is sexuality. Nature-cultures tend to have a far more direct experience of and an open attitude toward sex than those whose culture has been overlaid by a moralistic religious belief.

The cave and the rock, the dolmen and menhir, the mountain and valley, the serpent and the egg, the mound and stone circle, are all just too delicious to ignore as the landscape giants' equivalent of human sexuality. In Chapter 3 it was suggested that an elaborate sexual symbolism accompanied the mounds, dolmens and standing stones of the Neolithic age. Huge undertakings were carried out to express in the landscape the actions concerning fertility on the part of the cosmic giants. In order for the forms of earth and stone to resonate with the appropriate cosmic powers they were built to resemble the giants. This involved visual images: the male menhir, the female dolmen; shapes such as serpents, circles, triangles and spirals; alignments to stellar, lunar and solar events; and geometry, measure and relationship. New Grange is a classic example of all the above.

Similar patterns representing the fecund power of the cosmic giants were expressed in the great mounds and pyramids of the Americas. The Ohio Serpent Mound with the egg between its jaws is the microcosmic sperm fertilizing the cosmic ovum. At Chichén Itzá in the Yucatán Peninsula the builders of the great pyramid designed it with a giant stone serpent, descending from top to bottom of the stairway. On the equinox, this serpent is picked out by a triangular pattern of sunlight and shadow, thus making the serpent come alive as the sun moves along it. This extraordinary piece of engineering represents the return of Kulkulkan, the Mayan Quetzalcoatl, and honors the fertile union of earth and sky.

We have no reason to doubt that people were as fascinated by sexuality in the past as they are today. The human race has become very successful at reproducing itself and has become the dominant species on land. It could be argued that this has occurred precisely because of its sexuality. It developed an erotic organ over the entire surface of its body, though it had to give up the advantage of warmth and protection that a thick and hairy skin provided. It selected the unusual feature that the female was more or less always ready for mating. At the same time her breasts became larger than needed for purely biological reasons. The male saw no problem with that. Sexuality provided the body with hormones and the capacity for ecstatic pleasure to ensure the travails of reproduction were more than compensated for. The female had no problem with that. The clitoris appears to be the only bodily organ ever developed for the sole purpose of pleasure.

Humor, pleasure and sexuality always entered into the rituals of life. Judging by existing nature-cultures, ancient peoples were not as solemn about their rituals as are some Westerners today. The sexual innuendos of today's Pueblo Indian clowns during the most important ritual occasions of the year would seem out of place inside a church. The landscape of the Southwest is full of Native American names which translate as "Woman Who Spreads Legs Wide," "Big Penis," "Maiden's Breast" and "Tight Buttocks." These in no way diminish the sacred nature of the landscape or the importance of properly honoring those places. The Hopi say the world is held in balance by their prayerful and playful observation of the yearly cycle of ceremony. People who open to feelings and intuitions at ancient sacred sites report that they seem to access genetic memories of what actually happened there, such as people coupling by the thousands in emulation of the Avebury giants.

In Europe, male autocracies in ancient Greece and Rome focused on giant phalluses, sometimes decorated with wings and carried through the streets. Later, the phallic connotation of the Maypole, the bigger the better, was obvious enough to be noted with distaste by many a Victorian parish priest. But over centuries of persistent, punishing, puritanical teaching, sexuality went the way of the giants and the Great Goddess: down and out of sight. Today's religious processions in Europe and Latin America are likely to provide only a sterilized glimpse of the goddess, herself now a product of immaculate conception and her son a sexless product of virgin birth.

## SILBURY AND AVEBURY

In few places has Neolithic sexual symbolism been so elaborately developed and described as at Silbury Hill near Avebury in Wiltshire, Britain. The enormous mound, 130 feet high, was begun around 2660 BCE. The remains of plants and insects in the foundation show that it was laid during the first week of August, the feast of Lammas that signifies the start of the harvest season. The hill was subsequently added to only at that time of year.

In *The Silbury Treasure*, Michael Dames presents the startling idea that Silbury was made to dramatically illustrate the birth of a child by the Harvest Goddess—the bounteous form of the Great Goddess. The hill was placed and shaped so that during the Lammas full moon in early August, the play of moonlight over the contours of earth and on the water in the surrounding ditch successively illuminated the birthing process of a pregnant woman. For viewers on the hill slopes, the child emerged head first from out of the womb of the hill. It turned over in the course of the night to drink milk from its mother's breast. By dawn, the reflected moonlight spread outwards due to the carefully sculpted shape of the ditch:

> The genius of the Silbury designers is nowhere better demonstrated than in this use of moonlight and shadow to create an apparent outward flow of fecundity, where birth moved from the specific monumental Mother to the Mother in her extended form—the land awaiting the start of harvest.[2]

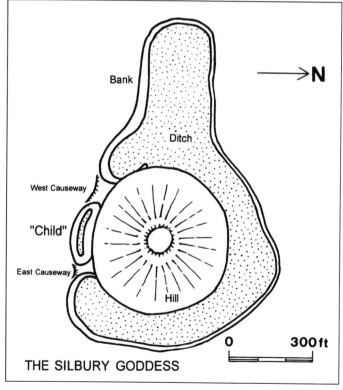

Bank

Ditch

West Causeway

"Child"

East Causeway

Hill

→N

0    300 ft

**THE SILBURY GODDESS**

In his second book, *The Avebury Cycle*, Mr. Dames expands his vision to include all the sites of the Avebury/Silbury area in one great "annual sequence

of human rites" aimed at bringing the Great Goddess to her "maximum vitality." We describe this more fully in our chapter on rituals. The Avebury cycle demonstrated "a common language valid through vast stretches of time and space, because it was based on people's common experience of the human body."[3]

We do not know if Mr. Dames' vision of the past is "as it really was." But it fits with what we know is there in the landscape, what has been handed down in folk tradition, and what sits well in the hearts and minds of those seeking an earth-honoring tradition today.

Even archaeologists who decline to interpret findings have noted the consistency of the sexual themes at Avebury. The stones of the extant eastern avenue are paired as lozenge and rectangle, which could represent female and male reproductive organs. The only two stones remaining of the western Beckhampton

*Paired "female" and "male" stones in the avenue at Avebury. 4th millennium BCE*

avenue are known as the Adam and Eve stones. Nearby West Kennet Long Barrow duplicates the shape of the goddess's womb as depicted in Neolithic sculptures. Darkened dolmen barrows and underground stone chambers might have been used by local women as birthing chambers. There they could bring forth from their wombs into the womb of the Great Mother.

Within the great circle of Avebury itself—originally 99 or 100 stones in an earthwork almost a quarter of a mile across—there are two smaller circles. In the center of one stands the remains of a "cove," stones arranged in a U formation. In the center of the other was once the tallest, most phallic stone on the site. It was known as the "Obelisk." This was the spot which later became the location for the village Maypole. This has led to the inner circles being known as the Women's and Men's Circles.

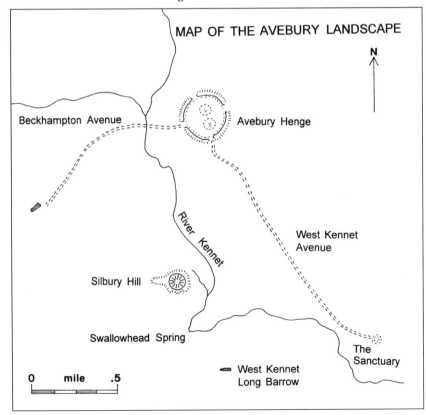

MAP OF THE AVEBURY LANDSCAPE

N

Beckhampton Avenue

Avebury Henge

River Kennet

West Kennet Avenue

Silbury Hill

Swallowhead Spring

The Sanctuary

West Kennet Long Barrow

0        mile        .5

People mated at sacred sites in order to enact and thereby demystify the great mystery of life as it was felt moving through the cells of their own bodies. They could see and feel the same processes taking place in the natural world. By representing these forces in the gigantic stone formations and mating within them, the ritual-sexual act revealed more of the purpose and meaning of the Great Round. It drew the power of life into the people themselves. It connected them to the greater forces of life, within and without.

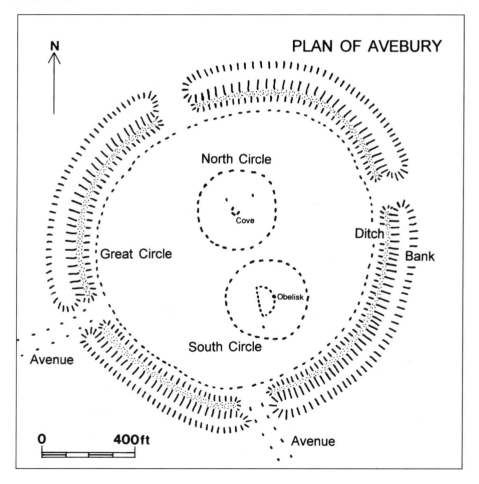

**PLAN OF AVEBURY**

N

North Circle

Cove

Great Circle

Ditch

Bank

Obelisk

South Circle

Avenue

0    400ft

Avenue

Sometimes the sympathetic magic being enacted was appropriately immense. The two sinuous stone avenues each extending for over a mile from the giant henge at Avebury not only represent serpents around the cosmic egg but also the open legs of the Cosmic Woman ready to be fertilized. Is Avebury a depiction of the female's reproductive system with its two fallopian tubes leading from the ovaries to the womb and vagina? The implanted egg of Silbury Hill lies in their center. The tall "Obelisk" in the Men's Circle may have represented the head of a phallus—or a sperm—activated by the annual men's procession to the henge. The men would have wound their way into the open mouth of the henge. A procession of women meanwhile would make their way along one or both of the avenues and on to the fertilizing uterus or cove of the Women's Circle.[4] A Neolithic couple mating within this sphere would understand that they were duplicating the cosmic mystery and contributing to the continuing presence of creation.

If Mr. Dames is anywhere near correct in his description of the drama of Silbury Hill as the goddess giving birth, then we can be certain that at other times and in other places equally dramatic depictions of the sacred-sexual cosmic giants creating life were made. The dolmens penetrated by shafts of sunlight, the total cosmography of Avebury, the pyramids of America uniting earth and sky, the serpent pattern of light on the pyramid at Chichén Itzá, provide insights as to how their makers connected themselves through sexuality to cosmic forces.

## GLASTONBURY

*T*he area of Glastonbury in south-central Britain gives rise to an amazing number of legends for such a small region. If you like magic, it is

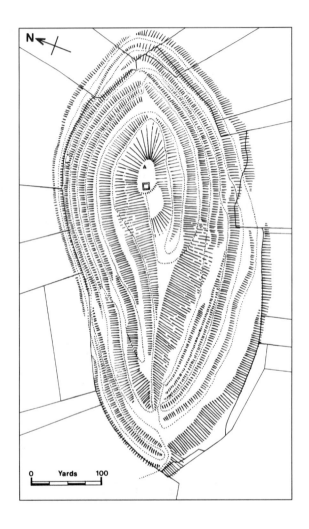

*Plan view of Glastonbury Tor. The dotted line traces the path of a labyrinth around the terraces. The straight lines are modern field boundaries*

the Isle of Glass, also known as Avalon where the souls of the deceased passed on. Only Druidic initiates could navigate through the mists. It has the fairies' magic mountain known as the Tor. It features the miraculous conversion of Christ's blood to the healing red spring water known as Chalice Well. It is where the staff of St. Joseph of Arimathea planted on Wearyall Hill turned into a thorn tree that blooms at Christmas.

If you like earth mysteries, there is the St. Michael Line that runs from Cornwall directly through the Tor and on to East Anglia. There is the spiral maze or three-dimensional pilgrims' labyrinth on the Tor. There is the Zodiac in the surrounding countryside as well as the complex geomancy of the Abbey. If you like traces of energy, there are unusual magnetic power points, multiple ley lines and reported UFO sightings.

If you like history, there is the thread connecting Cerridwen's cauldron in the Underworld beneath the Tor with the Quest for the Grail. The Arthurian knights lived in Camelot at nearby Cadbury Castle. The chalice from the Last Supper was said to have been brought to Glastonbury by Joseph of Arimathea. If you like physical evidence, there are the sacred Druid oak trees of the giants Gog and Magog, a burial place alleged to be that of Arthur and Guinevere, the ruins of the oldest and most powerful Abbey in Britain, and the omphalos or cosmic egg-stone on the Abbey grounds.[5]

This background shows the rich diversity of the region. But for the purposes of this chapter on sexuality in the landscape, we will concentrate on the hill known as Glastonbury Tor. Over the millennia this magnificent natural feature has been sculpted, terraced and honed to resemble from above, or below, the female vulva or yoni. The gigantic form set in the center of a level plain is explicit. Once, the way to the summit or the center was around the spiral paths which cover every flank. Two paths now lead directly to the summit. The longer, more gradual route follows the ridgetop which in the female parallels the erotic route from in front of the clitoris to the vagina. Many women have reported feeling sexually aroused when walking or standing on this ridge of the Tor. It is as if their own cliTORis is being stimulated. Men have reported feeling sexually aroused on the Tor without realizing that they are entering the gigantic yoni of the Mother of All. They also could be responding to the phallic tower of St. Michael the dragon-slayer, which is all that remains of a 13th Century church.

Like Silbury Hill, the Tor is representative of the Great Goddess. It includes both male and female. The encircling paths form spirals; these could reveal awareness of the processes of reproduction. The guardian of the Tor, Gwynn ap Nudd, the dragon whom St. Michael crushed, is to the earth goddess as sperm are to the egg. From the foot of the Tor gush two water sources, the Red and the White Springs.[6] It is natural to associate them with menstrual and seminal emissions. There is a legend that the Tor is the entranceway to the Celtic Underworld, a cosmic womb. The dead are taken in there and the living are born there—or rather reborn, as the Celts believed in transmigration of the soul.

The Christians saw Avalon as the home of the Holy Grail, originally a symbol of the Great Goddess. On the site where it was said the oldest Christian church in the world was built, now on the Glastonbury Abbey grounds, later Christians dedicated a church to St. Mary. The grail is to the Celtic cauldron of plenty as St. Mary is to the Great Goddess as the "oldest church" is to the place of birth and origin. The sexual imagery of Avalon is evident, in that it is the home of the goddess, the home of seminal dragons, and the home of the entrance to and exit from the Underworld.

The Tor used to be a major site for the fire-festival of Beltane on May Day. Fires were lit in line-of-sight across southern Britain, with the Tor being one of the most visible locations. This was a fertility feast, marking the bursting forth of the earth's plenty in blossom. It celebrated the cloaking of the earth with the green mantle of the Earth Goddess and the Green Man. People took this festival as a time to mark their own fertility. "Bale-fires" would be lit. Couples would form trust bonds by clasping hands and promising love and commitment to each other for a year and a day. After such "handfasting," they would leap over the fires naked as a public proclamation of their pledge. People left the fire-lit areas and mated lying on the earth. Some tales say that women could choose the men of their liking for this event, as in the American custom of Sadie Hawkins Day.

Additional evidence for the sexual nature of the landscape at Glastonbury comes from a giant form of the Mother Goddess giving birth. From above or from the surrounding plain—especially from the south—the ancient Isle of Avalon resembles a reclining woman. The form includes the Tor as one breast, Chalice Hill as her pregnant belly, Wearyall Hill as an outstretched leg and other undulating forms as segments of her body. Between her legs at nearby Beckery was a holy well dedicated to Bridget, the original Great Mother Goddess of the Irish. Some authors have suggested that in the giant Glastonbury goddess figure, Beckery or Bride's Mound forms the head of the newborn infant.[7] The Christians placed the phallic shape of the Abbey Church at the entrance to her vulva.

We can be sure that ancient peoples did attach sexual symbolism to their sacred sites. The character of the Tor as breast or yoni is sufficiently obvious. To this day the military pilots who use it as a landmark call it "the nipple." But we cannot be certain of the exact nature of ancient peoples' perceptions, intentions and ceremonies. Like the Glastonbury Zodiac, evidence for the ancient character of the Tor or the Isle of Avalon is not as important as the fact that people today are projecting onto the landscape the

contents of an earth-spirit cosmology. They are again thinking in terms of giants. This is all part of an important growth in the awareness of the intimate connectedness between humans and the landscape. In the same way as the intelligence of the cells in our bodies relate to us, people now seem to be responding to the living body of the earth with actions which are appropriate to Gaian consciousness.

## THE CERNE ABBAS GIANT

**H**t the village of Cerne Abbas in Dorset, southern Britain, there is an extraordinary figure cut out of the turf to expose the white chalk underneath. Known as the Cerne Giant he extends for 180 feet up the hillside. In his right hand he brandishes

*Glastonbury Tor from the west. (Photo by Joseph Zummach)*

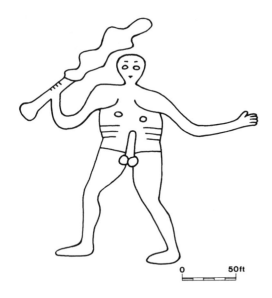

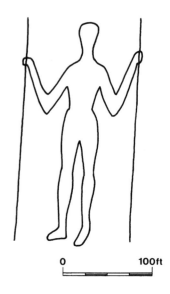

a knobbly club 120 feet long. A huge tumescent penis runs up from a pair of splendid testicles to the navel. It was believed a woman would have no difficulty in conceiving if she sat at the appropriate spot on the giant's anatomy. Some said lovemaking would have to happen there if the case was particularly dire. After all, the infertility problem could exist within the man. Until the last century the village put up its Maypole in the prehistoric enclosure above the giant, known as The Trendle, "circle."

The custom of putting up and dancing around a Maypole on the first of May is an ancient one. Where the event is still practiced it is usually accompanied by

the choosing of a May Queen. In pagan ceremonies—which may or may not be ancient—she is matched by the Stag King. As mentioned in the Glastonbury section, May first is the ancient festival of Beltane which means Bel's, Bale's or Baal's fires. It is the cross-quarter day between spring and summer. Traditionally a time of purification and putting animals back out to pasture, it is a fertility festival which, in some places, followed a time of ritual abstinence similar to Lent. The roots of the festival are obscured in the depths of European prehistory, but we can be fairly certain the erecting of the Maypole preserves a ceremony which ultimately finds its meaning in the symbol of the tree.

A reasonable interpretation of the Cerne Abbas giant is that it represents Hercules and dates to the time of the Roman occupation of Britain. The figure has parallels in Romano-British art and would have been associated with fertility. Hercules is often shown with a knotted club, and the extended left arm almost certainly was draped with a lion skin, another emblem of the hero. However a British equivalent of Hercules was Ogma, the Gaulish Ogmios, who also had a club. As an ancient giver of language and transporter of souls, Ogma was a culture-hero with giant status. His name includes the sound found in names of other giants—Og and Gogmagog. Local tradition favors the giant interpretation rather than the giant-killing Hercules.

Other fertility gods can also be associated with the club, such as tree deities, the Bachlach, the Fachan, Gruagach or Wild Herdsman. Whatever the case, whether the giant is extremely ancient or just very old, whether it represented one of these deities or all of them at different times, the association with sexuality and fertility has always been evident. It seems ancient people almost had a compulsion to depict sexual themes on a gigantic scale. This pagan practice continued in Medieval times with the parading of giant effigies. The phenomenon continues today with carnival events like Mardi Gras.

At one time there may have been many more hillside figures in Britain such as the Cerne Abbas Giant but they are now lost because the turf was not regularly "scoured" to retain their outlines. One that remains is the Long Man of Wilmington in East

*(Above) The Cerne Abbas giant. Dorset, Britain*
*(Right) The Long Man of Wilmington, Sussex. Although the figure may have an ancient origin, its present form dates to the 19th century*

Sussex. He towers 230 feet from toe to crown. Local lore says the giant is a silhouette because his flesh, blood and bones went to create the earth, rivers and hills. The slender Long Man is stylistically very different from the Cerne Giant. And the crude Cerne Giant is very different in style from another famous hillside figure, the Uffington White Horse in Oxfordshire. This gigantic figure is shown in Chapter 7. The horse was sacred to the Celts. Their feeling for the animal emerges in the abstract lines of the giant figure which flows gracefully across the hillside. The Uffington Horse is likely to have a first millennium BCE origin.

## THE GODDESS AND THE GREEN MAN

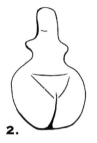

R eaders will recall throughout the book we made the point that the body is the means by which we describe and measure the world. Early people did not make a distinction between the world and their experience; they perceived each in terms of the other. They thus encountered the world as a living "I." Judging from Paleolithic and Neolithic art, men saw themselves in terms of the animals they hunted. Women saw themselves in terms of their reproductive abilities. But men are almost entirely absent in art. Where they do appear it is often in the guise of an animal or engaged in a hunt. Woman are depicted frequently in art but sometimes with sexual features so exaggerated that the head and other extremities disappear.

It is important to realize that men are not absent from these representations. They, in fact, occur as often as women do. It is the Great Goddess, who contains both feminine and masculine, who is represented over and over again. The goddess is the Great Round. Her mysteries of transformation are supremely inclusive. The cosmic template—when perceived in terms of the ever-changing dynamic of the womb of the Great Goddess—encompasses the All. She is the giant body in which unity, creativity, relationship and meaning can be found. There is no giant so vast who can geometrically encompass what the Great Goddess can cosmologically encompass.

As the urban-cultures developed, the son of the goddess literally grew up and took center stage. The Great Round worldview was gradually replaced by a linear one. Cyclical rebirth was changed to the linear concept of future temporal salvation. Group consciousness shifted to focus on the individual. Nature-cultures based on body-mind wisdom shifted to urban-cultures based on separation from nature. These changes often caused people to experience a lack of meaning and connectedness.

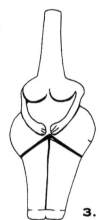

Throughout history attempts can be seen to recover the primal unity embodied in the cosmology of the Great Round. Many of the great world mystery traditions reveal the wish to restore the Great Goddess or Great Round cosmology. Isis weeps for her son and dismembered lover Osiris. Cybele searches for wounded Attis, Inanna for Dumuzi, Aphrodite for Adonis, Ishtar for Tammuz, Magdalene for Jesus. All the men are wounded, dying or dead. Only when masculine culture and energy is accompanied and infused by the sense of birth, love, death and rebirth of the Goddess can men find wholeness in the transformational mysteries of life.

In the Native European Tradition this mystery was represented by the passage of the god around the seasonal cycle. He waxed and waned with the vegetation cycle of the year. The tree became his symbol. He was known variously as the Green Man, Dionysus, the Horned God, Cernunnos, the Stag King, John Barleycorn. Remnants of him can be discerned in the

---

*Neolithic goddess figurines.*
(1) *c.* 4,500 BCE, 15cm, Bulgaria
(2) *c.* 6,000 BCE, 7cm, Bulgaria
(3) *c.* 5,000 BCE, 22cm, Romania
*After Marija Gimbutas*

elemental giants: the nature spirit Pan, the club-carrying Gruagach, the one-legged Fachan, the axe-wielding Bachlach, the farm-helping Fynnoderee and the forest-dwelling Wild Man. He was born from the goddess, he loved the goddess and he died in her arms. Only through this cycle could the linear character of masculine energy be incorporated into the cyclical nature of the feminine. Only through death and rebirth, through continuation of the information stored in the genetic coding of DNA and RNA could all be transformed and live on within the cosmic body—the womb of the Great Goddess. ▨

## CONCLUSION TO PART II

In this section on Energies and Patterns we have looked at giants as earth energy, dragons and serpents. We have followed the patterns created by dowsers, geomancers, architects and geometricians. We have described natural patterns shaped into zodiacs, chakra systems and landscape temples. We have critiqued attempts to build the ideal temple, city and cosmos. And we have given examples of the sexual face of the landscape in forms which juxtapose giant female and male symbolism.

Movement and form characterize the nature of the giants we have presented in Part II. Chapters 6, 7 and 8 center on movement, revealing that the earth is alive with fluctuating patterns of energy. Animals, dowsers and geomancers sense these energies and work with them. Giants and dragons are a good way to think about them.

After looking at prehistory and history, we propose a renewal of our worldview, where body and mind, matter and spirit are reunited into earth spirit. Where the earth spirit is kept free, it moves powerfully under, on and above the land in what all cultures have conceived as dragon currents. The elementals reveal this dragon power moving in tree and rock, fire, wind and water. Reclaiming the dragon will return to Gaia's children the cycle of rebirth, the balance of polarity, the joy of sensuality, the immanent sense of life, and the practice of the ancient serpent wisdom.

Form is the principle on which Chapters 9 through 12 center. Sacred and fractal geometry teach us that certain ratios and measures are bridges between dimensions. They hold true for the miniature and the gigantic dimensions. The microcosm and the macrocosm meet in the center, the human mesocosm. The same principles and proportions are found in natural landscapes such as Sedona, intuitively constructed formations such as Neolithic stone circles and the Avebury goddess, and intentionally proportioned structures such as cathedrals. We shall see that these proportions are occurring to this day in places where the concept of giants is again stirring.

# INVITING THE GIANTS TO AWAKE

CHAPTER THIRTEEN

# ACTIVATING THE

# BODY-MIND WORLDVIEW

he was pleased with all he had done to prepare for the gathering. As he approached the camp-site he noted with deep satisfaction that there was enough space and shelter for everyone. Fires were burning, pots were bubbling. Under the tall trees he could see people already gathering for the ceremonies. As yet there was no drumming or dancing.

He turned to go to his tent and get ready, when something in the sky caught his attention. He looked up, and saw two giant figures sailing like kites through the sky. They had on ceremonial dress. The huge figures were painting each other. They applied pigment to each other's brightly colored bodies with flat wooden sticks.

His composure shaken, he hurried to his tent. It was reassuring to see the cauldron steaming in the center. He began donning his costume. Just then there was a commotion at the entranceway. He was about to ask who was there, when the two giants from the sky entered. He felt he knew who they were.

"Who are you?" asked one of the giants. He was taken aback by the question, but stammered a reply. "Wh-why, I'm Jack Atkinson, professor of linguistic-biology."

"Brain on the table," said the other giant. Jack was too stunned to say anything. It sounded like a command. Before he knew it the two giants were beating a pulpy brown dough on the table with the paddles they had been using to paint each other.

After a while, the brown dough assumed a definite shape. It was spherical, hollow and fibrous with a bulge at the bottom out of which came two stems or root-like protuberances. "This is no good," said a giant, and picked up his paddle again. Jack was alarmed.

The giants beat the fibrous dough until some pulp came out of it. They then beat that until it separated into some dross, which they discarded in the cauldron. What remained formed a shape, like the first, but lighter and it only had one root. "Oh, this is good," said a giant. They prepared to leave.

"Hey, wait a minute," said Jack. "What do I do with this?"

"You put the one with the two roots inside this one." The giants left.

Jack picked up the two fibrous masses carefully. It didn't seem possible that the first one would fit inside the other. But it did. The two stems pressed together to fit inside the one stem. Jack was delighted. Now I can go to the dance, he thought.

"Now I can fly with the many-colored dragon!" he cried out loud.

_____

hen Nicholas, one of the authors, had this dream he was working on this chapter. The giants seemed to want to make something very clear to him: "Brain on the table!" Reflection suggested that the two-stemmed brain represented the right and left sides of the brain working separately. The single-stem brain represented all of the brain working together. The indications were that the separation of the logical-analytical and the feeling-intuitive hemispheres was an overlay due to cosmological and linguistic tendencies. It was not due to any deep biological cause. In the body-mind they would find union. The body-mind is the inherent intelligence of the total of a person's soma and psyche being.

## THE BODY-MIND INTELLIGENCE

The sensitivity of the body to subtle and complex phenomena is of an extremely high order. The senses of smell, touch, kinesthetics, spatial dynamics, rhythm, sight, sound, are fundamental to body intelligence. A cat hair, a thousandth of an inch in diameter, can be felt by the tongue and grasped by the fingers. Animals have a highly developed set of body communication functions. The body moves in space: to the right, to the left, up, down, ahead, advance, retreat. The actions are unequivocal. Basic sounds are universally recognizable throughout the animal world. Humans have built their languages upon the signalling systems of nature. No doubt this is the "linguistic-biology" said to be the study of the "professor" in the dream.

The body intelligence of those living close to nature is rooted in the direct physical experience and perception of the surrounding world. Such people are capable of differentiating thousands of scents, tastes, intonations and movements and determining their quantity, distance, depth and dimensions. Edward T. Hall calls these "high context" cultures, where the learner is in, of and on the thing being learned, much as a farmer's child learns to plow.

As humans moved away from the natural world an alternative mode of perception arose. Language and mental categories developed which were suitable for the abstract relations and concepts of urban life. This became especially pronounced as writing developed. The written word gave categories of thought a "real" existence independent of the realm of the thinker. In place of the direct sensory perceptions of the body-mind, the new worldview was intellectually sophisticated but perceptually limited. Edward T. Hall calls these "low context" cultures, where learning occurs through words and reason instead of through experience. Such cultures tend to reify—in religion and in law—black or white mental categories. They reduce nuances and codify responses. Low-context cultures split the mind from the body.

Over the past few millennia the concepts of a dualistic, urban cosmology, separate from the direct perception of nature, have deeply determined the lives of people in the West. Yet this history is very small compared to the life of humanity, the life of primates, the life of mammals, the evolution of cells and bacteria which constitute the total physiology of life itself. The history of Western civilization is but a veneer on the surface of the life of the body-mind. And it is this life with which we are interested.

The life of the body-mind has its roots in the source of primordial creativity. Its DNA has unfolded itself for a billion years or more. It encodes information on the growing edge of creation. The body-mind is neither mind nor matter, neither individual nor species. It is the result of the generative force. It is the unfolding of the wave of life throughout time and space, generation after generation.

As an example of the nature of this generative force we take the view that life is more than chance combinations of atoms and cells. To organize the parts which collectively enabled a bird to fly, or the human brain to form, there was an order which brought together the parts not by chance, nor by simple adaptation to external stimulus, but through intelligence. This intelligence is inherent throughout the multitudinous constitution of the universe.

The challenge is to listen to the intelligence of the body. This intelligence has never been forgotten, merely overlaid. The challenge is to be open. The challenge is to change our worldview, which means literally to change our minds. "Brain on the table!" The giants in the dream beat the brain on the table like dough. It seems hard to change. But the body remembers.

By relaxing into the body, by relaxing into the ground of our being, it is possible to reconnect to the intelligence of life. In this state, consciousness is connected to matter and matter to consciousness. There is nothing one has to do, but relax. There is no belief, religion or discipline to practice. In this state of openness and direct perception of the world it becomes natural to again think in terms of giants. The mind as body, the body as mind, creates an experience where the surrounding world begins to come alive. If this awareness of immanence is maintained, David Abram writes: "Birds, trees, even rivers and stones begin to stand forth as living, communicative presences."[1] The intelligence of life inherent in the forms of earth will move us, move through us, and inspire us to create a new multi-colored world. Then we can fly with the many-colored dragon.

In these next few sections of this chapter, as throughout Part III, we will be looking at ways to reconnect with the wisdom of our bodies. We encourage the reader to use dreams and visions, personal myths, meditation, intuition, ritual, music, art and action on a daily basis. We especially encourage walking, swimming, touching animals, camping, making love outdoors, just watching the sunset or the stars—to be all that you are when you don't have to do anything. Through these means we can discover the ways in which the giants speak.

## THE POWER ANIMALS

Animals are extremely helpful when it comes to reconnecting with our body-intelligence. Animals are central to the spiritual practices of nature-cultures. Animals are often perceived as the "allies" of humans. In Siberia and the Americas an animal may be seen by shamans in a vision. From then on it will be their ally or power animal. In Australia the animal ancestor may enter or "inspirit" the child in the womb. This determines the dreaming, the songs and thus the territory of the child when it is born.

Animals have power because they are at one with their being and their environment. Nothing obscures their instinctive wisdom. It is often apparent from birth. In contrast the human child has to be taught almost everything. The power of animals comes through the body-mind and their direct connection to the creative source. An animal is hungry. An animal is strong. An animal is fast. An animal flies, swims, sees for miles, hears over vast distances, smells a thousand scents. A human may have these qualities, but an animal *is* them. Animals provide a set of meanings, a vocabulary that is direct and real. Human meanings and vocabularies in comparison are abstract and separate from the source. When Native American or Siberian shamans seek an animal ally they are seeking for direct experience of the creative, generative source. When we ride horses, swim with dolphins, observe the birds, enjoy our pets, we move into the world of pure being.

Although it is hard to know what the ancient European traditions were, animals always played a vital role. Giant bulls run with deer, horses, woolly rhinoceros and mammoth across the cave walls of Paleolithic Europe. Whole bodies of sea eagles, dogs, gannets, geese, otters, salmon, oxen and deer were carefully deposited in the dolmens of the Neolithic era. Fantastic, otherworldly animals scroll their way across stones, mirrors, swords, brooches and other ornaments of the Celtic era. These later appear in the ornament of churches and documents.

*Bulls from Lascaux, France. circa* 17,000 BCE

In existing nature-cultures around the world the animal powers are very important. In them we find the sense of letting go and journeying into the chthonian world of the body. We discover the sense of relaxing into the pure experience of being which we share with our animal allies. It is possible that the shaman's journey to meet the power animal is a journey into the cellular memory of physiological evolution. The animal powers emerge from out of the body-mind as Jung's "archaic remnants." The body remembers those powers and through journeying into the archetypal realm it is possible to recall the somatic experience of every era, even the most archaic.

In the poetry of the Celtic tradition which has survived, there is a sensibility for such timeless omnipresence. The poems attributed to the 6th Century Taliesin often refer to metamorphosis. His "I am" refrain may sound like boasting, but with the poet we travel through every elemental and animal realm, and end up asking "who is the speaker?" One of the poems in this vein, *The Song of Amergin*, originates from deep within the Native European Tradition.

> *I am the wind upon the sea,*
> *I am a wave upon the ocean,*
> *I am the sound of the sea,*
> *I am a stag of seven points,*
> *I am a bull of seven fights,*
> *I am a hawk upon a cliff,*
> *I am a teardrop of the sun,*
> *I am the fairest of blossoms,*
> *I am a boar of boldness,*
> *I am a salmon in a pool,*
> *I am a lake on a plain,*
> *I am the mound of poetry,*
> *I am a word of skill,*
> *I am a battle-waging spear of spoil,*
> *I am a God who fashions fire in the mind.*
> *Who but I knows the secrets of the unhewn*
> *dolmen arch?*[2]

## CELLULAR GIANTS

The wisdom of the body-mind derives from inherent intelligence. How convenient it is not to have to think in order to walk, to run, to catch a ball and, once learned, to ride a bike. These things are "automatic." They reveal the wisdom of the body. Then there is the intelligence responsible for the working of the liver, the digestive system, the reproductive system or the nervous and the immune systems. And what about the brain? We know only a small amount about how the brain works. It is as though every brain cell is connected to every other cell in a neurochemical bath to create a system far greater than the sum of its parts. The intelligence for the function of all these systems seems to reside in the cells. White blood cells have motivation, memory and cognition. They perceive, learn, store information and communicate. The DNA within the chromosomes of the human sperm and ovum cells contains the information for the unfolding of the entire body.

Our bodies are organized combinations of cells, bacteria and other elementary life forms. These have been on the planet for billions of years. They could be said to constitute the life of the planet. As one species predominates for a few million years, then another replaces it, it is the cells which continue to exist in different permutations of form. All cells exhibit intelligence, contain information and can be said to possess cognition or mind. DNA is a repository of the whole history of evolution. It contains its information in a way that allows it to converse with the whole of its environment.[3]

The process by which cells maintain themselves, and especially how they have reproduced over millions of years, creates within us feelings and images. The microscope was invented only recently but the monsters of our dreams and our art have always had an alarming resemblance to the microscopic world. Users of hallucinogenic chemicals have reported vivid voyages into their own internal cellular structure. It may be that the earlier asexual and parthenogenetic processes of reproduction by the cells are recorded in our creation mythologies. The first goddesses give birth out of themselves in the same manner as simple life forms. Rapid cell development took place when the atmosphere changed and the amount of sunlight increased—dragons and giants brought fire to earth. These events were encoded in cell memory and may be responsible for stories like those at the beginning of Chapter 12. All these cellular processes are extremely similar to images which are found in art and in the landscape. The same images are found around the world because they are experienced as fundamental to the mystery of life. We may speculate that spirals record inner awareness of the structure of DNA.

The dolmens, henges, geoglyphs, songlines, serpents and pyramids in the landscape are in proportion to the body of the earth as individual cells are in proportion to the human body. To the cells of our body which constitute and maintain us, and through whose intelligence we have cognition and mind, we are giants. And to us, the world is a giant. Acting on that awareness we humans make representations of the giant in which we sense ourselves to live. Microcosm talks to mesocosm talks to macrocosm. The Universe communicates through the Underworld of the cells, the Middleworld where the humans live, to the Overworld of the cosmos—the realm of the giants. "As below, so above."

Wishing to express the mysterious felt connection between analogous dimensions, humans feel the urge, even the necessity, to create temples on a gigantic scale. Constructed by us on the body of the earth, these temples are in relation to the world as our body cells are to us. As we are giants to the cells, these landscape temples are cells to the giants. They appear on earth as the work of the Giants of Gaia. They are the connection to the next, greater dimension. "As above, so below."

If this view is correct, then in some way humans will always be impelled to express their awareness of multi-dimensionality on a gigantic scale on the body of the earth. Where is this happening today? Where is the inherent wisdom of the body-mind expressing itself on any scale? One answer may be in the renewal of interest in the landscape as a medium for the artist. Artists like Richard Long and Andrew Goldsworthy have taken ice, rocks, twigs and leaves—the elements of the natural world—and sculpted them into forms. These by their very nature might be gone with the next wind, rain or change in temperature. Some of their undertakings have approached the gigantic. Many magazines have pictures by an artist or an advertising company that use a country field to express themselves. The urge to write large in the landscape is very strong indeed.

There is a renewal of fascination with turf mazes. More labyrinths have been built in the last decade than at any other time in history. Running a labyrinth speaks directly to the body-mind and helps integrate the right and left hemispheres of the brain. Many people remark, upon seeing a labyrinth for the first time, that it looks like a brain. Build one in your own backyard and run it from time to time!

People are seeing huge figures in natural land forms, and are often compelled to enhance their form. Zodiacs are appearing. Chakra systems are being conceived of and built. Giants are being born. There is a perennial fascination in dinosaurs. Creatures the size of football fields are being etched in the vegetation of a passing season. In the tradition of the presidential figures of Mount Rushmore, a mountain is being sculpted into the head of an Indian in the United States. Such "artistic" endeavor is deeply satisfying, often intuitive, and sometimes quite beyond the conscious motives of the artist.

If it is true that cellular intelligence makes itself felt in humans in the same way as humans feel they are to the earth, then gigantic figures in the landscape are deeply expressive of a unifying principle of life.

At times, attempts to render this expression will be extremely strong. The conscious mind is struggling to articulate the inner experience of the body-mind. Movies like *Field of Dreams* have depicted this experience. In following inner feelings, in building a baseball field, the "giants" came. *Close Encounters of the Third Kind* revealed a similar experience. To the participants, the mountain which appeared in their dreams—and which some had to draw or sculpt—was the World Mountain, the omphalos on the cosmic axis. The encounter with "giants"—in this case extra-terrestrials—subsequently followed. The movie *2001: A Space Odyssey* had a similar theme. The appearance of the monolithic block heralded a "giant" step in evolution. Silbury Hill and the American pyramids and desert geoglyphs may have been built from a similar sense of imminent transformation. This was not imposed from above, from an intellectual idea or a belief, but from biological and genetic information emerging from within.

As artists, as creators, we shape the figures of earth, then forget it is we who made them. Another age comes along and attributes them to the gods. It makes sense to do that. We are the gods and goddesses to the cells. The planet is a deity to us. The figures on the surface of the earth appear as messages to and from the gods.

Today we are faced with cellular transformational issues. The DNA and RNA are always changing. Few species remain static on the planet for any length of time. AIDS threatens human life on a cellular level. Information in the immune system is somehow becoming confused. It is as though the quantum level of information inherent within the cells is changing. We also know from scientific research that the earth itself is changing. In the past the earth has regulated its homeostasis in order to maintain life. With the impact of human life on forests, deserts, oceans and the atmosphere the earth might do that again. It is on these levels that one of the latest manifestations of micro-macrocosmic "artistic" expression in the landscape can be addressed.

## THE CROP CIRCLES

The crop circles have struck a chord in the human psyche. Somehow, these swirling, cryptographic forms created overnight in the grain fields of the planet have made a deep impression on the mind. Thousands of people, chiefly in Britain, are drawn to go and walk inside these splendid swaths in the grain. Others are motivated to create these enigmatic symbols, or to imitate whatever is creating them. Every summer many people are "called" from their beds and out into the night.

Many of these symbols have appeared in conditions of absolute mystery. Some of the most spectacular formations—hundreds of feet across—reveal no sign of their makers. Their origin is imputed to UFO's, to angels, devas, fairies, meteorological vortices and humans. However these symbols are made, they confront us with a question of meaning.

Most crop circles fall into classifiable formations. At first, in the late '70s and '80s, there were simple circles. Now there are combinations of circles, rings, bars and other appendages, usually arranged in a linear pattern. Crop circles evolve from year to year, but "pictograms" composed of circles connected by bars are the most common form. All rings and circles are

*Crop circles from Britain, 1990 – 91. The body of the "Mandelbrot" on the upper right is 163 feet long*

formed in a swirled or spiral manner. Each year, some formations are on a gigantic scale and are magnificently complex. The crop circles can easily fit into our description of giants in the landscape. But what are they saying?

The symbols in the fields look like encoded information. Geometry is clearly an issue for their makers. Some resemble esoteric symbols. An atypical one depicted a figure from chaos theory, a Mandelbrot Set. The crop circles' resemblance in shape and scale to ancient sites has often been commented upon. The majority of them appear in the vicinity of Avebury and Stonehenge.

There are almost as many theories about them as there are crop circles. Working on the hypothesis that they are expressive of the awareness of analogous dimensions in the universe the crop circles could be about transformation. The perception of shifts, by the human body-mind, on every quantum level of the intelligent structure of the universe is directly transferred onto the landscape in a time-honored fashion. A canvas is not enough to express the analogical information on a sufficiently gigantic scale. Living crops express the nature of the living content. Due to awareness of AIDS the current sense of cellular transformation is strong. The advent of the virus and of the circles is similar in their time frame. Other microorganisms, animals and planetary

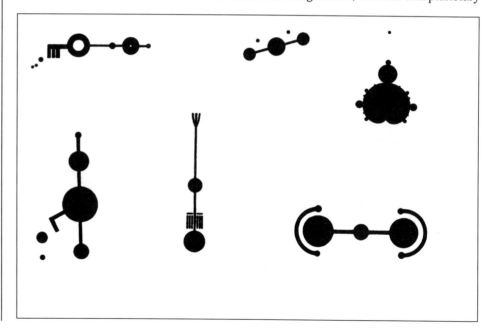

biosystems are also undergoing transformation due to human effect upon the environment.

The crop circles may represent the urge to reconnect with the multi-dimensional body within which we live. The perception by humans of giant forces moving through the world leads some to consciously manifest those forces in huge patterns on the earth. In the same way as children draw worlds in the sand the crop circles are drawings by the "finger of the giants." The analogy between cells and humans and humans and the world suggests that by working on one we affect the other. In the same way as AIDS or cancer is a malfunction within our bodies, attempts to heal our presently cancerous relation to the world finds expression in gigantic forms. Healing the earth, as giants, means healing ourselves, as cells. Healing ourselves, as cells, means healing the earth, as giants. "As above, so below."

Whether or not the giants of the environment, the cellular world, humans and the crop circles can be connected in this hypothesis, it is reasonable to assume that the crop circles find meaning through their congruency of gigantic symbolism, the living fields of grain and the sense of a transformational change resonating throughout every level of our world today. Considerable energy is involved in the creation of the crop circles. Many of the circle makers would be unable to consciously describe their motives. Many circles are intuitive manifestations of the inherent wisdom of the body-mind. Many commentators on the phenomenon speak about it in terms of world change. The enigmatic symbols in the grain speak to us as the monolith in *2001*, the mountain in *Close Encounters*, and as the Ohio Serpent Mound, the geoglyphs of the Nazca, the megaliths and other landscape forms did to their makers in their day.

## GIANTS AND GAIA

When the activity of an organism favors the environment as well as the organism itself, then its spread will be assisted; eventually the organism and the environmental change associated with it will become global in extent. The reverse is also true, and any species that adversely affects the environment is doomed; but life goes on.[4]

This is the opinion of James Lovelock, the scientist who first propounded the Gaia Theory. He is unhappy as a doom and gloom merchant. It is with reluctance, only following through on the logic of the theory, that he adds the second sentence. For him, and other biologists, the emphasis is on "life," the whole life of Gaia, rather than just on humans.

In this book we suggest that giants are a powerful key to the future for humanity. Giant thinking is a way of being with the forces of nature which makes them accessible, alive, meaningful and comprehensible, yet leaves them mysterious and unpredictable. Giant thinking is being aware of the communion of all life. Giants suggest the crossing over of psyche and soma, of mind and body. They suggest the use of the whole being in relating to the world. Giants suggest thinking in terms of analogous dimensions: atomic, molecular, cellular, somatic, planetary, galactic. They suggest an alternative way of seeing.

Whether the giant is seen as a weather front, in clouds, as a quantum potential, as the collective body of types of cells, in a river, a mountain chain, as part of a cosmology, as myth, or as a pattern determining the forms of life, it is a part of Gaia, the being in which we all live. Our mind-body wisdom is a part of Gaia also. By relaxing into the body, by allowing the body to speak, by honoring the life force, by living intimately with the forms of life as one body to another, then our activities will favor the environment as well as ourselves. Nature does not oppose self-interest when it is also collective interest. The future is in our hands. The giants will help if called.

In Doris Lessing's novel *Shikasta* the world order has collapsed. Humanity is reduced to bickering remnants, apportioning blame. Then a remarkable thing occurs. The giants return. The giants take the people away from the remnants of civilization into places which appear wild and remote. There they encourage the people to build. The people grumble and complain. Then they notice something. It seems that the stones with which they build fall into place. The work is effortless. The roads plan themselves. The people build with the environment rather than on top of it. They are working with the grain of life rather than against it. From out of the wisdom of their body-minds, in harmony with the forces of earth, the basis for a new way of life is rapidly established. After a while the giants take the people out onto the hills. They look down on the cities they have created. They see that without plan or pattern they have built in the shape of a star or spiral—figures emerging from out of the intelligence inherent in all of life.

This is the awareness of the giants that lives in our bodies. They come to help, to assist in creating figures of earth. They are the world-shapers that are also ourselves. Every culture has giants. They make the world. When we relax into our bodies, into the unfolding of the wave of life, we know them. They move in us. Life is our co-creation. ✻

### CHAPTER FOURTEEN

# RE-ENCHANTING
# THE LANDSCAPE

As I entered the jungle at Cobá I knew something was going to happen. A snake rustled through the leaves. Roots and creepers pried apart the stone walls of the ruins. The voices of the ancient Maya seemed anxious to burst forth again and reveal the mysteries of life. On the summit of a small pyramid I could see other vegetation-covered mounds. The city must have been huge. Standing above them all was the partially cleared great pyramid of Cobá.

I made my way to the great pyramid. The steps were steep. The day was hot and humid. It was hard going. Halfway up, a huge, luridly colored iguana basked in the sun. Its spines looked dangerous. As I came closer it nonchalantly moved to one side. On the summit the canopy of the sky met the round horizon of the jungle. I began to sing. It was a song that honored the power of Spirit and of Mother Earth.

Then I began to dance. My body moved to the right and left. The words of the song seemed to dictate that the part to spirit moved to the right and the part to the earth moved to the left. I became ab-

sorbed, taken up by the dance. But the words felt clumsy. The melody felt out of place.

I began altering the words and the melody. The rhythm maintained itself through the movements of my body. Soon I was just singing "Spirit..." to my right, "Earth..." to my left. The energy of each coiled around me... "Spirit...Earth..." I could see the swirling shapes of the dragons of earth and sky... "Earth...Spirit..."

The words were still not congruent with my experience. My dance began to slow. The words fell away. Their essence was contained within my dancing body. Soon it was all contained within my hands, which came to rest together above my heart. The energy of the dragon currents merged. Earth and spirit became one within my heart. My body rippled with the new information. Every cell was touched by the awareness of unity. Nothing remained the same.

---

Here in Part III the search for giants takes an applied approach. It will help if the reader feels personally drawn into the special realm that magic weaves. The authors invite the reader to feel and sense directly the path to finding giants. For this reason, "we" in the text will now include the reader as well as the authors.

## ENCHANTMENT AND MAGIC

The English word "magic" comes from the Persian word for sorcerer, one who practices wizardry and enchantment. Enchantment means to be under a spell, charmed, bewitched due to the chanting of magical words. Sometimes this is made to sound evil or at least foreign to Westerners, but that is not so. Magic is not evil any more than technology is; it depends on its use. Magic is no more foreign than flying; it depends on how we look at things. People who remain close to nature, whether they live now or lived five thousand years ago, practice an understanding of the way natural things work which is now called magic. Magical technology was common knowledge at one time and can be again.

Magic happens every day, if we look for it and allow it into our awareness. Magic happens to everyone, if we are open to it and allow it to manifest for ourselves. Magic can be direct and clear, not at all complex or mystifying. Magic *is*, all the time, all around us, just like electricity or magnetic fields or solar radiation.

In this book we use the word magic to mean the wondrous and unusual, the amazing and fortuitous workings of the universe. We use it to mean serendipity, synchronicity, luck and coincidence. Carl Jung wrote extensively on the value of these things.[1] We also use magic to mean the sensations and knowledge we get from intuition, sixth sense, gut feeling, lucky guess, split-second decision, corner-of-the-eye experience, heightened awareness, mental telepathy, knowing the future, and communicating with non-humans.

Magic happens when we know who is calling before we answer the phone or when a book falls off a shelf and opens to a page with just the information we were looking for. Magic happens when exactly the materials and tools we need to make something are the ones at hand. Magic happens when we are traveling and make a wrong turn only to come upon a most exquisite spot we would have missed otherwise. Magic happens when we sit next to someone on a train or plane whose interests mesh with ours in an uncanny way. Magic happens when we are feeling low and receive a spontaneous hug from a child.

People who want to recapture how it must have been to live magically do the most ordinary things. They talk with their animals and their plants, all of which thrive. They conduct their daily routines in a conscious way that is laden with alchemy: transforming gloriously colorful fresh food from garden to table to nourish those they love, exercising to revel in the sinuous, energy-building ability of the body, taking scraps and residue from nature and making personalized gifts, drumming and dancing to impress special occasions upon the body's memories.

In this book we have built a matrix of information and understanding which straddles the line between the ordinary and the magical. The book verges on the enchanted world of spirits and forces that are beyond the reach of the man-made. These include dragons which are depicted in all cultures, goddesses in megalithic chambers, giant forms in the landscape, spirals of coiled power leading to the inner world, sacred springs and wells where healing is reported, myths of superhuman giants that turn out to have a basis in fact. By now the reader is aware that one's worldview dictates whether something will be considered technology or magic, real or unreal. The authors have tried to create a bridge to cross easily between those two paradigms. We have also tried to go further and delete the dualism altogether.

## THE EYES AND EARS OF MAGIC

The hearth was the source of every human art. Around the fire spirit, people gathered to tell the first stories, draw the first pictures, sing the first rhythms, dance the first steps, perform the first dramas. Hearth is a metaphor for home and family. All the arts of the hearth, and all the sights and sounds of prehistory, can be used to re-enchant the landscape. Let us concentrate on two of them.

We see giants with the inner eye. Many examples throughout history tell of people seeing this way. At the end of the last Ice Age, people living near the Pyrenees Mountains in present-day France and Spain explored natural caves and "saw" shapes on the walls which they enhanced with charcoal and pigment. They saw the haunch of a large bison, the nose of a horse, and drew or carved the rest of the animal around that existing form. Later, people built gigantic representations across the landscape. They drew serpents, horses, lizards, giants and constellations of stars, following the shapes they "saw" in the terrain. During the Renaissance, Michelangelo "saw" the giant figures that wanted to emerge from each slab of marble he sculpted.

We hear giants with the inner ear. Listening with the inner ear connects us with others who heard this way far back in prehistory. Sound, rather than actual music, is common to all cultures through the use of drums, bells, flutes, chants and droning instruments such as the didgeridoo and tamboura. Many cultures have realized that chanting is the root of enchantment. Flutes spiraling, bells ringing, chants repeating, drones imitating earth and animal sounds—these are ways of expressing natural energies felt by all people in all parts of the world. Music is what feelings sound like.

Drumming is the sound of the earth, the heartbeat of creation. Drums require trees to give up wood and animals to give up skins. Drums carry sound far into the air but also carry sound and vibration far inside the body, affecting the central nervous system. Drumming to a very fast beat, as shamans do, transports the drummer to an altered state. In that state we can hear with the inner ear. Non-present drummers seem to join in, and exquisite chanting fills the space. Sometimes the drumskin seems to disappear and it feels as if we are making the sound by beating the air itself. Visions occur, leading the drummers off to places important to each person, as happens in dreams. At the right moment, all drumming stops simultaneously, spontaneously. The magic of the sound giant seems to be present.

Since the elements of nature are constantly putting out their sound and music, it makes sense they would enjoy receiving some back. Animals stay very still when someone plays music to them. They like classically ordered compositions such as music by Bach. All the elements appreciate their own sound mirrored back to them. Gurgling like a stream, cawing like crows, moaning like the wind, buzzing like bees, answering a whippoorwill, whispering like grain, clacking like stones, crunching like nuts, roaring like waterfalls—these sounds help us to actually sense elemental essences while we communicate with them.

## THE ENCHANTING LANDSCAPE

Once upon a time all land was alive and sacred and all plants and animals interacted with humans. The land, plants and animals are still out there and willing to continue this arrangement. It is up to us humans to put ourselves back into the enchanted landscape. As mentioned in earlier chapters, what we see out there depends on our heritage and the beliefs which form our worldview. Our mindset tells us what to look for. Every culture calls on magical external guides that match their unconscious, their dreams, their ancient images. The outside environment of a people therefore matches their inner landscape and way of thinking. When people can sense magic they can see giants, animal allies, dragons and elementals in the landscape.

All we humans have to do to re-enchant the landscape is to become part of it. Magic happens when we cooperate with nature instead of dominating it. If there are ants all over the patio, we can burn and spray and poison them, often failing to dislodge the creatures even though we are the giants. Or we can tell the ant elementals the difficulty it creates for the small children who play on the patio and give them a week to find another habitat. They will be gone in seven days.

If we need to move some rocks we can shove them around with mechanical devices, cursing and sweating all the while, or we can sit with them the evening before the big move and talk about what is needed. We can send an image of their new location and what the final arrangement will look like. There are energies which find rock-moving easy and they will help if asked. The next day even a ton of rocks will move easily and arrange themselves in a fine design. Sometimes a time warp seems to occur and we cannot recall doing each step of the process but we can see that it is all accomplished.

Weather witchcraft is part of landscape magic. Wind and rain and snow, clouds and thunder and hail are the giants of the sky. They need to live somewhere but they are not particular about which patch of sky and earth is home at the moment. If the soil is parched and the crops are wilting, these giants can be summoned to give a drink to the earth. If much planning has gone into preparing an outdoor ceremony that needs warm, dry weather, these giants can be asked to play elsewhere. When treated this way they may tease but seldom ruin an event.

Often when we feel depressed and abandoned, full of sadness or despair, we unconsciously go to the landscape giants to pray. We sit on a hillside or under a shady tree or beside a brook and ask for help in getting through the problem. When we get some relief we might attribute it to God, Goddess or a saint who answered our prayers. We could as well attribute it to the elementals of hill, tree and brook who listen intently to any genuine plea. They are very powerful and can offer their essence, which is free and whole and functioning perfectly within its nature. If we cannot get out of the city, we might gravitate to a park or the backyard to let the magic of nature flow through us. If even that is not possible, we can touch a cat or dog, a houseplant or fresh vegetable, stone or wood in order to connect to the universal *chi* or life force that flows through all things.

Magic pushes up against our ordinary borders and is waiting just on the other side. We are constantly sending and receiving on more levels than we might realize. Whenever we wish to broadcast out or beam in more consciously, we do it by giving time and space for that to happen. For example if we want to practice what Michael Roads calls "talking with nature," we can sit or lie quietly by a tree, rock or river and begin communicating.[2] At first, our left brain will whirl thoughts and messages claiming their importance upon our attention. We ignore these, noting that we can get back to them later. When the inner chatter subsides, the two-way communication can begin. We might notice a faint new awareness or a different sensation—a good sign to keep going.

Almost certainly we will get a new thought which has not appeared on our inner landscape before. When we get a new thought, it is probably a mixture of the outside essence from an elemental along with inside building material from our mind. Sometimes it is not earth-shattering, but subtle and gentle and therefore missable. If we have focused concentration on a particular question the answer might seem encoded like a Zen koan, yet it usually has a direct meaning if we search for it. If we have not asked a question, the thought we get might be quite unlike our usual ones, and then we know we are in touch with the elementals directly. Then we know we are in the enchanted landscape.

## FINDING PLACES OF POWER

The enchanted landscape seems to be more concentrated in certain areas. Let us examine why that might be so. The next sections will look at two concepts which have become popularized by earth-energy investigators: power spots and sacred places.

Power sites are places where the earth's energies concentrate to a noticeable degree. This power is measurable as extra amounts of electromagnetic energy, as underground veins of mineral ores, and as underground water which comes to the surface in wells, springs or pools. Power spots also contain invisible energy, not always detectable by modern gauges but sensed by living things in the vicinity. Plants, animals and humans all tend to congregate at power places.

Although places of power occur in all climates on all continents, they have several features in common: hills, water and rocks. A power place is either at the base or top of a hill, with other high ground around but not completely surrounding the site. There is natural fresh water, usually a spring. The sun can shine directly on the spot. Groves of trees and ample rocks marked such sites originally. Natural rock formations can be in the form of a cliff, free-standing boulders, a mountain, stony brook, cave, or grotto.

Plutarch, a biographer who visited Delphi in the century of Christ, wrote in *The Decline of Oracles*, "Men are affected by streams of varying potency issuing from the earth. Some of these drive people crazy or cause disease or death; the effect of others is good, soothing and beneficial." This notion is expressed in language: "malaria" means bad air, while "Buenos Aires" means good airs.

Some power spots have a beneficial effect on people who go there, some have a detrimental effect, and some have both. A site such as Stonehenge, which is known to have both positive and negative effects, might be storing the desirable and undesirable events that have happened there over the ages. We can surmise that the outcome depends partly on what feelings and intentions the visitor brings there, since a power site often intensifies the person's own condition.

Recently a few of us got permission from English Heritage to go into the center of Stonehenge after hours. We took rattles and flutes, feathers, blue corn meal and earth from other sacred places. We held a quiet ritual in the exact center. Then we each concentrated on the part that most appealed to us. Terry stayed with the altar stone, Joseph the bluestones, Marcia the Heel Stone, and Nicholas walked in and out of the trilithons. The sun set brilliantly, sighted between two stones of the outer circle. Stonehenge was benevolent that evening.

A site which has mostly negative effects on people has unpleasant geophysical concentrations. An example is Chaco Canyon in New Mexico. Chaco has high ionization due to one of the highest rates of lightning in the world, quick shifts in barometric pressure, and earth-generated radiation from uranium. This may be an apocryphal story, but an example of Chaco's geopathic nature is the collapse of the cliff face behind Pueblo Bonito when archaeologists removed the pahos, the prayer feathers, which were there. The authors have personally witnessed violent extremes of temperature, sandstorms, misplaced wallets, accidents, domestic violence, and even a death during a ceremony in the canyon. The best advice is to approach such places carefully, listen for warnings, and heed whatever you sense.

A site which has mostly positive effects on people is best described by sensations rather than in geophysical terms. The air "feels good," the waters massage the body curatively, the hills feel friendly, the place seems safe. People feel uplifted and purified and sometimes have transforming visions there. An example is Canyon de Chelly in Arizona, only 100 miles west of Chaco Canyon. The atmosphere is radiant, giving. Spider Rock generates energy, in contrast to the draining quality of Chaco. People want to return to Canyon de Chelly time and again, sometimes feeling compelled to go and renew themselves.

Places of power have been accurately identified through the ages by people from the locale. Their experiences have been passed down in storytelling and myth. Usually the tales describe physical sensations and emotional changes that occur in people standing at a power spot. The senses become heightened: the skin tingles or becomes chilled, the ears hear unusual sounds, the eyes perceive swift-flying lights. The elements of nature also seem to be obeying silent commands. Leaves move when there is no wind, rocks moan, water talks, birds hush, an insect pauses like a hunting dog ready to flush a covey.

Emotionally, people report that power spots intensify their feelings. Positive power spots make people feel peaceful, joyful, intuitive, ethereal and insightful while negative power spots make people feel nervous, fearful, upset and angry.[3] The following true story happened to Marcia, one of the authors, and exemplifies a negative or geopathic place.

## THE POWER OF PARICUTÍN

he central mountains of Mexico were having rainy, cold weather when I arrived for a month of intensive Spanish study. I joined a special busload of other adult students for a weekend trip to some rural places in Michoacán. I sat next to a blond woman about my age who laughed at how I wangled my way onto the already over-booked excursion. Her only name was Katya. Within 50 miles, she had so gained my confidence that I admitted to having "special powers" and strong connections to ancient Celtic times. Katya was certain I was a Druid witch, a fellow practitioner of wisecraft.

The hours on the bus passed in metaphysical talk while bouncing over uncountable potholes. After a succession of small hamlets and remote mountain passes, the bus stopped in the middle of nowhere. I had often wondered where that was exactly; it is on the territory of the volcano named Paricutín. The thirty of us from the bus were to mount small horses waiting with guides alongside the unpaved road, and ride a couple of miles to see the effects of the volcano's last eruption. Since there were not enough horses for everyone, Katya and I chose to walk. Katya liked to say "don't push the river," her version of going with the flow.

About 50 years ago, Paricutín had ejected lava over a nearby town, literally burying it under jagged black glassy rock. We were not going to climb on the volcano itself. I felt relieved because just seeing an aerial photo of the volcano had made me shiver at its sinister appearance. Paricutín volcano was a slick black lifeless cone whose crater looked like the mouth of hell.

The humidity was worsened by heavy gray clouds that hung close above us. We left the road and walked down a long, steep mountainside. The rough terrain was deformed with gullies and tree roots exposed as if by huge torrents of water. After this descent the route leveled out but was covered by volcanic ash that created a black, powdery moonscape. The earth did not look safe. Walking on that black powder, I had thoughts of being trapped in quicksand, I had visions of broken bones, I felt the fear of someone who is lost. When it began to drizzle, some people turned back to wait at the bus.

We came to an open area bordered by large bushes with red berries. One lone old man was selling *limonada* from a battered Thermos jug. The rain and the dense berry bushes kept us from discovering what was beyond the clearing. Once we struggled through the bushes we were looking straight up at jutting lava hills. Black masses of lava stretched for miles up to the volcano. The sight was so forbidding that most of the people stayed with the damp guides and horses in the clearing. As I look back on that moment, I have doubts about my own common sense, because I pressed on.

On the lava, the landscape became completely other-worldly. Fingers of rough porous stone, just a few feet across, but five to ten feet high, were poured one after the other. Some of us jumped from finger to finger, while others took the low road and climbed around each crag at its bottom. It was slow going and I felt like holding back. No obvious danger existed but it seemed I was being warned to keep out.

After we climbed in elevation we could see the whole disaster. The volcano had buried the town completely. It was as if a gigantic hand wearing a hard black glove had smashed down and crushed all the structures beneath it. Only the roof and one unbroken steeple of the Catholic church rose above the lava. I pictured the community thirty feet below me, and absently took out my camera as if to photograph it. For the first time, I truly became aware that I was standing over what had been a living town. Buried beneath my feet lay homes and shops and streets and clothes and cooking pans and toys and furniture and mementoes. I shivered and buttoned my jacket under the poncho.

Katya and I and three others decided to aim for the steeple to see if we could climb down into the church. The minute we voiced our plan, it became impossible to go on. As if calling up a weather guardian, the rain came down harder and the temperature plummeted. I put the camera away and concentrated on the slippery footing. We stopped calling out remarks to each other. I realized that I could no longer see the church. Someone shouted, "Let's go back!" The last remark I could hear from Katya was, "The gods must be angry." She was right, and they got angrier.

A tremendous deluge let loose. The rain doubled then doubled again. The storm was as violent as the hurricane I had experienced as a child. I was frightened by the deafening roar, a torturous sound as if the volcano was erupting again. Daylight vanished at two in the afternoon. My universe shrank to a black vortex of angry power, battering water, freezing howling wind. The rain drove me to my knees. In darkness and fright, I did not know which way to escape.

Katya had been standing on the adjacent finger of lava not six feet away when the deluge started. Now I screamed her name again and again but could not see her nor hear a reply. I worried about the others until I realized I had all I could do just to get through this myself. I had no idea how I would ever find my way back.

My heart raced and I almost panicked. Then I thought: I can move...blind maybe, deaf maybe, but at least I can feel my way along the spine of the lava to where I can go down into the crevices. So I did. I crawled in what I thought was the direction of the horses. If I came to red berries underfoot, I would keep going until I reached the bushes near the clearing. I felt like Gretel without Hansel. I crept and crawled along the jagged floor of the lava forest. I do not know how long it took, as my fear, while giving strength, robbed my sense of time. Finally I found a few berries, then more and at last the bushes and finally the empty clearing.

I saw Katya come into the same area, and after a bit the others arrived. We felt exhausted but halfway relieved. The guides with all the horses had abandoned us but who could blame them? We would have to find our own way back to the bus, unless that was gone too. Since Katya and I had walked in, we recollected what we could about the terrain we had covered earlier. Our basic plan, shouted over the roar of the storm, was to go against the water that was flooding the clearing from the mountainous slope above. To show the state we were in, it seemed insightfully brilliant to go up, since we had walked down to get there.

Visibility was so bad that we sometimes had to link arms to stay in touch. When we came to the black sand it was awash with new creeks, but at least we were on the right track. We slogged and slurched and slipped and cursed and cried and pushed uphill and fell and caught ourselves and kept going. We had to force against a tangible pull backwards from the volcano. After a long time, the foreboding effect of Paricutín lessened. Two people put up their umbrellas and the torrential rain came right through the fabric. The sight of the useless umbrellas struck us all as being wonderfully funny. We progressed more easily after that.

We topped out and were standing on a muddy road covered in a foot of water. We weren't safe yet but we felt as if we had been exorcised from evil. We had left a bad place. Something had lifted off us. We were relieved to feel only the wet and the cold. We pushed through calf-deep water along a straight space between the heavy undergrowth—the road that had carried horses and a busload of people only hours before. The bus wasn't there so we sloshed to the nearby village. The bus was just pulling away from the plaza! I now know that five angry, scared people can stop a bus with only a few words of the native language and a lot of intention.

Later I tried to say it was all in my imagination: that feeling of being warned, that tropical deluge that tried to sweep trees and hillsides and us away, that town that felt punished by tons of lava, that church that forbade all entry. No. It is fact: Paricutín is a geopathic area, a bad place. But after it taught its lesson, unleashing giant forces that nothing could withstand, it taught the solution. Get down, get genuine, get real, just as my power animal had told me once before. Out of panic I was led to cooperate with the elementals: follow the lava folds, find the red berries, remember how I had walked in, find the black sand, go back the way the water shows. And make the bus wait.

Each of us has been to a wilderness, national park or great cathedral for first-hand experience with power and spirit. That trip to Paricutín volcano awakened in me a sense of awe at the power of the giants—the lava from within the earth, the flood on the surface and the storm above. I began to pay more attention to Earth's messages and to seek out other places where this occurred. I had a lot to learn about power places, magical meanings and the ancient ways of enchanting the landscape before I could *see* giantically enough to do it myself. As Paricutín showed, experience was the best teacher.

## GIANTS AT POWER SITES

One of the signs that you are at a power site is finding a giant there. Of course, at some places giants have been constructed and are impossible to miss. Stonehenge, the Giants' Dance, has concentric circles of megaliths that stand out on the Salisbury plain from miles away. The outside of one stone has a giant's whimsical face upon it. Huge avenues lie close to Stonehenge. To the north is Avebury where, as we have described, gigantic goddesses, serpentine paths and fertility symbols await the visitor. In America, the network of "ways" at Chaco Canyon, the many mounds, the pyramid complexes and the colossal figures and patterned lines as in Peru and Chile, stretch for many miles in giant fashion.

*Stonehenge giant's face. (Photo by Joseph Zummach)*

However, many power sites are in a more natural state and the giants need to be discovered by the visitor. The zodiac around Glastonbury, the huge and beautiful rock shapes around Sedona, and the chakra system through Europe are examples of nature's giants. At Canyon de Chelly a running human figure hundreds of feet high exists naturally in the cliff to the right of White House ruins. Such simulacra are everywhere. Where wholesale destruction by humans has been avoided, power sites also are home to gigantic amounts of living things: migrating flocks of birds, herds of animals, earth-working insects, fungi which cover acres, native plants in abundance.

## FINDING SACRED PLACES

In the sense that the earth is alive, all land is sacred. But in the sense that some areas have been dedicated and set apart for reverence and rites, there are specific sacred places which the giants seem to favor. Not all power spots are sacred, but all sacred places develop at power spots. Power places receive their specialness from the earth, and the power was no doubt there before humans were on this planet. When many people over many years visit, worship or live at power places, they take the best of themselves and leave a trace. These traces accumulate and turn that spot into a sacred place. That is how the terms are used in this book: power spots get their energy from the earth; sacred places get their energy from human intention and ceremonies.

We are emphasizing power spots and sacred places because the reciprocal connection between earth and humans can be seen so well at them. Since sacred places are located at power spots, the effect is similar to focusing light through a lens or a laser on a target. At power spots, the earth stores, concentrates and pours forth the best of nature. Powerful spots become sacred because people conduct significant events there. Ceremonies are repeated on a power spot because people sense an extra intensity of earth spirit and obtain positive results. Each repetition of ritual multiplies the power and imbues that spot with a clear channel to other worlds. The purpose of sacred places is not to go there searching for some external power, but to go there because the energies more easily connect us to our true spiritual selves. In that sense, each one of us is a sacred place.

It is interesting that sacred places develop in a certain order. First a spring or well—a female symbol—becomes a place of veneration; often a special tree is associated with the water. Next, stone becomes involved. This stage can be marked by a holy crypt, cleft or cave. Later a megalith or other stone marker is erected on or beside the spring, penetrating the earth and connecting female power to male sky power. Finally, a church is built over the megalith or stone marker, sometimes using the ancient stones to construct the church.

The spring at a power spot comes to be revered by local people as a holy well. The holy water signifies a place where the earth mother consecrates her magic, and where her receptive spirit can be contacted through a watery hole into the underworld. Inside Christian churches, the holy water font brings the sacred well upstairs. Wells and groves of trees were sanctified long before the Druids were associated with them, prior to the arrival of Romans in Britain.

We can be sure that special trees were the forerunners of standing stones and menhirs, since they have the same ability to connect below-ground energy with above-ground energy. As time went on, elaborate structures were built to capitalize on power centers, and these evolved from open circles of wood and stone to enclosed stone temples and cathedrals. The innate power of stone is described fully in the chapter on Elementals.

This chapter has explained what to look for in the enchanted landscape inhabited by the Giants of Gaia. The next two chapters go further in applying the knowledge laid out in this book. Chapter 15 gives ideas about what to do when a special place is found, in terms of performing ritual and ceremony. Chapter 16 gives ideas about how to awaken your local giant. We invite the reader to continue this journey into the magical Otherworlds. As the 16th century chronicler Philip Stubb said, "You will not return home as you went." ❊

### CHAPTER FIFTEEN

# PERFORMING RITUAL AND CEREMONY

*I*t is long ago. You are inside a large cave, in the womb of the giant Earth Mother. The flickering orange light of the central fire bonds you to the others of your tribe. Drums sound the rhythm of the group's heartbeat. The chanting and drumming echo back from the high stone ceiling and resonate inside your bones. The skins you wear smell more of your body than of their original fox owner. The heavy musk of your clan joins with the odors of loamy herbs boiling, with burning wood, with lighted oil smoking in bowls outside the circle. The memories are old. You pray together often, when the sun shows her heat or hides it, when the moon shows her light, or hides it like tonight. It has always been this way. The drink is passed to you. The purification ceremony begins.

It is 12,000 years later. The sky is your roof. Crystal points of starlight dim as the moon rises full over the clan. You weave a serpentine pattern in and around the ring of gigantic, upright stones. You dance with the certainty of long-practiced tradition. You sing the old songs to call in magic. You smell the herbs prepared by the medicine woman. A fire is lighted in the center. The consecrated space works its power on you. An owl puts the question to the heavens. A spent owl feather is dipped into the sacred oil. The shamaness touches the feather to each forehead in the circle. The purification ceremony begins.

It is 3,000 years later. Small bone-fires, set in the four directions, ward against outsiders entering the holy place. Roman soldiers do not know of this grove in the northern forest. The great oak represents the giant Tree of Life, your connection to the sacred powers. The roots carry your prayers deep into the living underworld of the Mother. The branches speak for you to the moon and stars. You touch the trunk and feel its life-filled protection surrounding you. You all wear blessed stones and crystals. From the sacred well, the priestess draws holy water for you and the others to drink. The purification ceremony begins.

It is 2,000 years later. The time is now. You wear new clothes that do not smell of you. The place called church is built of stone. Coughs and shuffling feet echo back from the high ceiling. You are held by your godparent, surrounded by a dozen silent members of your clan. Light enters through the colored scenes of the past—blue, orange, red. The tree is now a cross. The crystals are now rosaries. The herbs are now incense. The bonfire is now two candles. There is no drum, no dance, no owl, no moon. The priest takes holy water from the font and wets your forehead. The purification ceremony begins.

## THE MEANING OF RITUAL

ach of these scenes is a ritual of baptism. Clearly much of the immediate, direct, natural, sensory meaning has been lost over the millennia. Fortunately, nothing prevents us from putting that meaning back when we perform ceremonies.

Rituals are ceremonies to formalize, commemorate or mark important events in a meaningful way. Rituals are outward expressions of the heart. Ritual can be a ceremonial act, a solemn procedure or customary practice. Ritual often, but not always, has a planned purpose and expected outcome.

What do rituals look like and sound like? When are they done, and by whom? When is ritual appropriate? Are they always formal and prescribed and serious, or can they be spontaneous, one-time, joyful events? Where can rituals be done? Do they require certain trappings, tools and dress, certain training? Can rituals be done "wrong" and if so, what happens?

Rituals can be long or short, planned or spontaneous. They can be done by anyone, solo or in small groups or with many people. They can occur inside or outdoors, day or night, summer or winter. All that is necessary is an intention and a feeling of spirituality. No special equipment, litany, books or sanctified space is required. Drumming, chanting and dance are often part of the ceremony. While practice and familiarity may bring a person to more frequent and comfortable ritual action, no training is necessary.

Ritual is appropriate any time we want to mark something as special: a life passage such as a birth, partnership or death, a new love, an age such as puberty, midlife or croning, a solar season such as winter solstice or spring equinox, a lunar cycle such as full moon, a transition such as a new home or job, a place such as a stone circle, mountaintop, spring, or a tree in the back yard. The Zuni Indians say people are born "raw" and only a rite of passage can initiate us into the "cooked" state of cultural and spiritual wholeness. To the Zuni, ritual is not incidental; it is essential.

Ritual can start with simply connecting with the natural world in a conscious way: greeting the dawn, being moved by a sunset, admiring a flock of flying geese or a cat stretching in a patch of sunlight, marveling at the tracery in a fading autumn leaf, sensing the memories of an old maple tree, admiring a giant's handprint made by inlets of the sea.

Rituals are not designed to supplant or contradict organized religion but to provide another type of spiritual experience. Ritual does what a sacrament does: it provides the outward, visible sign of an interior, spiritual transformation. The chief purpose of ritual is to transform ourselves, our perception, our emotions, our consciousness. Ritual helps because it shifts us from the mundane and ordinary into sacred time and space.

Let us look at some examples of shifting out of the mundane. Ritual changes the celebration called housewarming into the ceremony called house blessing. Ritual changes a fortieth birthday party from "over the hill" jokes into a rite of passage for midlife. Ritual changes divorce from a legal and financial decree into the closing ceremony of a relationship. Ritual changes birth from a medical procedure into the welcoming of a new spirit and a naming ceremony. Ritual changes a weekend of camping into a resurgence of earth energy through us and a chance to talk with animals and plants. In other words, ritual transforms special events in our lives into sacred celebrations.

Ritual has different meanings for individuals. Ritual is giving thanks for the beauty of the world. Ritual is energy and power. Ritual focuses power in a set place and time. Starhawk, author of *Truth or Dare*, sees ritual as "a patterned movement of energy to accomplish a purpose..." She adds, "The purpose of ritual is to create situations in which we feel the great tides moving through us."[1] *Yoga Journal* reports that "The purpose of ritual is to bring full consciousness to all our actions."[2] Dolores Ashcroft-Nowicki says ritual itself is only a tool, and that doing ritual with intention will focus the heart, mind, body and spirit in a concentrated way.[3]

The process of attuning to the heart, being conscious of the living power within everything in creation, occurs when doing rituals in nature. Nature rituals not only help to counteract the current domination and destruction of nature, they also help us to think in a larger way. Once we change the assumptions which predispose our way of seeing, we are often moved spontaneously to honor Gaia, the giant Earth Mother. We sense that the trees take a year for one huge breath, inspiring water, air and sun in early spring, and expiring in late fall as the sap and leaves settle to rest. We want to make music with the wind whose voice is heard over the planet. We start to talk with the stones which have recorded everything that has ever happened. We are able to journey inside rivers which are the bloodstream of the land. Ritual moves us out of the local and the ordinary, into the magic and magnitude of cosmic time and space.

## RITUAL, LANDSCAPE GIANTS AND SACRED SITES

he preceding section on meaning leads to the idea that ritual is spirit in action. Ritual is the energy that connects the spirit of a being to the spirit of place.

Ritual is done at sacred sites to recall their meaning and to work their magic. Ritual is done to connect with the huge landforms focused around earth energies. Ritual is done to sense the gigantic and elemental truths of water, stone, hill and tree. These are the "great tides moving through us" that Starhawk speaks of.

Let us take a closer look at how ritual connects us with giants in the sacred land. We will begin by looking at gigantic landscape patterns established by our ancestors that were activated through seasonal cycles of ritual. We return to the fabulous site of Avebury in central southern Britain.

Michael Dames has offered an ingenious and plausible interpretation for the phenomenal collection of Stone Age structures around Avebury. His interpretation is based on a ritual cycle of the year, where there is a parallel between the life stages of humans and of the Great Goddess and of the agricultural seasons.

As summarized in the book *The Avebury Cycle*, four thousand years ago Avebury was the metropolis of southern Britain. It featured:

> *the tallest man-made hill (Silbury), the largest henge or sacred enclosure (Avebury), the great chambered cemetery of the West Kennet long barrow, and the two stone avenues, each a mile and a half long, of West Kennet and Beckhampton....As the earliest farmers and pastoralists, the Neolithic people were worshippers of the Great Goddess, whose seasonal aspects were commemorated with appropriate temples.*[4]

Mr. Dames shows how these temples might well represent the giant images of the triple goddess moving through all her aspects annually. First in February she appears as the maiden at Imbolc, the "ewe's milk" time dedicated to the goddess Brigid. At spring equinox her pregnancy is apparent. Marriage follows on May Day/Beltane. Birthing happens either at the summer solstice or at Lammas in August when crop fruition represents the goddess as mother. Her later maturity is seen at the autumn equinox. Finally she goes into her underground-crone aspect from Samhain or Hallowe'en through the winter solstice.

As the seasons progressed, local people would perform rituals at the appropriate site to turn the wheel of the year. As described in Chapter 12, they would gather at Silbury Hill each Lammas to watch the Harvest Goddess give birth. Each season was equally important, equally honored and celebrated. The beauty of this system was that a single celebration could honor cycles deeply intertwined on three different levels: the human life cycle of birth, death and rebirth, the triple Goddess aspects of maiden, mother and crone, and the four seasons important to the growing of crops.

The vast images at Avebury contain coded information in symbolic form just as clearly as hieroglyphs, newspapers and computers contain decipherable information in written form. Our "prehistoric" predecessors knew how to portray images that would last across time and occupy great amounts of space. The symbology is based on the human body as representative of the Neolithic view of the divine energy. The West Kennet Long Barrow was the vulva of the Great Goddess. Silbury was her pregnant womb. The Avebury structures are living descriptions of the divine body moving through puberty to sexual maturity, maternity and completion—which leads again to the beginning of the cycle.

According to this system of giant formations around Avebury, the yearly cycle begins in the river Kennet at Candlemas on February second when the goddess returns from the Underworld. Brigid makes the dry river flow just as she makes the ewe's milk flow and the sap rise and the seeds stir. Evidence suggests that Candlemas also was marked by young girls entering a puberty hut at the Sanctuary positioned at the head of the West Kennet avenue of sacred stones. Here they prepared for the fruitful part of the Avebury cycle and their own life cycle by celebrating the first flow of their "moon blood." Towards the spring equinox, the two long stone avenues were activated through the energy of the serpents they represent. The avenues lead directly to the great Avebury henge, within which are two smaller circles, one for women and the other for men. As described in Chapter 12, a ritual connecting the female and male forces represented consummation of the sacred marriage on May eve.

Silbury Hill probably played several parts in this drama because its landform can represent several stages of the goddess, all of them in enormous proportions. The flattened top of the cone is her eye of wisdom, overseeing the whole cycle. Today the cone itself looks like a breast or a pregnant belly, but with the original irregular moat around it, the watery base formed a squatting goddess. Silbury Hill was her womb in the birthing position. The fruit of the goddess' labor was a divine child produced at Lammas early in

August, the same time as the fullness of the crops. Whichever interpretation one prefers, fecundity and sexual maturity are strongly suggested.

The final part of the drama revolves around the dark season of the year. Samhain or Hallowe'en occurs midway between the autumn equinox and the winter solstice. This passage must be made carefully by humans, as the Great Mother retreats into the Underworld. As we saw in Chapter 3, to the south of the Avebury henge and Silbury Hill lies the three hundred forty foot-long goddess implanted in the West

*Adam's Grave Long Barrow near Avebury*

Kennet Long Barrow, complete with womb. Neolithic long barrows often were named for giants, each a version of the Great Goddess. After a regenerating rest in winter, the long goddess returned to enspirit the form of the squatting goddess, and the annual cycle of fertility could begin again.

Michael Dames writes that the structures of the Great Goddess at Avebury had a collective purpose, namely to stage a spiritual drama which took one year to perform. Each structure took its turn as the special setting for celebrating a particular part of the year, matched to the mystery of life-death-rebirth. The rituals of the drama of life were joined together to make a cyclical play. The people understood how to mythically telescope a mortal lifespan into a solar year, while the goddess turned the year by changing from Maiden to Mother to Wise Crone.

In *The Avebury Cycle*, Dames lays out an even more complex vision of the Neolithic landscape that goes beyond Silbury hill, West Kennet and the great henge and stone avenues of Avebury. He envisaged the figure of a huge goddess made by the local land forms and a connect-the-dots pattern of ancient earthworks. He writes:

> Around this majestic inner group (Avebury)...is an extraordinary outer image comprising twenty seven Neolithic long barrows and circles arranged over fifty square miles, which mark the outline of a vast goddess figure as manifested in the contours of the landscape itself.[5]

It is impossible to say whether or not the Neolithic people were aware of and deliberately enhanced the presence of this gigantic figure. The undulating curves of the beautiful downland in this area do suggest the presence of a body. The long barrows on their ridges are enormously suggestive of the human anatomy. But it is possible to say that following the patterns physically present in the Avebury landscape, the people actively responded to them by means of ritual. Ritual immediately puts us into the spiritual realm and lets us share in the work of creation. The Neolithic people could directly perceive the gigantic designs in the landscape, understand the life mystery and enact it confidently. Every enactment of this cycle was important and regarded as being the first. The cosmos, the myths, and all of creation would cease unless this deeply meaningful round was continued year after year.

Through the Avebury colossi the Neolithic people of southern Britain built a permanent and gigantic sacred message. They perceived and created a magnificent synthesis between the landscape and the human figure, between the living environment and the culture existing there, between the external and the internal worlds, between the goddess in cosmic proportion and the divine image within. They used ritual to act out the dramatic connections. Through ritual they re-created their living world in an annual cycle of great congruency and meaning.

## WORKING RITUAL YOURSELF

have you ever felt at a loss when viewing the Grand Canyon or a waterfall or a site like Avebury or a cathedral, and wanted to do some special act? Have you ever felt something coming through your senses that you were moved to do, such as sing, sway, gather, light a fire, leave an offering at a site? That is why ritual exists, to let that something come through us in a powerful way. Ritual helps us to be personally and spiritually connected to a power spot or moved by an event. Ritual evokes deep meaning in the center of the self. When we do ritual with others it connects us to the heart of a group. When we do ritual at a sacred site it connects us to the spirit of place. That is why all cultures have ceremony.

Ritual intensifies our feelings and sensations, our spiritual urgings and connectedness. We open to ageless, timeless wisdom, to certainty of action, to emotions we normally might avoid. We come alive from deep within. We feel power arise from our core outward to places and people, and from our surroundings inwards. Everything is alive. This life force surges back and forth, filling us as little else can. Suddenly prayer, which may have been banned from our lips for decades, comes forth not from the head but from the heart. Suddenly meditation, which may have eluded us on demand amidst a restless and stressed existence, flows over us effortlessly, comfortably. Suddenly movement, which has waited out our stiffness, arises from our somatic memories and we can drum and dance.

Ritual is the action at sacred sites that recalls their original meaning and works the ancient magic. Some sites have been set up in gigantic patterns that were meant to be activated throughout the year, as at Avebury. We activate special places through ritual and the sites activate us. They connect us to the elemental truths of water, stone, hill and tree as enspirited in the giant landscape. The magical elements are coordinated through human patterns in fountains and wells, stone circles and cathedrals, mounds and tors, sacred groves and legends where giants were oak trees.

These planned configurations reflect more than the elemental truths of water, stone, hill and tree. When the sky energies and astronomy were added in by Neolithic people, along with line-of-sight fires and fire festivals, we see that they also worked with the four ritual elements used in magic, namely earth, air, fire and water. We can hear the parallel between humans and nature in the present-day chant, "Earth my body, water my blood, air my breath and fire my spirit." In addition, we can tell from the precise orientation of their structures that Neolithic people also worked with the cardinal directions. Native Americans add three other dimensions: above, below, and the sacred center. The elements and the directions are usually included in ritual today.

Rituals exist for four main reasons: for an effect such as healing or weathercraft or initiation; for calling people and objects to us which are lost or needed; for tapping inner resources; and for worship or blending with the infinite Great Spirit.

Dolores Ashcroft-Nowicki differentiates between *doing* a ritual, *performing* one, and *working* one.[6] "Doing" indicates that the rite is mainly a rehearsal or an introduction for newcomers to the power of ritual. "Performing" indicates ritual drama such as ritualizing the myth of Inanna or enacting a summer solstice legend. "Working" a ritual points to the hard work needed to prepare the place and the self, and signifies the deep mental, emotional and spiritual energies brought to the task.

Table 1 gives an overview of pre-ritual, ritual and post-ritual characteristics of cultures. History shows that the phases are cyclical and tend to repeat themselves. Cultures which have lost the value of ritual begin to move to the beginning of the cycle and reach for the fulfillment of the pre-ritual and ritual stages once again. Some explanation will clarify these three distinct phases.

Ritual today differs from the creation cycle described at Avebury. In that pre-ritual time, people believed that their very actions kept creation going. Their actions did not represent or symbolize creation, they

| Life Aspect | PRE-RITUAL | RITUAL | POST-RITUAL |
|---|---|---|---|
| SPIRIT | ALL IS SPIRIT. | SPIRIT IS CO-VALUED WITH MILITARY AND POLITICAL POWER. | SPIRITUALITY IS CO-OPTED BY FORMAL RELIGIONS, AND SEPARATED FROM OTHER ASPECTS OF LIFE. |
| MIND | NO SEPARATION OF UNCONSCIOUS AND CONSCIOUS. ALL TIME IS SACRED; ALL IS DREAM TIME. SINCE ALL IS RITUAL, NOTHING IS RITUAL. | SET TIME ASIDE FOR EMOTIONS AND HEALING. NEED SPECIAL CELEBRATIONS BECAUSE LIFE NO LONGER OCCUPIES OUR DAYS. | RITUAL IS SCORNED, FEELS STRANGE, NOT BELIEVED IN. HEALING IS CONDONED VIA DRUGS AND SURGERY. SCIENCE, LOGIC, MASCULINE VALUES PREDOMINATE. |
| EMOTIONS and MEANING | EMOTIONS, INTUITION, FEMININE PRINCIPLE ALWAYS ACTIVE. THE MESSAGE IS THE MESSAGE IS THE MESSAGE. | PERIODIC SANCTIONED EMOTIONS. SOME MEANING GETS LOST AS CONTENT GETS FORMALIZED INTO RITUAL. THE MESSAGE IS IN RITUAL. | UNEMOTIONAL. EMOTIONS ARE HIDDEN. INTUITION IS DISMISSED. THE MESSAGE IS GARBLED OR GONE. |
| BODY and LEISURE | DANCING, MATING, DRUMMING, CHANTING, BONFIRES, FASTS, FEASTS. TREK THE ANNUAL NOMADIC ROUTE, STOP TO WORSHIP AT SACRED SITES THAT ARE POWERFUL AT CERTAIN TIMES OF THE YEAR. | THANKSGIVING, BIRTHDAY PARTIES, FAMILY TRADITIONS. RITE OF PASSAGE. VISION QUESTS FOR INDIVIDUALS ARE THE ONLY NOMADIC FORM REMAINING. NEED RITUALS TO RETAIN OLD MEMORIES. | GO TO MOVIES. GO TO DRINK IN A BAR. GO OUT TO EAT. GO TO CHURCH ON SABBATH. SIT HOME AND WATCH TV. |
| FOOD and SURVIVAL | SEED IS FERTILITY. PLANT SEED IN ORDER TO KEEP CREATION ITSELF GOING. WHAT THE EARTH MOTHER GIVES IS ALL THAT IS ASKED OF HER. | AGRICULTURE, CROPS, ATTEMPTS TO INCREASE SOIL FERTILITY. SEED BANKS; STORE FOR NEXT YEAR. TRADE SEED WITH TRAVELERS. COMMERCIALIZATION OF FERTILITY. | POISON OUR FOOD SEEDS AND OUR SOIL. MANUFACTURE CHEMICAL "FOOD" PRODUCTS IN FACTORIES. NO RECOGNIZABLE CONNECTION TO THE EARTH. FOOD-RELATED DISEASES. |
| WORK | EVERY PERSON IS A PRACTITIONER, A PRIESTESS OR PRIEST. WHAT WE DO IS THE SAME AS WHAT LIFE IS. LIVE AMONG THE GREAT SPIRITS. | TRIBAL CHIEF, SHAMAN, HERBALIST, HEALERS ARE IMPORTANT LEADERS. WORK BECOMES SEPARATE FROM SPIRIT. PEOPLE INVOKE THE GREAT SPIRITS ON SPECIAL OCCASIONS. | ONE LEADER FOR EACH ENDEAVOR. WORK FOR MATERIAL SUCCESS. SPIRITUAL PRACTITIONERS MAY BE DRIVEN UNDERGROUND, RIDICULED, PERSECUTED, OUTCAST, KILLED. |
| STORIES | CREATION STORIES ARE ENACTED ANNUALLY IN ORDER TO MAKE THE YEARLY CYCLE HAPPEN. | MYTHS, LEGENDS AND FOLKTALES ARE SOURCES OF KNOWLEDGE. ALL WISDOM IS CONTAINED WITHIN THEM. TALES ARE BELIEVED. PEOPLE BENEFIT FROM TRADITIONS AND STORIES. | MYTH MEANS FALLACY. FOLKLORE AND LEGEND LOSE THEIR BASIS IN FACT AND BECOME SUPERSTITIONS. MEN WRITE MOST LITERATURE. SCRIPTURES ARE THE MAIN BOOKS. |
| STRUCTURES | MEGALITHS ARE EARTH POWER JOINED TO SKY POWER. CAVES ARE WOMBS. CIRCLES ARE THE MOTHER AND COSMOS. WORSHIP TAKES PLACE OUTSIDE. | OUR ACTIONS AND OUR "BUILT ENVIRONMENT" REPRESENT OUR BELIEFS. OPEN-AIR TEMPLES ARE BUILT ON POWER SPOTS. STRAIGHT LINES AND SQUARE SHAPES APPEAR IN BUILDINGS. | CHURCHES HAVE HIERARCHICAL DESIGNS AND ARE WALLED AND ROOFED, CLOSED OFF FROM MOTHER NATURE. BUILDINGS ARE NOT BASED ON SACRED GEOMETRY OR GEOMANCY. |

Table 1: The Phases of Rituals in Cultures

*were* creation. There was no separation of the physical from the spiritual, the unconscious from the conscious, the collective from the private. People dreamed while awake. They lived actively with the great spirits, and within nature. Therefore their actions were, strictly speaking, not rites, but embodiments of the totality and wholeness of life. In those days, every person was a spiritual practitioner, a priestess or priest.

In later eras and in some cultures today, ritual arose in order to remember, to retain the old memories of a previous era. Much of what was passed down was still believed, but was experienced as *representing* the divine and sacred, instead of *being* it. Such traditions carry on for many generations. People like them and benefit from them. People set time aside for healing and emotion and celebration because these things no longer occupy their days. But the meaning or content begins to get lost as it is formalized and divorced from its origins in nature and in communal life.

Finally, as in many Western societies today, ritual becomes scorned, disbelieved and unpracticed. Its role is replaced by science, medicine, logic, religion and hierarchical systems. Only a few people can be priests or healers. Life itself is not spiritual but material, and daily actions are undertaken to earn money rather than to become connected with the great mysteries of life. In such a post-ritual climate, creation is deemed "myth," ritual is deemed "superstition," healing is deemed quackery and folklore is deemed untrue or dangerous. At this point ancient wisdom is rapidly lost.

To illustrate these three phases (see also the "Cosmological Typology" given in Chapter 5), we can use the concept of pilgrimage. Originally, all our ancestors were nomads. They made an annual circuit to sacred places, not as ritual but as their life. Their territory was a giant spirit. They lived in a pre-ritual way. From then until now, people have taken pilgrimages to sacred places, setting aside time and leaving aside their normal life, expecting to encounter hardships and to perform certain acts in order to achieve a spiritual reward. They are pilgrims in a ritual way. Today in the post-ritual era we might take a vacation trip to a national park because we have an urge to connect with nature without knowing why, without knowing what to do there.

"Knowing what to do there" is the same as doing ritual. When we go to be with the giants in the landscape, anything we do in an honoring way is ritual, spiritual, and excellent. For those who prefer to have some guidelines, we offer the following information. (see Table 2)

Ritual traditions from various cultures can be gathered for use in modern times. It is impossible to reduce the power and magic of ritual to lines on a page, but Table 2 summarizes some of the important components of sacred ceremony. The sequence of Enclosure-Metamorphosis-Emergence is similar to the phenomenon of transformation that occurs in a chrysalis. By choosing aspects for your ritual from the Table, you will be in the company of rich tradition.

A ritual can be as simple as placing a shell in a natural hole in a cliff or chanting around a campfire during a full moon. A ritual can be as complex as an initiation rite, building a medicine wheel, or a ceremony for the winter solstice planned by many people, with costumes, instruments, dance, song, enactment, readings, symbolism and feasting.

## RITUAL STRUCTURE

Like an essay or a speech, ritual follows the pattern of having an opening, the body of the event, and a closing. Diane Stein in *Casting the Circle* explains the structure clearly.[7]

Opening a ritual involves creating a safe space and bringing any special objects or offerings into the space. The people present usually clear away worries, problems and ills, either by mentally calming themselves or by physically cleansing with incense, a sage smudge stick or salt water. If alone, one sets the boundaries of the special area. If in a group, everyone forms a circle to accomplish this. The final portion of the opening is called invoking. This means to call into the circle any person, trait, spirit, or being that is wanted but may not be physically present. Native groups often invite the cardinal directions and the four elements of earth-air-fire-water as well as ancestors and spirit guides.

The body of the ritual celebrates its purpose. Someone may state the reason for gathering, and might lead a meditation to center on the purpose. This portion often involves healing, change or transformation, and may last an hour or so. There might be two or three major components of the ritual during that hour. It is important to involve everyone actively so they do

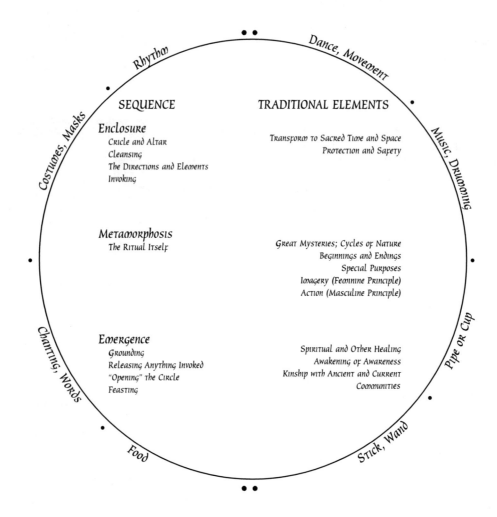

Along the circle (clockwise from top): Rhythm · Dance, Movement · Music, Drumming · Pipe or Cup · Stick, Wand · Food · Chanting, Words · Costumes, Masks

SEQUENCE

Enclosure
Circle and Altar
Cleansing
The Directions and Elements
Invoking

Metamorphosis
The Ritual Itself

Emergence
Grounding
Releasing Anything Invoked
"Opening" the Circle
Feasting

TRADITIONAL ELEMENTS

Transform to Sacred Time and Space
Protection and Safety

Great Mysteries; Cycles of Nature
Beginnings and Endings
Special Purposes
Imagery (Feminine Principle)
Action (Masculine Principle)

Spiritual and Other Healing
Awakening of Awareness
Kinship with Ancient and Current
Communities

Table 2: The Framework of Ritual

not feel like onlookers. Frequently this is accomplished by having each person say or do something. One example would be to put an object in the fire and say what transformation they are requesting.

Once a deep connection is felt between the self and the purpose, it is time to work with the energy. Directing and concentrating the power helps to complete the transformation. Using a sound is a favorite way to raise the power: chant, sing, hum, howl, dance, drum up to a peak. Work with the elemental forces which you can perceive flowing around you. Then stop. The energy will continue out from the group, creating the change that was named in the ritual's purpose.

To close a ritual, the people stoop down or sit and return any remaining energy and power back into the ground. The earth holds many currents of energy and always seems to have room for more. Grounding also returns the participants to normal earth awareness. Anything that was invited into the circle is thanked and released. The people disband the circle and then often enjoy a group meal.

## A RITUAL WITH GIANTS

**P**utting these pieces together, we will now walk through a ritual. This one will ask for positive attributes from giants in the landscape. It is important to bear in mind that giants reflect our intentions and interact with them. Giants are not external beings who live on a "higher level" of the universe. As with any spirit guide, they unfold their presence within us and on the planet to the extent that we engage with them. Tuning ourselves to this wonderful subtle order of subjective being is a great challenge.

It is helpful to find a place that represents both feminine and masculine properties. Some examples are a cave (yoni) with a tall tree (lingam) beside it, or a dolmen and menhir, or a favorite place in the desert where earth and sky come together, or water and fire at a hot spring, or actual figures created in the landscape.

Gather any people you like and items such as drums, rattles, bells, candles, favorite objects, fresh fruit/berries/nuts, wands, feathers, stones, shells, pictures, and anything else that comes to mind or wants to come along. At the exact spot that most attracts you, create a level area on which to place the objects, as on an altar. When the scene pleases you, the ritual can begin. The following structure is only a suggestion, awaiting your own ideas.

The group starts drumming and using other instruments to announce the transition to non-ordinary time and space. Ancient people around the globe used drums as

the voice that Spirit can hear. While drumming, form a circle around the altar. The altar marks sacred space; the circle makes sacred time.

A designated person is positioned at each of the four cardinal directions. Dividing the circle into quarters is alchemy for "squaring the circle." It represents the union of the irrational and rational, quantifiable and unquantifiable, infinite and bounded. The four directions are variously associated with elements, traits, animals, colors, time of day, time of year, and parts of the self. Common sense helps us to make these associations. Wherever you live, welcome water from the direction where a sea or river is closest to you, fire from the sunny south if you live in the northern hemisphere, earth from the direction of greatest land mass, and air from the remaining quarter. Each direction is activated as it is invoked, perhaps by pouring water, by lighting a candle, by pouring soil onto stones, by lighting incense or waving a feather. The designated person lighting incense for the east might say:

> *We welcome the East, source of sunrise, powers of Air. We ask it to illuminate our minds as it does the day, to help us make new beginnings, to bring the eagle's clarity. May we move as easily as air, change as readily as the wind, and breathe knowing we are the life force.*

As mentioned earlier, cleanse each person, and invoke anything or anyone whose presence is desired. Now begin the body of the ritual. Someone describes the purpose for gathering at this place where feminine and masculine aspects are shown in a huge way. For example:

> *Here beside this womblike cave and phallic tree, we wish to honor the balance represented by feminine and masculine energies. We come here to draw into ourselves your knowledge and peace, your ability to bring balance out of difference.*

*You, cave, are round and deep, dark and hidden. Sometimes we distrust the unconscious parts of us that dream in the dark of the night. We fear the old memories we have hidden deeply away. Help us to understand the wonders of the dark: the womb where we floated and first dreamed, the cave which shelters animals large and small, the night which births the day, the winter which seeds the summer. Help us to open to others and receive, as you let in air and light at your opening.*

*You, tree, are straight and high, green and exposed. Sometimes we shrink from speaking straight out, from appearing green and inexperienced, from exposing our feelings. We hide our lush foliage and bursts of color. You are a magician, attracting Water through your roots in Earth, mixing it with your blood sap to travel the roads in your trunk, pushing into Air where your branches catch the Fire of sun and transform into blossom and leaf and fruit. Help us remember we also are magicians who can transform thought into books and music and inventions and teachings, who can stay rooted during crisis and soar through our creativity and love.*

Ritual mixes quiet and active segments and uses great variety. There are many ways to have everyone participate and feel an important change. People might make a mask to represent a lost part of themselves, or dance to represent a different animal, or enact a myth, read a poem, change costumes, chant, or do anything else that is meaningful and effective.

In this ritual we are embodying the attributes of cave and tree. The cave remains still, the tree grows. We want to incorporate their lessons of being completely different yet complementing each other. So we will enact a cave and a tree. The cave can be any container, preferably a clay pot. We thank it for coming from the earth to form a useful and beautiful shape.

From the interior of the container we symbolically clean out unwanted debris: pain, unhappiness, loss, fear, failure. We can bury those things in the earth. Instead of being fearful of the dark hole, we fill it with new soil representing our growth, healing, relationships. We make a space and plant a seedling or flower to represent the flowering of our dreams. Thus we connect the still cave with the growing tree, a connection which seemed unlikely at first.

Next, we make ourselves into the Tree of Life. Starhawk describes this imagery in her book *The Spiral Dance*.[8] Stand erect as you imagine your spine is the trunk of a tree. Feel the ground with your feet as you let your roots go deep into the earth. Draw up power from the earth. With each breath pull the life force through you, feel the energy rising like sap rising through a tree trunk. Your head releases branches up toward the sky energies, sweeping in knowledge from the birds, the air. The breeze blows your branches so some touch the earth again, creating a cycle, returning, flowing, intertwining with the energy of everyone else present.

The core of the ritual may contain several more portions. One or more parts can include body movement, which is an excellent way to fill the participants with awareness of gigantic forces. It is best not to rush so people can feel profoundly transformed and touched by the purpose of the ceremony. Finally the power may be raised to a peak, and then grounded. Invoked presences are thanked and the circle is opened.

A very different ritual would be a perambulation of the landscape. You can walk or travel in a procession, circling around where you live. The perambulation might encompass up to thirty miles. You can honor the water, trees, earth, rocks, sky, plants, animals, the below and the above. Look for patterns and configurations of giants. Watch for place names that fit a giant's body. Look for chakra systems, rocks that are shaped like animals or humans, hills and valleys that form a huge reclining figure. Study a topographical map to see if a pattern emerges from the landscape, such as the bird at Sedona, or the Zodiac at Glastonbury.

You can stop at any place that appeals to you and interact with whatever is present. Sing, dance, drum, pray, move as you wish. You could read the perambulation of the giant goddess in *The Avebury Cycle* by Michael Dames, for further ideas. You could make a drawing of your own perambulation to keep in a special place at home. You could make a plumed serpent, or whatever is of your tradition, to keep as a reminder of all realms around which you journeyed—the earth and sky, feminine and masculine—and to bless the sacred center, which is the Middle World and the dwelling place where you live.

In closing, we now have the concept that ritual is any act of honoring that connects us with the spirit of place and with our inner ability to heal, change and transform. The landscape is a palette of natural and enhanced shapes that comfortably and patiently carry energies. The life force of giants and dragons flows throughout the landscape. We are the artists who activate the life force by our colorful rituals. We connect powerfully with this force if our ceremonies use all our senses, take place in natural surroundings, allow for magical occurrences, and trust that the enormous power and blessings of the landscape will come to us. Anything we choose to do in this manner will be an ideal ritual. ✹

### CHAPTER SIXTEEN

# AWAKENING YOUR

# LOCAL GIANT

"It's so huge! It should be called Giants' Canyon! Let's come up with our own giant creation myth for it."

We walked for miles along the south rim of the Grand Canyon, sensing, feeling, imagining. The red rocks and muddy river, the buttes and cliffs, the space and colors imprinted themselves on our minds and began to unfold their stories.

"Most myths have gods and goddesses. Where are they here? Maybe the rocks are male and the Colorado River is female. How about this: the Sky God traced his penis along the ground seeking the Water Serpent hidden inside the Earth Mother. When she opened to him it became the world's largest vulva."

"Ha! Like any good creation myth, sex is foremost in yours. That explains how the Grand Canyon looks but not how it feels. I have a strong sense that the canyon is not polarized, not in opposition. It seems like male and female merge here or even reverse their usual qualities."

"I see. The rocks, though hard and upward lifting, could be female and represent the labia of the vulva. The river, though soft and downward flowing, could be male and represent the sperm swimming inside the container of creation. I think your feeling holds true, that everything is reversed here. It's not

a sacred mountain. It goes down, although it looks like it goes up."

"Right. I wonder what legend the local Havasupai Indians have about the canyon? The Plumed Serpent probably figures in it, somehow joining the Above and the Below. That matches my feeling that female and male are meshed here."

"It fits! The Colorado River is a giant serpent bringing forth water from below. Its plumes are the pink rock walls of the canyon up above. Then what are all the descending layers of ledges and strata of different kinds of rock? They must have their story."

"Each layer is a skin sloughed from the serpent over the ages. Each stratum is the skin remaining from the living serpent as it created all the climates, the flora and fauna of the planet. Here we can look into the story of the making of the entire earth."

"I like it. But what still puzzles me is that many legends do describe a polarity, like the contest between the red and white dragons of the Arthurian legends. If we were to pursue the red and white analogy, here everything is red and nothing is white."

"True. 'Colorado' means red so the river is the Red Serpent. Perhaps the native people identify the canyon with the mineral giantess, Copper Woman, or the red cliffs with Red Shell Man. Of course, the canyon is the first emergence place for the Hopi. Wait, I've got it! The White Dragon is the Sky! It could be clouds and rain, but since the daytime sky is so blue here, it could be the Milky Way at night."

"Good. Remember that photo of the Grand Canyon taken from space? How huge it was? How easily seen from above? Let's end our legend with a modern twist: 'And then the Beings of Earth lifted off their planet into space. And they saw how the Red Serpent Canyon had made itself into the shape of its lover, the White Sky Serpent, and so attracted its mate to come to earth so they could join and bring forth life in the Middle World'."

"Very nice. Let's ask the canyon how it likes our story."

———————————————

## LOOKING FOR GIANTS IN THE LANDSCAPE

Although giants come in every elemental form, we will first use a few stories about trees to illustrate how to find giants in the landscape. Halfway between Isleta Pueblo, inhabited for over 600 years, and Old Town in Albuquerque, established in 1706, is a giant cottonwood tree with enormous girth. It is the Gog of the Albuquerque area and the Druids would have loved it. Next to the cottonwood is a 200 year old adobe house. Records show that the tree was already present when the house was built.

Tradition says that the Hispanic settlers and Pueblo Indians from the Isleta area going to Old Town for supplies stopped at the halfway tree for prayers and *siesta*. They created a shrine at the base of the tree where they left offerings. To them every day was sacred, as was every journey, every purpose and every living thing. They honored the cottonwood and understood its giant energy. Today, people who are in the presence of that tree, without knowing the local tradition, spontaneously remark how special it feels there.

You can learn to look around and see in the same way. You can go to your favorite tree and sense why you like being there. Then walk around it and look up in it for giant shapes. The Druid oak trees at Glastonbury, Gog and Magog, have uncountable figures in them: tree deities, woodsy human faces, animals large and small which seem to move as the viewer catches them from different angles. In Cornwall, a photograph we took in the ancient circular graveyard of Sancreed showed, partially concealed in a tree, a leprechaun complete with hat, beard, white collar and green jacket! We went back the next year for another look; the leprechaun was not there, but neither was the tree.

People used to "think in giants" all around the planet. Anywhere people lived they originally coexisted with giants in the landscape. Fortunately, some places have living descendants who maintain this practice. New Mexico, where the authors live, is called the Land of Enchantment and giants are at home there. The original inhabitants consecrated every mountain, named every butte, honored every river, blessed every mesa, prayed in every arroyo, asked permission from every deer whose life they took. The present-day Indians still do. Some people visit New Mexico and fear the vast empty spaces, the scrub desert, the apparent harshness. Other visitors see it once and change their lives in order to come back and live in its beauty. It all depends on your point of view.

New Mexico itself can be seen as a gigantic cathedral: the Rocky Mountains are the spires, the Rio Grande valley is the nave, holy water comes from the *Rios* named Pecos, Puerco and Jemez. The pews are shaped like barrancas and chasms, the altar candles are sunfired, snow-capped peaks, the blood of Christ is the sunset color of the Sangre de Christo Mountains, the manna and host are the plentiful gypsum at White Sands and the organ is the wind sounds over the Continental Divide.

If a line is drawn through the earth, the Colorado Plateau which contains New Mexico would be at one end of the line and the Tibetan Plateau would be at the other. Tibet and New Mexico share numerous parallels in architecture, food, decorative colors, ritual dances, chanting and beliefs. The Hopi word for sun is similar to the Tibetan word for moon and the Hopi word for moon is similar to the Tibetan word for sun. These parallels give rise to the idea that special places resonate as harmonics of each other. You may be able to find equivalent resonances for places you like by finding connections on maps and globes. Perhaps these actual, gigantic global links underlie the theories that there are invisible networks surrounding the planet.

When looking for giants in the landscape, not only maps but also aerial photographs are helpful. The view from above can quickly reveal a large pattern in the landscape. Understandably, many natural formations such as rivers, mountains and volcanoes reveal connections and undulations from the air that take on recognizable shapes. More amazing is the fact that many human-made formations such as those at Avebury, Atacama and Nazca can only be seen in their full scope from the air. The repeated occurrence of only being able to see a complete human-made pattern from above leads to the speculation that many ancient peoples were able to lift off this planet in mind or in body, as happens in the ending of the story that opens this chapter.

## STARTING SMALL

 hen creating special places, we suggest that you go for the gigantic in some form. One way is to find a natural spot of large size such as a cave, mountainside or waterfall. But if you are among the many people who do not have access to expanses of nature, you can invite the power of giants into a smaller space. You can create your own space in an area as small as under a backyard tree or in a part of the garden where earth-air-fire-water energy can circulate.

First, take a look for what is already there. We created an inviting, organic terrace beneath a favorite mulberry tree so we would spend more time within its enchanting canopy. At its blessing ceremony, a Tibetan friend said, "Look at the elephant guardian up in your tree." Sure enough, one fat branch had a bulge for the head, a definite pachyderm eye, then it arched like a good-luck trunk up into the sky. People had always gravitated to sit under that tree and now we knew why. To balance the giant elephant force in the air, we placed a sinuous, earthy dragon at the base of the tree, surrounded by quartz stones which serve as dragon's eggs.

Second, think of building something that will attract giant forces. Through working with things with elemental qualities—wood, earth, plants, stone—the design will come to mind, the materials will come to hand, and the project will almost build itself. A friend named Peter built a spiral in his yard that coils four times and ends in a meditation space. By the time one processes into the center, the body tingles with powerful energy and feels like it has just climbed a long mountain path. Similarly, some Gothic cathedrals had labyrinths inlaid into the marble floors and a mini-pilgrimage around its lines was meant to represent a trek to Jerusalem. Power greater than the pattern's size can be accumulated in coils.

There are other shapes that capture giant power. You might build a circle of stones so you can wind in and out in serpentine fashion. This builds up energy which the stones can hold for a long time. Or you may prefer to construct a sundial to focus the solar-giant energy. The right idea will come to you. In Brittany we saw a newly drawn earth-and-stone wheel for the four directions on the path to a Neolithic mound. It was a silent reminder that we were entering sacred ground. Lacking land, you can bring giants right into the home. A practitioner of Celtic spirituality installed floor-to-ceiling posts in a circle around his living room and attached a handmade goddess, god or mask to each. Admittedly, it was overwhelming to enter that room!

Third, work with the senses. The giants can be summoned by a group of people drumming and making music. The giants, angels, dolphins, subtle forces—whatever the energy is called—infuse people who are dancing freely. The giants can be attracted by the profuse colors of vegetables and flowers in the garden. All kinds

*A giantess in the landscape. Embodying aspects of the Pictish Goddess, she is located in a grove near the Maiden Stone, Chapel of Garioch, Aberdeenshire*

of giants seem to attend large, noisy, fun-filled outdoor gatherings; maybe that is one reason why big picnics and reunions are such memorable occasions.

Fourth, images and symbols can bring giant forces closer. An office wall with a picture of the Taoist yin/yang symbol will help to create balance between polarized forces such as dark and light, feminine and masculine, earth and air. People who have found their power animal frequently keep it close by means of jewelry, fetishes, statues and pictures. In this way, the animal's traits can be drawn upon: courage, speed, transformation, memory, strength. Statues and icons of a favorite deity can bring its special attributes directly into the personal environment. A garden with a large Kuan Yin statue will call forth her traits of peace and compassion. Many Christians appeal to the giant St. Christopher when traveling, or the goddess in her Mary-form when in need of a miracle cure.

Fifth, ritual can concentrate giant forces and then let them go. For ceremonies, you might want to call in the directions, the seasons, the elements of earth, air, fire and water, the energies of sun, moon and stars, people past and present, spirits and patron saints, power animals, and any other helpful presence. Chapter 15 offers detailed suggestions for connecting ritual with landscape giants.

Sixth, the elements of tree, crystal, rock, hill, fire and water can be used. Chapter 8 explains the elemental giants and how they are revered in many cultures. Even a small quantity of these contains the "elemental" of the entire realm. Elemental forces have the power to enter into their own kind no matter how scattered they may be, although it helps to use local stone and plants. An oak tree, for example, can reverberate with the power that is found in an entire oak forest. Once an element is worked with, that power remains. A stone or tree once loved will always carry that love. Experiments using electron microscopes have shown that elemental substances such as the wood of a piano or violin continue to resonate for hours after the strings of the instrument are muted.

Bringing your favorite elements into your environment allows their attributes to surround and empower you. People often have an affinity for one more than the others, and that is the one to concentrate on. For example, the authors have similar Celtic heritage, yet Nicholas is inspired in the presence of trees and Marcia in the presence of stones and water. Someone else might be drawn to laying out large designs with crystals. If your friends have a special elemental affinity that differs from yours, perhaps you can show each other how to see and feel giants in the other forms.

## LARGER GIANT EXPERIENCES

Going further afield than the home, giants can be found on a larger scale. Having the intention of finding giants and staying open to impressions will make them more visible. An experience of the authors will serve as an example. In the Sandia foothills east of Albuquerque there are many canyons leading into the curves of the mile-high "Turtle Mountain." We noticed that one canyon has a clear approach like a courtyard, then a narrow entry like the door to a church, marked by a solitary tree that acts as a guardian. Next comes a confined passage up a watercourse sometimes fed by snow melt to create waterfalls. This is the nave. After a hundred feet of climbing, a sandy level area spreads out to form the transept. High above, outlined against the deep blue sky is a semi-circle of boulders that form a natural bridge. They create an apse, which curves and faces east just like any proper apse. Rocks perched on either side form gargoyles and flying buttresses. Our giant is a cathedral!

The impression for some hikers might be that this same canyon is shaped like a bear. Others might sense that it is like a birth canal with the trickling water forming the umbilical cord to the navel of this part of the earth. Every one of these sensations is right, and every one awakens the giant.

Not far from Carlsbad Caverns in southern New Mexico is Lechuguilla cave in the Guadalupe Mountains. Only a few have been inside, as it is not open to the public. At its mouth, the wind blows with the force of a giant's breath. This particular giant is 1600 feet deep and its labyrinthine length has yet to be measured. Cavers say that Lechuguilla feels like "home." Park rangers say they never want to be transferred elsewhere and geomancers say the earth energies emanating from the cave are geo-beneficent.

Lechuguilla is a macrocosm of the human body's microcosm. Photographs show that the cave looks like an enormous three-dimensional version of the inside of our bodies. The passageways seem like magnified arteries and capillaries going off in all directions. An outstanding feature is the feathery calcite formations which look like the fimbriae fronds that sweep the monthly egg from an ovary into the Fallopian tube of female mammals. Like an underground Tiffanys, there are jewels of selenite and aragonite (calcium carbonate) which very few eyes have seen. Like costumes at Mardi Gras, there are twenty-foot plumes of shining white gypsum reflected in a fairy-tale lake. Like the night sky, there are cavities so vast that floodlights cannot touch the walls.

We are using many examples from New Mexico not only because the authors are familiar with them and the area is famous for its attractions, but also to illustrate the endless number and variety of giant forms that can be found in a defined geographic area. No matter where you live, if you use a giantic way of seeing you will find the giants.

At the end of the last chapter we mentioned the idea of a pilgrimage or perambulation. This is an excellent way to discover giants. You may choose to begin with an examination of maps and a study of local folklore and traditions. Place names are a giveaway. If you sense that a valley, hill, ridge or mountain range forms the body of a giant, you are in luck! Try to assess the qualities of this giant as a whole. Is it a dragon? If so, where is its head, heart, wings and tail? Dragons like to follow water courses or rocky ridges. In Chinese geomancy, the dragon's heart is usually a knoll in the center of a level area or valley. Dragons tend to be very energizing. They also tend to be huge. Since they are usually seen out of the corner of the eye their shape might not be explicit, but their character and pattern of movement is unmistakeable.

If you find a landscape giant, knowing the location of its head and heart can lead to finding all seven chakras. The chakra centers of a landscape giant may be fairly small, while their area of influence may be quite large. Establishing or "opening" a chakra in the body or temple of a landscape giant can be done in stages. Rituals to open each center could be done over a cycle of a year, then maintained as a pilgrimage cycle. Or a particular chakra, once it is discerned and established at least in the mind, can be visited any time it would be useful. If balance is needed then a visit to the solar plexus becomes meaningful. If acuity and inspiration are needed then a visit to the third eye chakra is in order. If communication is felt to be blocked then a visit to the throat chakra and a ritual of opening it will be useful. Fair warning: the congruence of inner and outer worlds could lead to excessive groundedness at the root chakra or more energy than bargained for at the sex chakra or the heart!

The chakras of a landscape giant or temple may not be in linear order. If the giant figure is explicit, though, the chakras in the landscape usually correspond to their location in that body. The location of chakras may be determined by elevation and vegetation, or astronomical and geometrical considerations. All seven chakras might not be present; there may only be the head of a giant with throat, third eye and crown chakras. In other cases, the body might be featured. The body of the "Shining One" at Callanish stone circle in the Outer Hebrides is described by the movement of the moon over low hills during its major standstill. The chakras of this giant are not perambulated but honored through ritual observation from one location during the course of the night.

Geometrical figures in the landscape also indicate the presence of giants. These may be configured by astronomical lines of sight or by features of the landscape, natural and human-made. These may not yield up chakras so much as other qualities of magic and energy. The center of a pentagram may be very grounding or very sexual. A circle may be extremely open or closed, unifying or excluding. The quality of such places will be established and strengthened to the degree that the elements of the area become imbued by ritual intent. They will become instruments, that over a lifetime can bring their players into congruence and thus meaningful relationship to the greater whole.

We recommend that if you recognize sites in the body of a natural landscape giant, you keep them in their original condition. Only after extremely careful consideration would it be appropriate to mark the spot in some special way. It takes time and much listening to recognize whether a site should be altered from its natural state. It is not appropriate to heave rocks around into whatever configuration strikes the visitor at the time. In moments, this destroys the elemental order which took millennia to create. It is precisely this elemental order which makes the spirit of place. It can be enhanced, especially if damaged, but this implies restoration rather than construction.

## INTERPRETING LOCAL LEGENDS

Place names and legends are excellent ways to understand the qualities of the landscape. Many names have ancient origins, and have arisen from direct experience of the quality of the place. On the East Coast for example, many rivers retain their Indian names. Some of them, along with islands like Martha's Vineyard, are said to have been made by the actions of giants. Ancient myths, folklore and legend tend to be localized and geomythically congruent. They may describe the actions of a hero, lovers or something apparently trivial, but they contain the information which can reveal the geomantic signature and giantic character of place.

Navajo mythology tells of a giant in the landscape of what is now New Mexico. Eighty miles west of Albuquerque near Grants there are coiled black lava beds deposited centuries ago when nearby Mount Taylor last erupted. The lava flow was named Malpais or Badland by Hispanic explorers. Northeast of Mount Taylor is a remarkable feature, a massive volcanic plug shaped like a sombrero and appropriately named Cabezón (a type of sombrero; *cabeza* means head in Spanish.) It is called Giant's Head in Dineh'. The Navajo myth explains that a giant lived in Mount Taylor. When it was slain by the twin war gods, its curdled blood oozed and circled to form the lava beds while its head rolled some distance away and formed Cabezón. Not much interpretation is needed for this tale. The lava coils and volcanic plug are so startling and unusual, that local people would need to account for their presence in some way. The authors have hiked and flown over this area and have felt its compelling attraction and primordial power.

Caution must be used when interpreting legends that come from an old culture if another culture has overlaid the area since the myth originated. In the example above, the Spanish replaced the Giant's Head with a hat. But a more common overlay of ancient chthonic traditions is the apellation "Devil." It is a truism: "The gods of the old order become the demons of the new." Hence giants like Nimrod, Bel, Grim, Woden, Wade, Völundr and all dragons became identified with the devil.

Another case of overlay occurs in the legend of Saint Christopher, the giant "Christ-carrier." He very likely represents the much older archetypal motif of the Giant Ferryman. Buried in the Christian legend is the ancient pagan custom of invoking the aid of a giant when crossing water. The character is dimly present in the figure of Classical mythology who ferries the souls of the deceased. Saint Christopher's chthonic origin is suggested by the various tracts which say he was originally a Cynocephalus, that is, a dog-headed giant.

## CREATING LEGENDS AND MYTHS

At the beginning of this chapter a creation myth was given that the authors derived from their senses and feelings while standing on the edge of the Grand Canyon. The reader can see how we resolved apparent contradictions in female-male, red-white, high-low, soft-hard characteristics, guided by the fact that the canyon is incontrovertibly there and nature resolves all contradictions.

It is no more difficult than that to create your own myths about giants. Simply be in a place, open yourself to a free flow of input and output, and cross over. Conscious attention and awareness allow the body-mind to perceive reality directly. Then it is possible to walk between the worlds the way giants do. Read the landscape and all its features exactly for what they are. Observe the wildlife. Imagine yourself to be a ferret or owl or oak tree. Imitate the sounds of the place. Sit on a rock and ask what it has seen and heard. Then speak from inner knowledge of how it must have come to be. And you will create mythology.

We have explored in this book how myths explain nature, humans, relationships, mysteries, the universe. Myths explain birth, life, death, rebirth, the origin and history of people. Myths embody the actual experiences of ancient people and the encoding of their reality. In like fashion, you can create myths that embody your experiences and your reality. If you feel a place is lion-like, it is, and its story will be about a lion. We can know what our ancestors knew: that the giants moving through our minds and nature are the powers which shape our minds and our world.

## CHECKLIST FOR FIELD WORK

how do we go about finding giants? How do we know when they are near? Are there giants everywhere? What do we look for? In this section we provide guidelines for field work in giant questing. The suggestions are derived from the previous chapters. The checklist is open-ended and we hope readers will add their own signposts.

❋ Check for physical signs. How does a place make us feel? What is the nature and mix of earth-stone-air-fire-wood-metal-water? Giants get us into spontaneous action and movement, like rolling down a big, grassy slope or dancing and swaying to music instead of sitting immobilized in a concert hall. Giants arouse our tactile sense, so we pet animals more, give more massages, feel the velvet of a rose. Giants help us climb to the top of hills and mountains so our sight can reach out for a hundred miles around. Giants help our hearing attune to the voice of eagle, brook and tree.

We can concentrate on places that feel good and look for giants there. In terms of geomancy, these are geo-beneficent or earth kindly. Because they are user friendly, they are easier to re-enchant. In previous chapters we have mentioned the attraction of Canyon de Chelly in Arizona, revelations from the Grandmother stone at Carnac, the relaxation that comes over visitors to Boscawen-un stone circle in Cornwall.

❋ Watch for sensations: physical, emotional, psychic. Do you feel like meditating at a certain spot? Does your body want to sleep? Do you get more insights somewhere? Is your intuition in high gear at a certain place? Do you get into an altered state? When you sit or lie quietly, does a powerful vision come through your mind and inner eye? These are signs of being touched by the great forces of the universe, of being washed by the great tide, of bearing the fruit of the Tree of Life.

❋ Look for signs that others have treated the place specially. Under the sundial-like center stone at Boscawen-un, we found seashells, ribbons and wild flowers. At Madron and Sancreed sacred wells in Cornwall, the pilgrims leave prayer ties and flowers. Under a fairy bush atop a fairy mound in County Clare, Ireland we found leeks, onions and quartz offerings. In each of these places we also left gifts—sometimes blue corn meal, sometimes Southwest red ochre, sometimes feathers or flowers. Giants are afoot where there are signs that people care, or that a place is sacred or enchanted. There may be ruins or a current building that feels special. There may be symbols in stone, turf or wood. It may be that the well is clean, or the path is unlittered. The giants, deities and devas like that. (Many sites contain a magnetism of their own and special care should be taken not to alter their existing vibration.)

❋ Find out what ancient people used to do at a site, and do the same to re-enchant it. Use ritual, myth-making, story-telling, drumming, music and dance, sleeping on the earth, dreaming, and other actions that feel right. If the ancient tradition is unavailable it can be re-membered, recreated from the inner source.

❋ Look for animals. Animals always reveal the character of place. Geomancers watch for the auspicious sighting or act of an animal when studying a place. Some animals might be made out of earth, like the effigy mounds of North America. Some might be carved, like the serpent on the pyramid at Chichén Itzá in the Yucatán. There may be animal petroglyphs. Some creatures might occur naturally in rocks and be positioned for all to see, like the Avebury stones. And some might have rarely been noticed before you find them.

❋ Look for evidence that the tree, rock or water elementals are powerfully present in a place. If sap is oozing, if a rockfall has just occurred, if spring runoff is around, the elementals are at work.

We can trust our creative imagination, which is always ready to see giants, fairies, elementals and dragons. Do not discount the possibility of finding them on film, even if they are not seen with the outer eye.

We can sense if weather elements are particularly active. While writing this book, we camped in bone-dry mountains with a hundred others to celebrate Beltane or May Day. All ritual plans for Maypoles, handfastings and jumping bale fires were jettisoned when snow, sleet and hail fell for the entire day. We renamed the event "Snowtane," and listened to and learned from the message of the elemental wild giants.

❋ Study the morphology of a landscape. Place names will reflect that others have seen giants there in the past. Look for chakra points in the landscape. A strong sense that the spirit of place is of the heart may indicate the heart chakra. A desire to sing may indicate the throat chakra. The qualities pertaining to other chakras may be nearby. If the idea of chakras does not appeal, then find where the head, the wings, the feet or other features of a landscape giant are located.

⚹ Look for unusual juxtapositions and lines of sight. Plan to be at special places at dawn and sunset. At these moments of transition it is easier to experience the qualities of the elemental world directly. At a solstice, equinox or cross-quarter day, note the features of the landscape marked by the rising and setting sun. Star rise and fall and lunar extremes were also keenly watched by our ancient ancestors. If you are an astrologer then you possess the knowledge to make meaningful pilgrimages to solar, lunar, stellar and zodiacal sites at auspicious times.

⚹ Search for places where you feel dragon energy. Placenames that include variations on serpent, devil, demon, St. Michael or St. George may help you. Places rich in dinosaur fossils may be good candidates! Try dowsing for ley lines or other signs of the life force in the earth. When the earth spirit is unfettered, it runs free along the paths that giants walk. Where the Great Goddess was honored, look for spirals and serpents, eggs and circles.

⚹ Open yourself to magic. Hear and see with your inner ears and eyes. Look for magic happening about you, for synchronicities. Ask for enchantment. Imitate the sounds of nature. Swim with dolpins. Go to known power places and sacred sites. Let your intuition and senses inform you of the events that have occurred there. Be aware of what the place might need at that moment, such as music, or silence. Pray. Do rituals and ceremonies. They are powerful pathways that have stood the test of time as bridges from the ordinary to the extraordinary, where giants exist. ⚹

## CONCLUSION AND CALL TO GIANTS

*T*he academic approach to giants is that they are ideological figures, through whom cultures represent their most compelling fears and aspirations.[1] The medieval carnival giants, for example, were made to be burned. This made fears evident, unified the people against a common foe made large, then destroyed the fears and the foe. To this day the custom of burning giants continues. In Santa Fe, New Mexico, a popular festival was created around the giant Zozobra. Every year the burning of his effigy destroys "Old Man Gloom."

In literature, authors such as Rabelais plucked their giants from the collective unconsciousness of the people and made them parables of good overcoming bad. The Christian giant Gargantua, as the hero of Gallic culture, defeats his gigantic heathen opponents. Biblical and folk traditions reinforce this theme, often with a dimiscule culture hero overcoming the wicked alien giant. In this view, giants help define "Us" and the "Other." However, as any child knows, giants are much more than this.

Giants became identified with the evil "Other" only with the advent of a cosmological dualism which saw earth and spirit, mind and matter in a crude opposition. In this worldview giants were made to suffer and be under the dominion of humans. As natural forces they are imprisoned, chained, buried, defeated, killed, made stupid, made objects of contempt, and forced back into the evil-identified chthonian depths from which they sprang.

We argue in this book that giants are merged with nature. This is the original view of giants. They are the elements, the orders, the intelligence and the forces inherent in the world. They are the "Giants of Gaia."

Where the culture is earth-based, giants are good. Like Prometheus, they are helpful, they are even the creators of humanity. America attempted to produce such a giant in the stories of the forester Paul Bunyan and his blue ox, Babe. It was unfortunate he was cutting down the very forests which gave him life. For the Native Americans, giants lived in the sky, the earth, the rivers, the mountains. They were vast, indifferent, arbitrary; but if respected their aid could be invoked. The Australian Aborigines have maintained their giants as beneficent, creative, world-sustaining ancestors for over 30,000 years. Humans and giants together establish congruence, meaning and harmony in the world.

Symbolically and mythologically giants hold the key to our return to a holistic cosmology. Giants embody a cosmos where nature and human are one. Giants exist. They are present in the interaction between the mind and the world. They are of the generative order which is both mind and world, energy and matter, earth and spirit. In the same way as Michelangelo released the form of his sculptures from within their marble blocks, so too can we release the giants within the earth.

At present, the giants in the landscape are only as alive as our relationship with the earth is alive. When the organic and flowing forms of nature are released from grids, the giants flow. When the complexity and diversity of life is acknowledged, the giants appear. When the earth, its elements and animals, are viewed as living teachers instead of raw resources, the giants instruct us once again. When myth is held to contain all the truths of the universe, the giants emerge to tell their stories. When geomythical resonance between place and language is renewed, the giants speak their magic. Right now, as the dialogue with the earth is growing, the landscape waits. The giants remain asleep.

Through cooperation, interaction and conscious awareness, the giants will stir. Through ritual honoring, geomythology and pilgrimage, the giants will awake. Through direct body perception and listening to the figures of the landscape of earth, the giants will get up and walk. They will be liberated from the sleep imposed upon them. Their power and intelligence will again be felt in the world. The giants are the blueprint for the building of the living temple of life on earth. The Giants of Earth arise from the depths of our creative mind-body consciousness. They walk wherever we create total wholeness between earth and spirit.

Giants awake! Arise!

# END NOTES

**PART ONE**

CHAPTER 1

1. See *Giant: The Pictorial History of the Human Colossus*, by Polly Jae Lee, A. S. Barnes and Company, 1970.
2. From Lynn Margulis and Dorion Sagan, *Microcosmos: Four Billion Years of Evolution from our Microbial Ancestors.* New York: Summit Books, 1986, pp. 214–15.
3. Claude Lévi-Strauss, *The Savage Mind.* London, 1966.
4. David Bohm, *Wholeness and the Implicate Order.* London: Routledge, 1981.
5. James Lovelock, *Gaia, A New Look at Life on Earth.* Oxford: Oxford University Press, 1982.
6. Rupert Sheldrake, *A New Science of Life.* Los Angeles: 1981.

CHAPTER 2

1. Hesiod, *Theogony*, 207–239, 617–735, 807–814.
2. Hesiod, *Ibid.* 116–187, 616–23.
3. Homer, *Odyssey*, 9. 105–542.
4. Aeschylus, *Prometheus Bound.* Heisod, *Theogony*, 507–616, *Works and Days*, 47–105.
5. Apollodorus, 1.6.1–3.
6. Gregory Bateson, *Steps to an Ecology of Mind.* New York: Ballantine, 1972.
7. Susan Stewart, *On Longing: Narratives of the Miniature, the Gigantic, the Souvenir, the Collection.* Baltimore: Johns Hopkins University Press, 1984, p. 347.

CHAPTER 3

1. John Michell, *The New View Over Atlantis.* London: Thames & Hudson, 1983, p. 83.
2. For a good, illustrated introduction to dolmens and their carved symbols see Jean McMann, *Riddles of the Stone Age.* London: Thames & Hudson, 1980.
3. See *The Boyne Valley Vision* by Martin Brennan (The Dolmen Press, Ireland, 1980) for a fuller view of this.
4. The Irish Gaelic "Nechtan" is closely related to the Scots Gaelic "Naddair" from which we get "adder." All the rivers: Arun,

Avon, Adur, Axe, Exe, Esk, Ouse, Tyne, Trent, Wye, Wyle and so on, have names which can be traced back to ancient European words for "serpent."

5. Martin Brennan, *The Stars and Stones*. London: Thames & Hudson, 1983.

6. See Barry Fell, *America B.C.* New York: Pocket Books, 1976, for an exciting if sometimes misleading look at American megalithomania. There is no doubt that ancient megalithic sites do exist in America, the site of Mystery Hill, New Hampshire, being one of them. But much more research needs to be undertaken before any conclusions can be arrived at.

7. For an excellent guide to the megalithic sites in Brittany see Aubrey Burl, *Megalithic Brittany*, London: Thames & Hudson, 1985.

8. For the excavation evidence see Stuart Piggott in *Antiquity*, 1958, vol. 32, or in *West Kennet Long Barrow Excavations*, 1955–56, 1962, and J. Thurnam in *Archaeologia*, 1860, vol. 38.

9. Michael Dames, *The Avebury Cycle*. London: Thames & Hudson, 1977, p. 29. For the goddess images of Brittany, Aubrey Burl, *op. cit.*, p. 148 and 162.10. Geoffrey of Monmouth, *The History of the Kings of Britain*. New York: Penguin Books, 1966 [I.16]. This work, as much fiction as fact, was completed in 1136 CE.

11. *Ibid.* [VIII.9-12].

12. John Michell, *op. cit.*, pp. 72–80.

13. "How Culhwch won Olwen," *Mabinogion*. Trans. Jeffrey Gantz, Penguin Books, 1976.

14. "Lludd and Llevelys," *Ibid.*, pp. 130–33.

15. Geoffrey of Monmouth, *op. cit.*, [VI.16–19, VII.3].

### CHAPTER 4

1. Franklin Folsom and Mary Elting Folsom, *America's Ancient Treasures*. Albuquerque: University of New Mexico Press, 1983, pp. 307–322.

2. *Ibid.*, pp. 232–261.

3. Told by Mary Little Bear Inkanish in, Alice Marriot and Carol K. Rachlin, *American Indian Mythology*. New York: Thomas Y. Crowell Company, 1968, p. 54.

4. Kathryn Gabriel, *Roads to Center Place*. Boulder: Johnson Publishing Company, 1991.

5. E. W. Gifford, "Northeastern and Western Yavapai." *University of California Publications in American Archeology and Ethnology*, volume 34, 1936. Also, Gifford in *Journal of American Folklore*, volume 46, 1933.

### CHAPTER 5

1. Bruce Chatwin, *The Songlines*. Penguin Books, 1987. This novel by the now-deceased British author is an excellent introduction to the songlines. "Creative spirit ancestors" is a phrase used by Robert Lawlor in his superb books.

2. Catherine H. Berndt, "Australia." In *An Illustrated Encyclopedia of Mythology*, editor Richard Cavendish, New York: Crescent Books, 1980.

3. From "The First Australians." *National Geographic*, February, 1988, p. 278.

4. These ideas were first written in Nicholas R. Mann, *His Story: Masculinity in the Post-Patriarchal Era*, St. Paul: Llewellyn Publications, 1995.

## PART TWO

### CHAPTER 6

1. Janet and Colin Bord, *The Secret Country*. Paladin, 1978, p. 202.

2. For an excellent critique of "Earth Mysteries" and a good summary of prehistoric research, see Ronald Hutton, *The Pagan Religions of the Ancient British Isles*. Oxford: Blackwell, 1991.

3. Paul Devereux, *Places of Power*, London: Blandford, 1990. Other books by Paul Devereux, such as *Earth Memory* and *Symbolic Landscapes*, are also available.

### CHAPTER 7

1. Francis Huxley, *The Dragon*. New York: Thames & Hudson, 1989, p. 7.

2. Apollodorus, 1. 6.3.

3. Quote from *Ireland of the Welcomes*, November–December 1976, vol. 25, no. 6, p. 21.

4. J. E. Cirlot, *A Dictionary of Symbols*. New York: Philosophical Library, 1962. Translated by Jack Sage.

5. Cirlot, *Ibid.*, pp. 62–63.

6. Marion Zimmer Bradley, *The Mists of Avalon*. New York: Ballantine Books, 1982, p. 60.

7. Hunbatz Men, personal communication, Arizona, 1989.

8. Francis Huxley, *Op. cit.*, pp. 62–63.

9. Michael Page and Robert Ingpen, *Encyclopedia of Things That Never Were*. New York: Viking Press, 1985, p. 190.

10. Francis Huxley, *Op. cit.*, p. 11.

11. Francis Huxley, *Op. cit.*, p. 36.

12. Jennifer Westwood, ed., *The Atlas of Mysterious Places*. New York: Weidenfeld & Nicolson, 1987, p. 5.

13. Janet Hoult, *Dragons, Their History & Symbolism*. Glastonbury: Gothic Image, 1987.

14. Jennifer Westwood, *Op. cit.*, p. 5.

15. Francis Huxley, *Op. cit.*, pp. 58–59.

16. Cirlot, *Op. cit.*, p. 84.

17. Page and Ingpen, *Op. cit.*, p. 78.

18. G. Elliott Smith, *The Evolution of the Dragon*, 1919. Quoted in Janet Hoult, *Op. cit.*, p. 20.

19. Francis Huxley, *Op. cit.*, p. 11.

20. Nicholas R. Mann, *The Red and White Springs*. Glastonbury: Triskele, 1993.

21. "Killing the Dragon" was once an integral part of the ancient pagan yearly cycle. The dragon died to be reborn. By taking one piece of the ancient tradition and impaling the dragon forever the new non-cyclical cosmology ensured that the light-identified hero could reign supreme. Christ's resurrection "once and for all" broke the cycle of change. Such vicarious redemption and transcendent linearity creates an imbalance in the psyche faced with the perpetual reality of change.

22. John Aubrey, in "Verses that I Remember Somewhere", *Remaines of Gentilisme and Judaisme*, 1686–7.

## CHAPTER 8

1. W. B. Yeats, *Irish Fairy and Folk-Tales*. London, p. 2.

2. W. Y. Evans-Wentz, *The Fairy-Faith in Celtic Countries*. Gerrards Cross, England: Colin Smythe, 1977. From Foreword by Kathleen Raine, pp. xi–xii.

3. Michael J. Roads, *Talking with Nature*. Tiburon, CA: H. J. Kramer, Inc., 1987.

4. See Jennifer Westwood, *Albion: A Guide to Legendary Britain*. London: Paladin, 1985, p. 281, for a full picture of the association of the smith giants with elves and dwarves.

5. Unlike some authorities, the authors see the Wild Man and the Green Man as the same. The Wild Man and Woman went the same way in the Western world as the giants; that is, they were depicted as grotesque and stupid because of their association with nature. In a little known tradition, the sage Merlin went clad in nothing but leaves when he dwelt in the forest to learn his wisdom.

6. "A. E." George William Russell, "The Hazel." Quoted in Ross Nichols, *The Book of Druidry*. Wellingborough, England: Aquarian Press, 1990, pp. 292–293.

## CHAPTER 9

1. Adapted from E. W. Gifford, "Northeastern and Western Yavapai Myths," *Journal of American Folklore*, Vol. 46, 1943.

2. Mircea Eliade, *Myth and Reality*. London, 1964, pp. 5–6.

3. Mimi Lobell, "Spatial Archetypes." *ReVISION*, Vol. 6, No. 2.

4. Father Charles Moore, conversation, Sedona, 1990.

5. Robert Lawler, *Sacred Geometry*. Thames & Hudson, 1982, p. 5. This book is an excellent study in sacred geometry. All the concepts briefly mentioned here can be pursued in its pages.

6. See John Michell, *The Dimensions of Paradise*. New York: Harper and Row, 1988, pp. 67–68.

## CHAPTER 10

1. For Stonehenge see the works of John Michell. For Woodhenge and other sites see Alexander Thom, *Megalithic Sites in Britain*. Oxford: Oxford University Press, 1978.

2. A. Thom and A. S. Thom, *Megalithic Remains in Britain and Brittany*. Oxford: Oxford University Press, 1978.

3. Jeff Saward, "The House of Iitoi." *Caerdroia 1989.*

4. John Michell, *The Dimensions of Paradise*. New York: Harper and Row, 1988, p. 34.

5. E= Mc$^2$ where "E" is energy, "M" is mass or matter and "c" is the constant or the speed of light. Thus the energy in matter is equal to its mass multiplied by the speed of light squared.

CHAPTER 11

1. Is a similar shift happening among the Yavapai in the story of the grandson's body in the landscape rather than the Grandmother's? It is he who goes up to heaven and returns with medicine power.

2. W. Y. Evans-Wentz, *Cuchama and Sacred Mountains*. Athens, OH: Swallow Press/Ohio University Press, 1989.

3. For very readable descriptions of the new physics see F. David Peat, (1) *Synchronicity: The Bridge Between Matter and Mind*. New York: Bantam New Age Books, 1987. (2) *The Philosopher's Stone: Chaos, Synchronicity and the Hidden Order of the World*. New York: Bantam Books, 1991.

4. Carl G. Jung, *Man and His Symbols*. New York: Anchor Press/Doubleday, 1964, p. 211.

5. For a stunning picture of the cellular nature of life see Lynn Margulis and Dorion Sagan, *Microcosmos: Four Billion Years of Evolution from our Microbial Ancestors*. New York: Summit Books, 1986.

6. W. Y. Evans-Wentz, *The Fairy-Faith in Celtic Countries*. Gerrards Cross, England: Colin Smythe, 1977, pp. 191–193.

CHAPTER 12

1. From Yavapai sources. Quoted in Nicholas R. Mann, *Sedona Sacred Earth*. Albuquerque: Zivah Publishers, 1991, pp. 10–13.

2. Michael Dames, *The Silbury Treasure*, London: Thames & Hudson, 1976, p. 172.

3. Michael Dames, *The Avebury Cycle*. London: Thames & Hudson, 1977, p. 11.

4. *Ibid.*, p. 144.

5. Frances Howard-Gordon, *Glastonbury, Maker of Myths*. Glastonbury: Gothic Image, 1982.

6. Nicholas R. Mann, *Glastonbury Tor, A Guide to the History and Legends*. Glastonbury: Triskele, 1986.

7. Kathy Jones, *The Goddess in Glastonbury*. Glastonbury: Ariadne Publications, 1990.

**PART THREE**

CHAPTER 13

1. David Abram, "The Perceptual Implications of Gaia." *The Ecologist*, 15, 3 (1985), p. 100.

2. Based on John Matthews, *Taliesin: Shamanism and the Bardic Mysteries in Britain and Ireland*. London: The Aquarian Press, 1991, p. 55.

3. F. David Peat, *The Philosopher's Stone: Chaos, Synchronicity and the Hidden Order of the World*. New York: Bantam Books, 1991, pp. 107–108.

4. James Lovelock, *The Ages of Gaia: A Biography of Our Living Earth*. Oxford: Oxford University Press, 1988, p. 236.

CHAPTER 14

1. Carl C. Jung, "Synchronicity: An Acausal Connecting Principle." *Collected Works, vol. VIII*, Princeton University Press, p. 419ff.

2. Michael J. Roads, *Talking with Nature*. Tiburon, CA: H. J. Kramer, 1987.

3. Cynthia L. Corbett, *Power Trips*. Santa Fe: Timewindow, 1988.

CHAPTER 15

1. Starhawk, *Truth or Dare*. San Francisco: Harper & Row, 1990, p. 98.

2. *Yoga Journal*, January/February 1991.

3. Dolores Ashcroft-Nowicki, *First Steps in Ritual*. Wellingborough: The Aquarian Press, 1990.

4. Michael Dames, *The Avebury Cycle*. London: Thames & Hudson, 1977 from the jacket cover.

5. *Ibid.*

6. Ashcroft-Nowicki, *Op. cit.*, p. 14.

7. Diane Stein, *Casting the Circle. A Woman's Book of Ritual*. Freedom, CA: Crossing Press, 1990.

8. Starhawk, *The Spiral Dance*. San Francisco: Harper & Row, 1989, p. 58.

CHAPTER 16

1. See, for example, Walter Stephens, *Giants, In Those Days*. Lincoln, NE: University of Nebraska Press, 1989, p.11.

# SUGGESTED READING

Janis L. Pallister, "Giants," in *Mythical and Fabulous Creatures: A Resource Book and Research Guide*. Edited by Malcolm South, New York: Greenwood Press, 1987.

Sarah Teale, *Giants*. New York: Abrams, 1979.

J. B. Friedman, *The Monstrous Races in Medieval Art and Thought*. Cambridge: Harvard University Press, 1981.

Bruce Chatwin, (1) *In Patagonia*. London: Jonathan Cape, 1977. (2) *The Songlines*. New York: Viking Press, 1987.

Morris Berman, (1) *The Re-enchantment of the World*. New York: 1981. (2) *Coming to Our Senses: Body and Spirit in the Hidden History of the West*. New York: Simon & Schuster, 1989.

David Abram, "The Perceptual Implications of Gaia." *The Ecologist, 15, 3,* 1985.

William Irwin Thompson, *The Time Falling Bodies Take to Light*. New York: St. Martins Press, 1981.

David F. Peat, *Synchronicity: The Bridge Between Matter and Mind*. New York: Bantam Books, 1987.

Susan Stewart, *On Longing: Narratives of the Miniature, the Gigantic, the Souvenir, the Collection*. Baltimore: Johns Hopkins University Press, 1984.

# GLOSSARY

A word in SMALL CAPS within a definition has its own entry in the glossary.

ALBION - An ancient name of Britain when it was inhabited only by a race of giants. The giant personifying the spirit of Britain.

ALCHEMY - From the Arabic for "art of transmutation." An analogy for changing from matter to spirit, from the outer to the inner world, or for self-transformation. Any seemingly magical power or process of transmuting.

ANIMUS MUNDI - "World Spirit." The animating spirit of the world.

ANTEDILUVIAN - "Before the deluge." The time in the Bible before Noah and the flood. One of the purposes of the flood was to destroy the chthonian giants, but Noah himself is sometimes referred to as a giant.

ARCHETYPE - The name coined by C. G. Jung for the "archaic remnants" or patterns, ideas, images in the COLLECTIVE UNCONSCIOUS which can manifest in the individual consciousness with great influence and power. Examples: mother, father, sun, animal, hero, goddess.

AXIS MUNDI - The "world axis" around which the cosmological order turns. Often represented by the GNOMON or the TREE OF LIFE.

BACHLACH - A club- or axe-carrying mythological being associated with trees and cattle who appears in early versions of the story of the Green Knight to challenge heroes to a beheading game.

BARROW - A round earthen mound sometimes containing a DOLMEN, chambers, burials and artifacts. Long barrows are elongated and date from the NEOLITHIC AGE. Round barrows are usually BRONZE or IRON AGE.

BCE - "Before the Common Era." Replaces B.C.

BLIND SPRING - A powerful confluence of underground streams of water-created energy.

BODY-MIND - Used throughout this book to mean the whole being. The intelligence of the psycho-somatic processes inherent in every living being as a result of millions of years of evolution.

BRONZE AGE - An inexact archaeological term for a period in

European prehistory more recent than the NEOLITHIC and prior to the use of iron, when weapons and implements were made of a copper/tin alloy. Approximately 2,000 BCE to 800 BCE.

CANON - Derives from the Greek for a measuring rod. Used in this book to refer to the principles established in the ancient world concerning measure, number and proportion.

CARTESIAN - The mechanical interpretation of physical nature pertaining to the logical methods and philosophy of René Descartes.

CE - "Common Era." Non-religious designation for years since 0. Replaces A.D.

CELTS - The people who once lived in most of Europe. The Celts benefited from the achievements of much earlier traditions, and their own culture peaked in the IRON AGE. Their power was destroyed wherever the Roman Empire reached. They are now best represented by the Irish, Welsh and Basque. See DRUIDS.

CEQUES - Lines between sacred shrines or HUACAS which represented the spatial dimensions of the Inca Empire. Many converged on the capital of Cuzco. Their origin may lie in the lines and patterns traced in the Nazca highlands of Peru or the Atacama Desert of Chile.

CHAKRAS - Centers of subtle but vitalizing energy in the human body. An Eastern concept which finds its equivalence in Western mystical traditions where a halo may represent the Crown Chakra and the solar plexus the chakra of power, feeling and will.

CHAOS - From the Greek, describing the original condition of the universe. The opposite of the order of COSMOS. According to Hesiod's *Theogony*, first there was Chaos, then Eros, Tartarus (night, space, age, sleep, dreams, etc.), and the Great Goddess, Eurynome. Through parthenogenesis (self-creation) Eurynome brought forth GAIA. Gaia also through parthenogenesis made the Earth, then the Sky, Ouranos. Their union brought forth the Cyclopes and the TITANS such as Phoebe, Themis, Rhea, Hyperion and Cronos. The castration of CRONOS made Gaia bear the GIANTS. The union of Cronos and Rhea created the Olympian deities. Zeus proceeded to seduce the ancient Titan-esses, for example Themis, to produce the Fates, and even Eurynome to produce the Graces. In anger at Zeus, Gaia mated with Tartarus to produce the monstrous Typhon. See SENSITIVE CHAOS.

CHAOS THEORY - The study of shapes in nature - jagged, turbulent, twisted, fractured, tangled, fluctuating, random - for which there is no deterministic predictability, but for which there exists an organizing structure. Some of the most spectacular structures lie on the complex boundaries between orderly and chaotic behavior; for example, freezing water in air obeys mathematical laws to form the growth patterns of a snowflake, but no two snowflakes are the same.

CHI - or Ch'i - The Chinese name for the subtle energies of the body and of the surrounding world. Linked with breath, perfect chi means the balance of the complementary polarity of yin and yang.

CHTHONIC - Greek for "under the earth." Pertaining to the deities and spirits arising from the earth. Used in this book in contrast to the idea of transcendental order imposed from heaven upon the earth.

CIRCLE - The primary figure of SACRED GEOMETRY, representing the quality of completeness, entirety, eternity. It is the symbol of the cosmos. See GREAT ROUND.

CITY OF REVELATION - The name for cities such as St. John's NEW JERUSALEM or Plato's MAGNESIA which are built according to the canons of cosmic proportion and divine law.

COLLECTIVE UNCONSCIOUS - A term from Jungian psychology which refers to the contents of an individual's psyche which are culturally or racially inherited, possibly from the extremely ancient past. This group content usually remains below conscious awareness. It contains ARCHETYPES and other embedded material that form an individual's COSMOLOGY.

COSMIC MAN - The human as the microcosm of the macrocosm. The proportions and nature of the human body are analogous to the principles pervading the cosmos. See PURUSHA.

COSMOGRAPHY - The spatial dimensions or "map" of the world according to a culture's COSMOLOGY.

COSMOLOGY - *Cosmo*, Greek for "world order," -*logy*, Greek for "study of." Used in this book to mean a culture's view of the nature of reality, structured by language, images, ideas, myths and beliefs. A cosmology makes actual the reality which it purports to describe. See WORLDVIEW.

CRONOS, Cronus or Chronos, "time" - The TITAN persuaded by GAIA to rebel against his father. He castrated Ouranos, married Rhea and assumed the rule of Olympus. This was said to be the GOLDEN AGE. From the blood of Ouranos' wounds falling on Gaia, the giants were born. However, like his father, Cronos confined many of the Titans, the Cyclopes and the giants known as the Hundred-Handed, and did not allow his mate to reproduce. He swallowed Rhea's offspring. Eventually Rhea and her mother, Gaia, tricked Cronos and produced Zeus. But when Zeus defeated Cronos, he too assumed the dominant role. See CHAOS.

CROSS QUARTER DAY - The four days midway between the solstices and the equinoxes, occurring approximately the first of February, May, August and November. These were important festivals of the Celts and probably of the prehistoric European people.

CYCLOPEAN - Of the Cyclopes, the race of one-eyed giants. Also refers to construction employing large stones that fit well together.

DEVA - From the Sanskrit for "divine" and the Persian for "shining one," corrupted to mean devil. A nature spirit. Used to mean the IMPLICATE ORDER or morphic field which unfolds the explicate patterns of particular species.

DOLMENS - "Dol-men" in the Celtic language of Brittany means "stone table." Refers to MEGALITHIC construction where typically a large cap stone was placed on top of ORTHOSTATS and usually covered with a mound. A womb-cave symbolic of the birth and death mysteries of GREAT ROUND societies.

DOWSING - the art of using a divining instrument such as a forked branch or a pendulum to attune the body to its subtle sensory abilities in order to locate underground water, minerals, LEY LINES etc.

DRAGONS - A mythological composite creature able to enter every ELEMENTAL realm. Used in this book to mean the energy of the universe. Often conceived of as a dynamic, opposing polarity.

DRAGON CURRENTS - A term from GEOMANCY meaning the currents of subtle energy which flow over the earth. In FENG-SHUI they are the LUNG-MEI.

DREAMTIME - A literal translation of the Australian Aboriginal word for the time of the creation when the ancestors sang the world into existence. The time of the past-present-now.

DRUIDS - Knowers of trees, from the Indo-European root *deru* for "trees." The priests, priestesses, prophets, healers, bards, historians, magicians, law and lineage keepers of the Celts. Originally like SHAMANS, but by the IRON AGE they had affiliated into organizations which maintained strict standards of education and initiation. See TREE ALPHABET.

DRYADS - Tree spirits. Greek *drys* = oak tree.

EARTH ENERGIES - The unquantifiable forces which animate the spirit of the earth. The CHI of Chinese geomancy. Represented in most cosmologies by the DRAGON. Strongest at springs, fissures, caves or other openings into the earth.

EARTH MYSTERIES - A multi-disciplinary approach to deciphering knowledge and structures left by ancient people who interacted closely with the earth. The study of LEY LINES, EARTH ENERGIES, and anomalies, synchronicities and psychic phenomena at sacred sites.

EARTH SPIRIT - The living earth. The planet as alive and intelligent. The working of currents of subtle energy, often conceived of as a DRAGON, which ensure the well-being of life on earth. In most cosmologies this is secured by making the terrestrial realm the mirror of the divine. For URBAN-CULTURES the building of the TEMPLE with its AXIS MUNDI ensures the meeting of heaven and earth. For NATURE-CULTURES re-enacting the drama of creation secures the powers of the earth spirit.

ELEMENTALS - The basic qualities of creation, namely wood, stone, earth, metal, water, fire and air, animated by hard-to-see beings such as DRYADS, gnomes and giants.

EXPLICATE ORDER - A concept arising from the work of David Bohm to describe the structure of the material world as a result of the informative content of the IMPLICATE ORDER. The explicate order of substance unfolds from out of the implicate order of information and is at length enfolded back into it. See QUANTUM THEORY.

FACHAN - The Scottish Cyclopes. A large, one-eyed, one-armed, one-legged, club-carrying, wood-dwelling nature spirit. See GRUAGACH.

FENG-SHUI - The Chinese system of GEOMANCY. Meaning "wind-water" it is the study of the balance of subtle forces, the CHI, which emanate from and flow over the land. The two primary forces are yin and yang which flow around the landscape in courses known as LUNG-MEI. Yang energy is found in rough, mountainous terrain, yin in plains and gentle terrain. Yin and yang seek balance, and in their movement they give rise to other forms of chi known as the five elements: earth, fire, wood, metal and water. When these forces are in ideal relationship, perhaps effected by human intervention, the DRAGON CURRENT or EARTH SPIRIT flows for the benefit of all life.

FYNNODEREE - An extremely large, usually naked, hairy WILD MAN from the Isle of Man, whose help can be enlisted on the farm, provided clothes are not left for him in payment.

GAIA or Ge - Greek name for the Earth Goddess. It was her dance which created the world. Out of her union with the Sky, Ouranos, she made the GIANTS and the TITANS who then assisted in the finishing of the creation. See CHAOS.

GAIA THEORY - The idea, conceived by James Lovelock, that the earth is a self-regulating living organism, whose intelligence is to be found on a quantum level or in a GENERATIVE FIELD, and whose object is the development of its life. The theory suggests that humans are evolved hosts for cooperating cells, who thereby benefit more than they could as singular organisms. The theory suggests that when a constituent part is not acting beneficially for the whole, new adaptations in life on earth will occur.

GENERATIVE ORDER - A name used in this book to describe the order of information in the universe from which mind and matter derive but which is neither mind or matter. A quantum field: see IMPLICATE ORDER and MORPHOGENETIC FIELD.

GENIUS LOCI - The particular SPIRIT OF PLACE, either personified into a being, or simply perceived as the impression it makes on the mind.

GEOCENTRIC - A view which places the earth at the center of creation. Thought to be "primitive," but the view in terms of human evolution is essentially correct.

GEOMANCY - The divination of the earth. The means by which the character of place is determined. A holistic practice, geomancy works with mind and matter to enfold humans and landscape into a meaningful pattern of correspondences. See FENG-SHUI, EARTH ENERGIES, etc.

GEOMYTHICS - The relationship between earth and myth, between the world and language. Through geomythics the inner and the outer worlds are brought into meaningful correspondence.

GEOGLYPH - A "figure of earth." Sometimes referred to as an "intaglio" when the design is formed by removing the surface material to expose a different underlying layer. Using that distinction, the figures in the Atacama Desert, the Ohio Serpent Mound and the Effigy Mounds are geoglyphs; the Nazca figures, the hillside figures of Britain and those in the Mohave Desert are intaglios.

GIANT - Used in this book to mean any being in human or animal form of great size. In Classical mythology the *Gigantes* were the offspring of GAIA with human heads and serpent limbs or bodies. Although it is only the TITANS who are human in form the term "giants" has come to include them. In Western religion and literature giants are associated with the ANTEDILUVIAN world and so became wicked and evil, but popular mythology has many examples of good giants. See CHAOS.

GIANTIC - *Gaiantic* - Of the nature of the GIANTS of GAIA.

GNOMON - A stick or pole placed in the ground in order to denote the world center or OMPHALOS and to determine and establish the surrounding world order.

GOLDEN AGE - A mythical age preceding that of iron, bronze and silver (the first two having quasi-historical reality), in which divine order prevailed and from which the human race has declined. The perfect world, whose order may one day return.

GOLDEN MEAN, SECTION OR PROPORTION - The ratio (phi) between two parts in which the lesser is to the greater as the greater is to the sum of the two. A:B::B:A+B.

GREAT GODDESS - Used in this book to refer to the primordial essence of reality rather than to a localized goddess. Early representations suggest the Great Goddess was seen as the GREAT ROUND inclusive of every gender and denomination. (A mythical term for the GENERATIVE and IMPLICATE ORDERS of the quantum physicist.)

GREAT ROUND - (1) A culture or a cosmology whose bearers perceive and directly experience creation in a constant state of flux, creativity, change, even CHAOS, amid unity. (2) IMMANENT spirituality, with no distinction of body and mind, earth and spirit. Usually honoring the GREAT GODDESS, the art of Great Round cultures is replete with spiral, serpentine and circular images. See OUROBOROS.

GREEN MAN - An early European deity with connections to Cernunnos, Dionysos and Pan who was honored with the vegetation cycle of the year. Later, the Green Man was represented as a head disgorging vegetation. This may be a vestige of a Celtic cult where the head was seen as the source of creativity and language. See BACHLACH.

GRUAGACH - A huge, hairy, sometimes leaf-covered, club-carrying WILD MAN of Northern Europe. Appears in literature as a guardian, a forest dweller and as the Wild Herdsman, protector of cattle. Related to the FACHAN, the BACHLACH and maybe to the GREEN MAN.

HENGE - A large, usually circular earthen bank and ditch, sometimes enclosing circles of wood or stone, e.g. Stonehenge.

HUACAS - Shrines at places of especial power such as unusual rock formations, earth chasms, forests and springs in Peru. The Inca people connected these shrines through the construction of CEQUES.

IMMANENT - Used in this book to mean indwelling, inherent, CHTHONIC. The opposite of transcendent.

IMPLICATE ORDER - David Bohm's description of the GENERATIVE ORDER of reality. The information which has a formative effect on matter, on the EXPLICATE ORDER.

IRON AGE - The age of iron in Europe, approximately 800 BCE to 0 CE. The age of the Celts and Druids.

KUNDALINI - The Hindu name for the energy, often represented by a serpent, which lies in the root or base CHAKRA.

LABYRINTH - A labyrinth is a unicursal pattern that can be laid out on a scale for people to negotiate. It is not a problem-solving maze. In this book the labyrinth is taken to be a representation of universal information from the level of IMPLICATE ORDER unfolding into the world of EXPLICATE ORDER.

LANDSCAPE TEMPLES - A naturally occurring set of features in the landscape which contain in microcosm the order attributed to a culture's view of the macrocosm. The COSMIC MAN in the landscape. A manifest form of the COSMOGRAPHY.

LEY LINES - Alignments between natural and/or human-made features in the landscape. Coined by Alfred Watkins to describe straight lines or trackways between sites, the word is now applied to other kinds of lines. These include the Chinese LUNG-MEI which are not necessarily straight but follow the undulations of the land, lines of dowsable energy, and global MERIDIANS which link sites across the world in great circles.

LUNAR EXTREMES - The extreme azimuths or rising and setting points on the horizon which the moon reaches in its 18.6 year cycle. There are eight of these known as the Northern and Southern Major and Minor Standstills.

LUNG-MEI - The lines which carry the CHI or the DRAGON CURRENT around the landscape. See FENG-SHUI.

MAGIC - From the Persian *magus* meaning "sorcerer." The practice of using charms, spells and rituals to invoke the supernatural, effect transformation and control events in nature. See SYMPATHETIC MAGIC and ALCHEMY.

MAGNESIA - Plato's perfect city built and governed according to the ideal principles of SACRED GEOMETRY and divine law.

MEGALITHIC - Literally "large stone." Used to describe places, people and a period in the European NEOLITHIC age when structures were built using large stones. Approx. 4,500 - 1,800 BCE.

MENHIR - French for "long stone." A standing stone erected in the European MEGALITHIC age.

MIDDLEWORLD - A cosmological term meaning this world. Midgard in Scandinavian mythology.

MORPHOGENETIC FIELD - or morphic field. The name biologist Rupert Sheldrake uses to describe the field of information underlying form and matter. Once a process has occurred, a morphic field is created which informs the constituent parts of the process, such as a molecule, how to do it again. The more it is done, the stronger the field and the easier the process. See GENERATIVE ORDER.

MYTH - A traditional story originating in preliterate society, dealing with supernatural beings, forces, ancestors, heroes, heroines. Myth explains origins, nature, relationships and all the important questions of life and death.

NATURE-CULTURE - A term used throughout this book to refer to those cultures close to nature with little urban development. Generally their WORLDVIEW will be unifying, IMMANENT and accommodating of change.

NEOLITHIC - The "new stone" age, as opposed to the PALEOLITHIC "old stone" age. Approximately 7,000 BCE to 2,000 BCE depending on area. Saw the domestication of animals, permanent settlement, first cities, writing and agriculture.

NEW JERUSALEM - The CITY OF REVELATION described by St. John. The precisely ordered heavenly city. The celestial cosmology translated into terrestrial cosmography.

NEWTONIAN - Of Isaac Newton, philosopher and mathematician. Used in this book to describe the CARTESIAN view of the universe. In this view, mind and matter are quite distinct, and everything in the universe can be understood and manipulated through application of mechanical laws.

OGHAM - A cryptic script possibly invented by the DRUIDS and used as a secret code for private signalling. Could be signalled through the fingers or carved on wood or stone. Akin to runic. See TREE ALPHABET.

OMPHALOS - Greek meaning "navel" or "center." The world center, through which passes the AXIS MUNDI. The cosmic egg, often represented by a stone. See SIPAPU and OUROBOROS.

ORTHOSTAT - An upright standing stone used to support a capstone in a MEGALITHIC structure such as a DOLMEN.

OUROBOROS - (1) The world serpent, wrapped around the cosmic egg, around the world boundary, or the TREE OF LIFE. (2) Of the cyclical view of life, ouroboric cultures honor rebirth, immanence and transformational powers.

OVERWORLD - The world above the human. The realm of heavenly beings, such as the Thunderbirds and the gods. Asgard in Scandinavian mythology.

PAGAN - Probably derives from *paganus*, Latin for "country dweller." A person with PANTHEISTIC spiritual views, who keeps the earth-based, CHTHONIC traditions alive, in contrast to the transcendent spiritual practices of the urban dweller. Formerly any non-Christian.

PALEOLITHIC - the "old stone" age. Preceding the NEOLITHIC this is a huge period stretching back from about 7,000 BCE into the remote past. The "Middle Paleolithic" (70-40,000 BCE) had the first well-developed flint industries and elaborate burial ritual. The "Upper Paleolithic" includes the period of cave art.

PARADIGM - A set of ideas, a context, a pattern or a WORLDVIEW which creates a set disposition toward the world, requiring a radical shift to understand any alternative view.

PANTHEON - The gods, goddesses and other deities of a cultural mythology.

PANTHEISM - A COSMOLOGY which identifies nature with the divine, and thus may have many deities and SPIRITS OF PLACE. (*Pan* - Greek for "all," *theism* - "belief in god.") Akin to paganism.

PETROGLYPH - a carving on stone.

PHI - The ratio or proportion known as the GOLDEN SECTION.

PICTOGRAPH - a painting on stone.

PLUMED SERPENT - The feathered or horned serpent deity of the Americas, known as Quetzalcoatl to the Aztecs and Kulkulkan to the Maya. Akin to the DRAGON.

POWER SPOT - A place on the earth where an amplification of energy is experienced. Often located near openings into the earth, the experience of the place may include increased ionization, barometric changes, electrical and magnetic anomalies and other unusual phenomena.

PROMETHEUS - "Forethought" - One of the second generation of TITANS. It was his particular task to aid in the creation and development of humanity. His gifts included fire, handicrafts and art.

PURUSHA - The Hindu name for COSMIC MAN. In his myth Purusha assumes the form of a giant. Slain by the gods his head became heaven, his navel the atmosphere and his feet the earth. He embodies the divine proportions upon which the TEMPLE is built.

QUADRATURE - The fourfold pattern for the laying out of the TEMPLE. Using a GNOMON the VESICA PISCIS is twice drawn out, unifying masculine and feminine principles. It is aligned to the four directions and creates the square of wholeness.

QUANTUM THEORY - A theory about the nature of reality in which atoms and molecules are composed of even smaller elementary particles. See section in Chapter 11.

REFLEXIVE - A concept used in this book to mean the capacity of the universe, by virtue of its infinite nature, to accommodate within itself every possibility. A COSMOLOGY projected onto the world will therefore find proof of itself as the universe shapes itself in the image of the cosmology.

RELIGION - Used in this book to mean a set of organized and codified laws and beliefs, usually practiced in urban settings.

RELATIVITY - The theory formulated by Albert Einstein, that space and time are relative and not absolute concepts. All movement in time and space can only be defined relative to the frame of reference.

RITUAL - (1) A ceremony to formalize, commemorate or mark important events. A patterned movement of intentionally focused energy to accomplish a magical or spiritual purpose. A means of transforming the mundane into sacred time and space. (2) A ceremony sanctified by RELIGION to reinforce and legitimate the social system of power.

SACBES - The ceremonial routes of the Maya, often taking the form of raised linear causeways aligned to their pyramids.

SACRED GEOMETRY - The theoretical systems which, through study of forms in the world, attempt to describe the pure spatial, geometrical order which underlies, and perhaps causes, those forms. See CANON.

SENSITIVE CHAOS - A phrase used to refer to the apparently chaotic patterns of flux in the natural world, but which reveal an order CHAOS THEORY is just beginning to describe. Sensitive chaos can be considered in contrast to the fixed order of SACRED GEOMETRY, and is used to describe the GREAT ROUND cosmologies of NATURE-CULTURES.

SHAMAN - A priest or priest-healer (of the tribes of Siberia and North America), whose powers exert an influence on the spirit world.

SIMULACRA - Likenesses, usually in nature, which resemble something other than themselves. Singular: simulacrum.

SIPAPU - (1) The hole in the floor of a kiva representing the place of emergence of the people of the Southwest. (2) The place of emergence in the landscape itself. The OMPHALOS or AXIS MUNDI representing the point of communication with the spirit world or with EARTH ENERGY. The circular, subterranean kiva symbolizes the womb of Mother Earth.

SOMATIC - Of the body. *Soma*, Greek for body. (Psychosomatic, of mind and body.) See BODY-MIND.

SONGLINES - The paths taken by the ancestral beings of the Australian DREAMTIME. The song the ancestors sang created the nature of the land.

SPIRIT - Latin for "breath." That which is believed to be the vital, animating force in living beings.

SPIRIT OF PLACE - The nature of a place as determined by the cosmology of the perceiver. See GENIUS LOCI and GEOMANCY.

SYMPATHETIC MAGIC - The concept that through similarity otherwise separate objects can affect each other. The "sand story" or map of a SONGLINE drawn on the ground is not just a representation to the Aborigines, it *is* the land the song is about. See MAGIC.

TELLURIC - Currents of EARTH ENERGY which concentrate at POWER SPOTS. The earth goddess of the Romans was Tellus or Terra.

TEMENOS - Greek for a ritually created boundary around a sacred enclosure, e.g. a temple.

TEMPLATE - The cosmological pattern for the design of a TEMPLE. The blueprint for all sacred time and space. Latin for time is *tempus*.

TEMPLE - A sacred space modeled upon a culture's concept of the nature of the divine. The cosmology in microcosm.

TITANS - Ancient nature deities. In Classical mythology the Titans are the children of Ge or GAIA and Ouranos. They include Oceanus, Iapetus, Eurymedon, Cronos, Phoebe, Rhea, Tethys, Themis and her children, Prometheus and Atlas, Hyperion and his son, Helios. After the war in heaven, most of the Titans were confined to Tartarus. See GIANTS and CHAOS.

TREE ALPHABET - A lost, oral alphabet of the DRUIDS whose nature derives from the trees. Probably possessing twenty components, the alphabet had a host of associated meanings: calendrical, directional, animal, mineral, magical, which made it a complete cosmological system. Written "alphabets" such as the OGHAM and runic scripts have been preserved, but the richness of their total meaning also died with the cosmology in which they were embedded.

TREE OF LIFE - The World Tree. The AXIS MUNDI connecting all worlds. Yggdrasil in the Scandinavian tradition. It represents the continuity of the genetic inheritance of life on earth.

UNDERWORLD - The world "below" the human. Utgard in the Scandinavian cosmology, Annwn in the Celtic. The dwelling place of souls awaiting rebirth, as well as banished giants, CHTHONIC deities and ELEMENTALS.

URBAN-CULTURE - A term used in this book to mean those cultures who have developed an urban environment. This is usually accompanied by a fairly rigid, hierarchical and dualistic cosmology and RELIGION where natural forces are perceived as wild and "Other" and the urban world as safe and "Us."

VESICA PISCIS - Two equal circles drawn so that the center of each is on the circumference of the other. The vesica created is in the shape of a fish, hence *piscis*. Its geometry creates a succession of polygons, its proportions the square roots of 2, 3 and 5, and thus it is considered as being supremely generative. See CIRCLE.

WAR IN HEAVEN - The battle between the children of GAIA and the Olympian deities. The myths have several episodes. First the TITANS attack Olympus, then the GIANTS and finally the monstrous Typhon. Even after this some of Gaia's offspring continue the assault.

WILD MAN OR WOMAN - A figure from European folklore, usually portrayed as forest-dwelling, naked, hairy and stupid. The wild man suffers from Western and Christian dualism which attributes inferior status to the natural and chthonian. Originally a cousin of the GREEN MAN, the GRUAGACH, the FACHAN, the BACHLACH and the GIANTS, the wild man is part of a rich tradition of nature initiation.

WORLDVIEW - The inherent pattern of ideas and beliefs which predispose a people to view the world in a certain way. See PARADIGM. Used in this book interchangeably with COSMOLOGY.

YONI - The Hindu name for a woman's vulva and womb. The vesica in the center of the VESICA PISCIS.

## About The Authors

Dr. Marcia Sutton graduated from the School of Foreign Service at Georgetown University. After conducting biomedical research for NASA she switched careers and earned her Ph.D. in Educational Psychology from the University of New Mexico where she has taught courses ranging from <u>Stress Management</u> to <u>Dragons, Druids and Sacred Stones</u> for the past dozen years. Her academic work is balanced by research into her Celtic roots and native European spirituality.

Dr. Sutton has financed her wanderlust by teaching English in Mexico, Colombia, Europe and Mongolia.

Nicholas R. Mann was born in 1952 in Sussex, England. He graduated with a degree in Ancient History and Anthropology from University College, London. In the early nineteen eighties, during his research of prehistoric sites of the British Isles, he experienced the very real subtle forces and presences that make up the esoteric world of ley lines, giants and the ancient gods. His further work in geomantic and geomythic studies around the world have confirmed similar forces at work.

He is the author of eight books, including *Sedona: Sacred Earth* and *The Isle of Avalon* and currently resides in the mountains of North-central New Mexico.